The Sorcerer's Apprentices

The Sorcerer's Apprentices

A Season at **elBulli**

Lisa Abend

SIMON &
SCHUSTER

London · New York · Sydney · Toronto · New Delhi

A CBS COMPANY

First published in Great Britain by Simon & Schuster UK Ltd, 2011
This edition published in Great Britain by Simon & Schuster UK Ltd, 2012
A CBS COMPANY

1 3 5 7 9 10 8 6 4 2

Simon & Schuster UK Ltd
1st Floor
222 Gray's Inn Road
London
WCIX 8HB

www.simonandschuster.co.uk

Simon & Schuster Australia, Sydney
Simon & Schuster India, New Delhi

Book design by Ellen R. Sasahara

A CIP catalogue for this book is available
from the British Library.

ISBN: 978-1-84983-322-6

Printed and bound by CPI Group (UK) Ltd, Croydon, CRO 4YY

To my mother, who taught me to cook,
and my father, who taught me to eat.

contents]

	Introduction	1
One	June, or the Machine	9
Two	July, or Achievement	55
Three	August, or Discipleship	89
Four	September, or Risk	130
Five	October, or Expression	166
Six	November, or Sacrifice	195
Seven	December, or Reputation	229
	Epilogue	263
	2009 Brigade	276
	Acknowledgments	278
	Index	282

On November 20, 2009, Ferran Adrià pulled me aside and asked to see my notebook. We were standing in the kitchen of elBulli, each of us in our normal positions: he at the end of the pass, where he could oversee testing of the new dishes that his second in command, Oriol Castro, was developing; I closer to the center where I had a clear view of the long middle table where the bulk of the restaurant's apprentices spent their day doing prep work. I was a bit surprised by the request: I had been in the kitchen for weeks each month since elBulli had opened for its 2009 season in June, and until now Ferran had never expressed any interest in what I was writing. But it was his restaurant, so I did as I was told. He started flipping through the pages, but it soon became clear he wasn't reading any of my scribbled observations; he was looking for a blank space. When he came to the first one, he pulled his pen from behind his ear, and wrote, in letters large enough to fill the page: November 20, 2009. "Remember that date," he said, handing back the notebook. "It's the day we decided. A few months from now, you'll understand what I mean."

When, in January 2010, Ferran announced that he would be closing elBulli for two years while he transformed it into a think tank for gastronomic creativity, the news shook the culinary world. The most famous chef in the world, a holder of three Michelin stars, a five-time winner of the title Best Restaurant in the World, the person single-handedly responsible for transforming the meaning of cuisine and broadening its possibilities, was announcing that elBulli would no longer be a restaurant. The speculation started immediately. Was he having financial problems or health issues? Was it true that his former partner was thinking of suing him? Was he simply—gasp—tired of cooking? In the midst of the firestorm, I ran into a friend who has never cared very much about food or restaurants. "I don't get it," he said, referring to the media explosion surrounding Adrià's announcement. "He's just a cook. It's just *food*."

We live in an age in which food, and those who prepare it professionally, are the focus of unprecedented attention. As a society we are newly obsessed not with the securing of food (which would be natural enough and which remains a pressing issue in much of the world) but with the consumption and celebration of it. We track down the best artisanal cheeses, make lists of restaurants where we must eat before we die, and blog about the short ribs we cooked for dinner. We eagerly follow the business ventures and love lives of favorite chefs. We watch television stations devoted to round-the-clock food programming, and read websites that fawn over every seasonal ingredient to appear at the farmers' market or that send reporters to stake out zoning meetings so that they're the first with news of a new restaurant. Food has become a major source of entertainment, in other words, but it is hardly just that. As increasingly large segments of the population seek to reduce the power of the corn lobby in Washington, to reform school lunches, and to encourage those around them to "vote with their forks," it has also become a political issue. Yet those who find this obsession perplexing, or silly, or possibly indicative of the imminent demise of civilization, can always dismiss it with a single phrase: But it's just *food*.

I wrote this book because I wanted to find out why it's not *just* food. Certainly the things we eat and how we eat them have always been about more than just the substances consumed. Throughout history, food has been a source of nurture (and not only nourishment). It has shaped culture and informed local and regional and national identities.

But in recent years the list of things that food is called upon to do—its meanings, in other words—has dramatically expanded. These days, food and the cooking of it can be a form of self-expression or a remnant of sexist enslavement, a glamorous means of obtaining wealth and attention or a time-consuming chore, a sign of individual status or a source of collective identity, a vector for politics, an intellectual exercise, a subject for scientific inquiry, an expression of love. Food is all this, remarkably, while still doing what most of us want it to do, which is to taste good.

Many people have played a role in this expansion of food's meanings, but few have been more influential than Ferran Adrià. Hyperbole may be the preferred rhetorical device of today's hothouse food culture, but it is no exaggeration to say that Ferran is the most significant chef of our time. Since he began, in the mid-1990s, to experiment with food's possibilities, he has transformed elBulli into the locus of a culinary revolution. Whatever one may think of "molecular gastronomy" (a term that Ferran reviles), it represents the most dramatic change to restaurant cooking since Escoffier. The techniques and ingredients Adrià has developed in his restaurant and equally famous workshop just off Barcelona's Boqueria market—the foams, the sands, the liquids turned into tremulous globules via the magic of spherification—redefine what eating (or at least eating out) means. Chefs around the world have adopted not only his dazzling, delirious inventions but his ethos: to bring science and cooking into closer relationship; to use food not only to please and satiate but to amaze and provoke; above all, to constantly reinvent. "What we've done," Ferran likes to say, "is create a new vocabulary, a new language, for cooking."

That new vocabulary has produced some startling metaphors: "dragon" cocktails that make the drinker breathe smoke, "caviar" made from tiny spheres of olive oil. But it is his grammar—that is, the way he puts plates together—that is most astonishing. Hot turns into cold, sweet into savory, solid into liquid or air. Adrià's cooking plays with the diner's expectations, undermines established categories of taste and texture, and constantly, miraculously, continues to surprise. In the end, it is this intense creativity that distinguishes him. His mantra is "Don't copy," which means that not only does he not copy other chefs, he does not copy his own ideas. Each year, he and his team roll out new techniques developed in their test kitchen and create a new menu from scratch, incorporating new ingredients discovered in the previous months' travels (in 2009, Japan still played a major role, though a few ingredients from the Amazon also worked their way in). It's as if Adrià has internalized Ezra Pound's famous dictum to artists: Make it new!

The acclaim Adrià has received for his work is similarly unprecedented. *Restaurant Magazine* has elected elBulli the best in the world five times. Fellow Michelin-starred colleague Juan Mari Arzak unabashedly refers to Adrià as "the most creative chef in history." Polls put Adrià as one of the most easily identified figures in Spain—ahead of the prime minister (Rafael Nadal and Pau Gasol, however, still have him firmly beat). He has been on the cover of *The New York Times Magazine, Time* magazine, *Le Monde,* and hundreds more; on the elBulli website you can search for articles about him in twenty different languages. And each year, every single reservation for the thirty-course extravaganza that constitutes dinner at elBulli disappears in a single day (yes, 2011 is fully booked, too). Somewhere between 500,000 and two million people apply; for the 8,000 or so who get in—from renowned chefs to anonymous gourmands—elBulli's small, unassuming dining room is the object of culinary pilgrimage.

In part, then, this is a book about elBulli. By now, there are enough chefs' memoirs and kitchen exposés and seasons of *Top Chef* and *MasterChef* and *Iron Chef* available that anyone with an interest in what goes on behind the swinging door can easily find out. The long hours, the scars and burns, the knife skills, the verbal abuse, the perfectionism, the flavor profiling—even the most casual foodie is now fluent in the phrases and contours of kitchen life. Still, there is something different about elBulli. As Adrià himself repeatedly says, it is not a "normal" restaurant. From its ability to continuously reinvent itself to its astounding dishes to the system he and his chefs have devised for running the kitchen, elBulli maintains a mystique unmatched by any other restaurant. Admirers, and even some detractors, frequently refer to Adrià as a magician or a sorcerer, someone who performs alchemy with even the humblest of ingredients. If Ferran is indeed a modern-day incarnation of the Wizard of Oz, this book is, in part, an attempt to answer the question: What's behind that curtain?

Ferran Adrià oversees the first step of the artichoke rose's preparation. (Francesc Guillamet)

At elBulli, there is no hoax, no quaking charlatan pretending to be powerful. Ferran Adrià really is working wonders with food, the likes of which have never before been seen. The only trick—if that's the right word—is that he is not doing it alone. Behind the curtain, dozens of others cooks stand with him: in recent years, there have been about forty-five people at a time working in elBulli's kitchen, and since most of them stay only one season, the total over the course of the two decades since he began experimenting with food reaches high into the hundreds. Some of them are permanent staffers, but most are young cooks who give up six months of their lives to travel far from home and work long hours for no pay. These stagiaires—the apprentices to Adrià's sorcerer—are following the most time-honored method of becoming a chef: volunteering to do hard, tedious labor in the kitchen of an established chef in order to acquire the skills, and perhaps a little of the philosophy, he has mastered.

Yet if elBulli is not a normal restaurant, neither are the stagiaires it attracts. For one, they are much more qualified: in most restaurants, stagiaires have little or no professional experience beyond what they may have picked up in their culinary schools' practice kitchens. But at elBulli, the apprentices are hardly newcomers; most have already worked in some of the best restaurants in the world, often for pay. And they will go on, once they leave elBulli, to work in many more. In fact, many of the world's greatest chefs—René Redzepi, Andoni Luis Aduriz, Massimo Bottura, Grant Achatz—have spent time in Adrià's kitchen, and all, without exception, were changed by their time there. This is the other great distinguishing factor of a *stage* at elBulli: it has launched the most glorious careers.

Training at elBulli, then, may be transformational for a young cook; it may help her get a prime position later and may, indeed, open up a world of professional opportunities that would otherwise be closed to her. But there is no guarantee. However long its list of dazzling alumni, elBulli has far more former stagiaires who are still toiling as line cooks in no-name restaurants or who have dropped out of the industry altogether. Cooking is a notoriously brutal profession, and even a stint at the best restaurant in the world cannot change its inherent difficulties.

So why do so many want to do it? Why are applications at the Culinary Institute of America up 50 percent in the past six years? Why do 30,000 aspiring British chefs apply to be on *MasterChef*? And why is a *stage* at elBulli even harder to secure, as Ferran likes to say, than a reservation? The exalted position of food within a certain segment of Western society helps explain why so many of us now shop at farmers' markets, tweet the details of our latest meal, take the occasional butchering class, and plan our vacations around tapas bars in Barcelona. But cooking is not like going to medical school: there is no guarantee that you're going to make a decent salary down the line. And as any well-regarded chef who has occasionally been treated as "the help" can tell you, the status that comes from cooking the right food is far less stable than that derived from eating it. Cooking is work—and ill-paid work at that.

In the course of researching this book, I learned that if you ask aspiring chefs why they chose the profession, they will invariably tell you that they love cooking. But this seems to me a tautological response: *You cook because you love cooking? That's it?* I wanted to know *why* they love cooking, what past longing it satisfies, what future they imagine it promises. I wanted to know, in other words, what it *means*. If we are to understand why food plays the pronounced role it does today, it seems to me that we have to be able to answer this single, critical question: Why cook?

"Look, I know. This isn't solving climate change or curing cancer. We're just feeding people," pastry chef Mateu Casañas says. He and I are sitting on the bench outside elBulli's kitchen on the last day of service for the 2009 season. Like the other chefs de cuisine, Mateu has spent his entire adult life working at elBulli, so I have a special interest in understanding why he does what he does. He nods thoughtfully as he pulls off an apron still immaculate after six hours of service, before repeating words I have heard before: "Here at least we know we have been a part of history." He means, I think, the history of cuisine; already the dishes he and his colleagues prepare have become part of the canon of professional cooking, pored over and replicated by other chefs, before finally serving as inspiration for their own dishes. But he could just as easily have meant history in general. Given the importance we impart to how and what we eat, there is little doubt that someday, some doctoral student in cultural history will study elBulli's menu for clues about our time and place. And what she will learn is that here at least, in this restaurant on the Catalan coast, at the end of the twentieth century and beginning of the twenty-first, food could do and be almost anything. It is that range of possibility that makes the stagiaires of elBulli, in the words of Claude Lévi-Strauss, so "good to think" when it comes to this strange modern phenomenon. Drawn by elBulli's reputation, they come from around the world—a truly global class that testifies to the newfound power of haute cuisine. Their motivations, as well as they things they discover, differ from apprentice to apprentice. But all of them are attracted by the radical opening that elBulli represents, by the promise that there they can find their own meaning.

One day in 2011, when elBulli has served its last meal as a restaurant, those young men and women will still be cooking. They will scatter back around the globe and go on to work in other people's restaurants or take the helm of their own places. Down the road, they may labor in temples of fine dining, grill steaks at some neighborhood bistro, invent whole new venues and styles, or maybe even find themselves in a world that no longer cares quite so intensely about the food they produce. But they will continue to take the things they learned at elBulli—perhaps the techniques and ingredients, but certainly the philosophy, the freedom, and, above all, the ability to explain why it's *not just food*—and make them their own. They will continue, in other words, to shape the future of this fascinating, complex thing we call cuisine.

one

June, or the Machine

"*Q uemo. Quemo. Quemo, quemo, quemo. Quemo. QUE-mo!*"

The most important thing the stagiaires learn on their first day at elBulli is this word: *quemo.* Literally, it means "I burn." The ones who don't speak Spanish don't know that, however, and so, as they mouth the strange word in the early days before it becomes reflex, it comes out a question, one often formed, it seems, in their own language: Kay-moh? Quémeau?

At the restaurant, *quemo* is an all-purpose warning: behind you, coming through, hot stuff, watch your back. There is no room for variation in this kitchen, where forty-five chefs and cooks and stagiaires and dishwashers from different countries are constantly moving, and so one word must carry the burden of many kinds of caution. If you listen closely, you'll hear it in the background of the louder, more obvious din created by the Thermomix whirring and coconuts being cracked and orders being fired and marrow bones being sawed apart and the occasional plate crashing to the floor. It is always there, like a looped soundtrack, this steady chorus of *quemo*s.

The cooks are supposed to say the word as they round the treacherous bend between the small kitchen and the main one or step through the portal that divides the hot stations from the cold—an alert on a blind curve. Some, however, repeat it as they pass through any crowded area of the kitchen, rhythmically announcing each step— "QUEmoQUEmoQUEmo"—so that the word becomes a mantra against accidental bumping and other calamities. Admittedly, this produces something of a boy-who-cried-wolf situation: how do you know when something really *is* hot? For that, the kitchen has spontaneously devised variations: *quemo mucho* for when a cook takes a hot pan from the flattop and turns around to empty its contents at his station—in other words, when something really *is* hot.

Except for when it isn't. Aitor Zabala, the chef de partie of Cold Station, says, "*Quemo mucho*" as he takes a tray of Ponds, delicate glass bowls of ice that will become one of this year's stellar dishes, and moves them from one freezer to another. In other words, he says "*Quemo mucho*" not when he is burning a lot but when he is freezing. The other variations are a little more reliable: *quemo máximo* is used for pots of boiling oil and other potentially disfiguring substances. And this being elBulli, at least twice a day comes the warning *quemo nitro*, as two of the cooks—protective goggles strapped to their heads, a cloud of smoke trailing behind them—haul a tank of liquid nitrogen back to the cold station.

Quemo has its personal variations as well. Katie Button never completely loses the querulous tone of the first day; for her, *quemo* will always be a question. Luke Jang puts the accent on the second syllable, which has the effect, like so much of what he does, of making his version seem faster, more efficient. For Luis Arrufat, *quemo* is a kind of personal manifesto, a bellowed *I am here!*, as if he were the lead in a musical who, having already walked onstage and puffed out his chest, still feels the need to signal that he is about to commence singing. The chefs de cuisine, Eduard Xatruch and Oriol Castro, get away with not saying it at all; it's a sign of their authority that they can assume that any person with whom they might collide will say it first. When they do use the word, it carries a distinctly didactic tone, as if to say, "Remember? This is how you're supposed to do it." Ferran doesn't have to say "*Quemo*" either, of course, but he often does, accompanying it with a swift flick of his hands, so that it takes on a meaning unique to him: *Would you please get the hell out of my way?*

The stagiaires learn another word today, too: *oído,* or "heard." Used the way an English speaker might say "roger," *oído* is an acknowledgment that you've heard what the speaker has said. At elBulli, *"oído"* is what you say when you are chef de partie and the person expediting has just called an order that will come from your station—you're acknowledging that you heard the request, and you've started working on it. But since *oído* is a hierarchical signifier—you say it only to those above you—the stagiaires say the word a lot more than anyone else. After all, they are the ones doing the restaurant's grunt work—cleaning schmutz from the rabbit ears that will be fried into something resembling potato chips, splitting open tuna spines to release the translucent blob of marrow, turning dozens of pieces of rhubarb into something resembling sea cucumbers.

When the stagiaires receive instruction or criticism (*We need more ears. You call that a sea cucumber? That's a fucking zucchini!*), they are supposed to reply with *"Oído"*—I heard you, got it, I'm on it. Sometimes Ferran will make a suggestion to the group and then, like a mostly benevolent drill sergeant and his "I can't HEAR you!," will ask, *"Oído, cocina?"* On those occasions the stagiaires will respond in unison with their own robust *"Oído!"* But usually the word is uttered by an individual, with varying intonations of enthusiasm or resentment, to demonstrate that he understands what the next task is. For despite the fact that many of them have cooked in important restaurants around the globe—Tetsuya's, noma, the French Laundry, Alain Ducasse—the thirty-two stagiaires in elBulli's kitchen are now on the bottom rung of the most famous restaurant in the world. And on the bottom rung, there is always something else to do.

∘ ∘ ∘

A table at elBulli is the holy grail of reservations for food lovers around the world, but a *stage* there is even more desirable for young, ambitious cooks. Each year, roughly three thousand apply for the privileged opportunity of passing six months as stagiaires—technically the word means "interns" or "apprentices," but it translates metaphorically as "kitchen slaves"—at its stove tops. The high regard in which the restaurant is held, as well as the chance to receive instruction from Adrià and his chefs, explains why apprentices travel, at their own expense, from Seoul and Bologna and Los Angeles and Caracas to the tiny, overbuilt town of Roses on Spain's Costa Brava. It is also why they agree to work fourteen hours at a stretch in exchange for one meal a day, a bed in an unattractive apartment, and exactly no pay. It is why they stand practically still for seven of those hours, their feet planted at the center counter, squeezing the germ from thousands of kernels of corn or trimming the slime off anemones. If they make it through the six months that elBulli is open, they are able to say that they have worked in the best restaurant in the world. Luca Balboni, one of 2009's three Italian stagiaires, puts it like this: "A *stage* at elBulli is like a baptism. Without it, you're not really a Christian."

Yet it wasn't that long ago that a *stage* in Spain would have been more like an excommunication. "It would be like saying you were going to go train in Turkey or someplace," says chef Dan Barber of New York's Blue Hill restaurant. "Interesting in an ethnographic way, but it would have meant you weren't serious about cuisine." Indeed, as late as the 1980s, Spanish food had almost no reputation at all; when expatriates such as Gerry Dawes and Janet Mendel began writing about it, they had to persuade skeptics that there was more to Spanish cuisine than paella and gazpacho. That Spain is now the most exciting and admired place to work for a serious student of cuisine is the result of the labor of dozens of innovative chefs and hundreds of exceptional producers. But in its origins, the phenomenon is almost entirely attributable to Ferran Adrià.

o o o

The *stage* is a remnant of Europe's medieval guilds. In fact, it is older than restaurants themselves and in its traditional form more akin to the voluntary indenturing that a young man would undertake in order to learn to print books than anything you might see on *Top Chef*. These days, a formal apprenticeship is no longer mandatory for an ambitious chef, and the modern incarnation of the *stage* is most often an internship arranged by his culinary school—with all the abuse-avoiding oversight and regulation that implies. Or it can be an impromptu passage: a young cook asks to spend a week or a month in the kitchen of an established restaurant, doing the drudge work—peeling the potatoes, cleaning the snails, chopping the garlic—in exchange for the chance to learn from a chef he admires.

But at elBulli, the *stage* remains a formal training period, with a beginning and end that coincide more or less exactly with the six months that the restaurant is open. Prospective stagiaires send in their applications a year in advance, so that a few months before the season begins, the restaurant has compiled a collection of cooks eager to indenture themselves. With only thirty-two slots to fill, the odds are against most of them. Those who do get in have Marc Cuspinera to thank.

For years, Marc was elBulli's chef de cuisine, but these days he oversees an odd combination of administrative and design work for the restaurant. With his longish sideburns and gently ironic sense of humor, he could be running a retro record shop in Brooklyn selling vinyl records. Instead, he is in charge of a broad category of tasks at elBulli that include scheduling photo shoots of each new dish for that year's catalogue, commissioning local artists to design the plates and bowls that the restaurant uses in its new dishes, and constructing the wooden separations that divide the compartments of the box of chocolates that goes out at the end of each meal. He also designs the silicone molds the restaurant uses to make one thing look like another—the "mimetic" peanuts (and almonds and pistachios) made from nut praliné, the roses made from frozen whiskey sours. "Marc," Ferran says, "is the MacGyver of elBulli."

Along with his other responsibilities, Marc has been in charge of the *stage* program for the past three years. When he himself started at the restaurant twenty years ago, he was one of only seven stagiaires (more than one person tells stories of elBulli's early days, in which Ferran would beg people he met on the street to come work for him), but these days, the number stands at around thirty-two, which means that Marc now spends the better part of the months prior to the restaurant's opening weeding through those three thousand applications, securing student visas, and convincing landlords in Roses that they do indeed want to rent their apartments to a small horde of mostly twentysomethings who all return home simultaneously to troop up the stairs at two each morning. As a result, he's acquired the weary tolerance of a longtime dorm mother: this is a man who has seen everything, from fights in the kitchen to the occasional arrest. (In fact, in 2009, he will be rousted from bed one night when the neighbors in a building that houses eleven stagiaires call to complain about the noise levels. This is after they have pelted with eggs and oranges the offending stagiaires, who were drinking on the terrace of their apartment.) Marc is the first person from elBulli with whom the stagiaires will have contact, and, should anything go wrong while they are working there, he will also be the last.

Selection is an inexact calculus, based more on instinct than on anything resembling a formal hiring process. In fact, elBulli doesn't interview its prospective stagiaires; Marc makes the call largely on the basis of how an applicant fills out a form. Most gush about their desire to work with the greatest chef in the world; many demonstrate an intimate knowledge of Ferran's career and recipes. But Marc is not swayed solely by enthusiasm. Experience counts; elBulli prefers its full-season stagiaires to arrive with significant work experience not only because it makes things run more smoothly but because the restaurant, in order to maintain good public relations, fills some of its slots each year with students from the local culinary schools. "And that," says Marc, "is as many beginners as we can handle." He tends to prefer younger cooks ("A forty-year-old won't last the six months," he says. "I know, because I'm forty") and ones who come from restaurants—Per Se, Alinea, the Fat Duck—whose level he considers roughly comparable with elBulli's. A chef may have years of experience at the top restaurants in, say, Malaysia, but if those restaurants are not familiar to Marc, the chef in question will receive the "We'll keep your name on file" letter rather than the one that reads, "The season begins on June 10."

Those chosen are supposed to arrive speaking at least some Spanish, although in practice not all of them do, and some, like the French-speaking Gaël Vuilloud, blatantly lie about their language skills in the hope of securing a spot. Men outnumber women, although in 2009 Ferran was proud to have seven female stagiaires. And although the restaurant likes to maintain a healthy mix of nationalities, there are certain limits. Spaniards always predominate; in 2009 there were generally fifteen of them at a time. The rest came from Canada, Switzerland, Italy, Portugal, Venezuela, Mexico, Ecuador, Colombia, the United States, Japan, India, Brazil, and South Korea. For the last few years, none, pointedly, has been French. "It's the attitude," Marc admits with a shrug when confronted with this apparent oversight. "They never seem to work out."

o o o

On the first day, the stagiaires appear one by one on Roses' boardwalk, dragging their suitcases and backpacks behind them in the bright morning sunlight. The ones who arrive first grab an outdoor table at the beachfront café, and order coffee or beer, depending on how they spent the previous night and how cocky they are feeling that morning. With each new arrival, the seated ones squint up into the blinding sun and offer a wary hello. A small group of the Catalan stagiaires—some cooks, some servers—know one another from culinary school and chatter together happily, but the rest sit awkwardly at the edge of their circle, introducing themselves, then falling into nervous silence. It feels like the first day of summer camp.

There is always a photographer or reporter around at elBulli, and even on this first day, a German documentary crew films every move as the stagiaires are ushered inside a dining room at the same café and take seats in straight-back plastic chairs. Through the windows they can see fat, sunburned tourists stroll happily down the boardwalk in their bathing suits, but inside the mood is tense and no one says a word. Marc takes his place at the front and begins to enumerate the rules: no facial hair, nails clean and trimmed, no wearing your chef's jacket outside the restaurant, and, by the way, you're responsible for laundering it yourself. No kidding around or practical jokes in the kitchen; we don't want any misunderstandings. Pants and shoes should be black; you should have a small offset spatula (a flat, angled knife with a rounded tip) with you at all times. No drinking on the job or showing up late; do the latter more than once, and you'll be sent home. Marc tempers his sternness with a little encouragement: "You're with us for 196 days, and 54 of those are days off. So take advantage of your time here, take advantage of it fully." But then, almost as an afterthought, he turns gruff again. "I've got a list of three thousand people who want to be where you are," he says, jutting his chin in the direction of his audience, whose members look decidedly stricken. "So if I have to throw you out, I've got plenty of people waiting to take your place."

After a lunch of chorizo sandwiches and local apricots, the apprentices have one last thing to do before heading up to the restaurant. Instructing them to grab their chef's coats, Marc breaks the stagiaires into groups and takes them to their new accommodations to drop their bags. Not only does he assign them an apartment—with anywhere from four to eleven housemates—but he assigns them their rooms ("If there's any damage, I want to know who to blame"). Their selection may have depended on a good deal of luck, but now that the stagiaires are part of elBulli, nothing they do will willingly be left to chance.

The route that leads from the town of Roses to Cala Montjoi, the jewel-like cay where elBulli is located, is seven kilometers of the most narrow, tortuous road you would ever want to travel. For clients, the location is part of the restaurant's allure—isolated, not easily reached, along a road that is as beautiful as it is dangerous. But for the stagiaires, the drive is more complicated. For the next six months, beginning around 1 P.M., a small line of cars will bear them up the mountain and, fourteen or so hours later, back down again, passing vistas of vineyards on the one side and the sparkling Mediterranean on the other. It's a bittersweet journey: all this beauty, yet not theirs to enjoy; unlike the cars they pass on the way, which inevitably contain vacationers with lobster-colored skin on their way from another beach, the stagiaires take the road only to work. And on this first drive, piled into cars for what is, for most of them, their first trip to the restaurant, those feelings are even more confused. "I was nauseated the whole way up," confesses Ralph Schelling, a young cook from Switzerland. "But I couldn't tell if it was nerves, excitement, or car sickness."

Soon, all thirty-two are standing around elBulli's stove tops with the thirteen permanent staff, including Ferran Adrià. As professional kitchens go, it is beautiful: broad and airy, with a large window in front and a glass wall in back that lets in the speckled Costa Brava sunlight. Erect in their still pristine white jackets, with long blue aprons around their necks, the stagiaires line the kitchen's edges like soldiers nervously awaiting inspection. Marc has traded his T-shirt for a chef's jacket, and he makes some initial comments as several of the stagiaires strain to keep their eyes focused on him, rather than trying to take it all in. "All I kept thinking was 'Oh my god, oh my god, oh my god," says Colombian-born Andrea Correa. "It was all I could do to stand still."

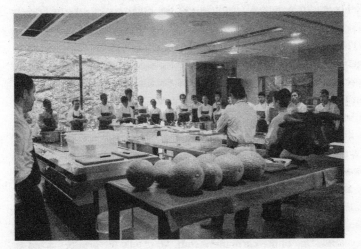

Chefs de cuisine Oriol Castro and Eduard Xatruch lead the meeting that starts the stagiaires' workday. (Francesc Guillamet)

Introductions come first. In any restaurant, identity stems from where you have worked, which is why Luca Balboni, the tall, handsome pastry chef from Milan, begins by saying he is from Massimo Bottura's Osteria Francescana. Short and wiry, Sungho Jin—he invites everyone to call him Sunny—worked at Tetsuya's in Australia. José Luis Parra nervously adjusts his red-framed eyeglasses and blurts out that he was at Biko in Mexico City. Perfectly erect, Kim Floresca quietly says, *"Per Se, en Nueva York"*; for Roger Alcaraz, part of the Catalan contingent, it is *"La Broche, en Madrid."* Tall and smiling, Katie Button exercises her fledgling Spanish and says painstakingly, *"Yo trabajo con José Andrés, en El Bazaar."* Gangly Luke's Spanish isn't much better, but he manages to get out "Mugaritz," the same as the raven-haired Begoña Martínez, standing next to him. Swallowed up by her jacket, the petite Andrea whispers that she worked at noma. And so it goes, a virtual who's who of the world's best restaurants: Txema Llamosas is from Arzak in San Sebastián; Emmanuelle (Emma) Leftick, who wears a tiny silver chef's knife around her neck, comes from the French Laundry. With virtually no knowledge of Spanish, Gaël Vuilloud manages nervously to get out only his age (twenty-two), until one of the other cooks asks in French where he last worked: Denis Martin in Vevey, Switzerland.

The permanent staff then introduce themselves. In contrast to the stagiaires, they come from mostly one place: elBulli. There is Oriol Castro, the kitchen's thirty-six-year-old second in command, who has been with Ferran for fourteen years. Mateu Casañas, thirty-three, has just been put in charge of Pastry—or "the sweet world," as it's called at elBulli—after working at the restaurant since he was twenty. Now twenty-nine, chef de cuisine Eduard Xatruch has been with the restaurant since he was seventeen. Sous chef Eugeni de Diego, twenty-five, joined when he was twenty-one. And all of the chefs de partie—Luis Arrufat, Andrés Conde, Aitor Zabala, Toni Moraga, Anthony Masas, Sergio Barroso, and Pablo Pavón—have also put in years at elBulli, sometimes exclusively. Every single one of the permanent staff, Marc tells the group, started as a stagiaire.

Finally Ferran speaks. Dressed in sandals and jeans, his dark, curly hair beginning to gray and his round belly straining against the confines of his T-shirt, he is not an intimidating figure, at least not until he begins to speak. In his staccato voice, he delivers a speech that is half pep talk, half hellfire and brimstone. He begins by welcoming them and emphasizing what a remarkable opportunity they have before them. "We're going to explain creativity to you," he declares. "Each year we become more and more like a university. You're going to learn a lot. And we don't expect you to know everything, not now, not today. We"— and here he gestures to the other chefs—"don't know everything. At this point, we don't even know what the menu is going to look like. We're all starting at ground zero."

This appeal to a common starting point is reassuring to some, but it raises mild warning signs for Sunny. After all, he is thirty-two years old and has worked in restaurants since he was nineteen. And not just any restaurants: he followed his stint at Tetsuya's with one at Thomas Keller's French Laundry, which is considered by many the best restaurant in the United States. He prides himself on his hard-won skills, and this suggestion, that experience doesn't matter, doesn't coincide with what he's learned. "Either you know what you're doing or you don't," he says later. "The recipes may be different, the plating may be different, but if you know what you're doing, your knowledge, your skill—they'll carry you through."

Ferran continues. Some of the things he says they've heard from Marc already: the unquestionable importance of arriving on time, the absolute need to drive carefully on the perilous road that leads to and from the restaurant. He reiterates that cell phones are prohibited in the kitchen and that anyone caught taking photos there will be summarily fired—the restaurant has had more than one bad experience in which stagiaires have posted a new or developing dish on the Internet. He tells them to buy a notebook and bring it every day in order to keep track of the new things they learn. Then he adds one item that comes as a surprise to those cooks who have worked in other highly regarded places: "I don't want to hear any screaming in this restaurant. No one insults anyone else, no one belittles anyone else. If you have a criticism, you raise it calmly, in a meeting. We're a team. And if I hear of anyone insulting anyone else, they're out." Can this be true? A few of the more experienced cooks look at one another questioningly. "When I started," Ferran continues, "insults, shouting, outbursts were normal. But by now we've created an environment of respect so that when others come here, they admire us." At this, chefs de cuisine Eduard and Oriol exchange a knowing glance. But Ferran, always speaking a mile a minute, has moved on.

"We're like the Barça," he says, making reference to Barcelona's beloved soccer team. "Maximum seriousness, in order to have a good time." With a warning that they are to be at work at ten the next morning, on time and dressed in their jackets and aprons, he dismisses them to their cleaning tasks. Then, thinking better of it, he calls them back for one last message. "Remember," he says, raising his index finger to a spot between his eyebrows in a gesture that will soon become familiar. "The recipes aren't the most important thing to take from here. What you have to take is elBulli's spirit."

As José Luis goes to hunt for a mop, he shakes his head with a mixture of awe and joy. "I can't believe I was just standing next to Ferran Adrià," he says. "I can't believe I'm here." But excitement is not the only emotion rippling through the crew. As the stagiaires scatter to their tasks, wiping down shelves and sweeping under the countertops, a thin wire of tension runs through the kitchen. Certainly none of them ever wants to arrive late for the start of the workday; Ferran has made it clear that more than one tardy arrival will mean automatic dismissal. (In fact, no less famous a former elBulli cook than José Andrés—today a chef and the owner of top restaurants in Washington and Los Angeles and a close friend of Ferran's—was fired on the spot when Ferran arrived at the Barcelona bar where they had agreed to meet at a certain time, and discovered that José Andrés had not yet arrived. The fact that Andrés had gotten there an hour early, after an eight-hour bus ride from Madrid, and stepped out to a phone both to call Ferran, apparently made no difference. The two fought, and Ferran told him to leave. "Four days later, I flew to America," says Andrés. "If that hadn't happened, I'd still be in Spain, probably still cooking at elBulli.") But their doubts, almost palpable, run deeper, expressed silently in the sideways glances they cast at one another as they check to see if anyone is working harder, then redouble their own efforts if they suspect someone is. They all know the names of the now-famous chefs who have passed through elBulli's kitchen, and they've all heard stories about people who couldn't cut it. So there are questions in their eyes: *Who is going to stand out? Who will fail? Is there a future great among us?* And the question that worries each of them the most: *Am I good enough?*

○ ○ ○

Like most serious European and American restaurants, elBulli operates according to a strict hierarchy that is militaristic in origin. Indeed, a kitchen staff is referred to as a "brigade," a name that comes from Auguste Escoffier, the fin-de-siècle French chef who not only transformed French cuisine but created the modern restaurant system as well. As a young man, Escoffier had cooked in the army during the Franco-Prussian War, and he recognized that many of its protocols were well suited to the kitchen (which, not unlike the battlefield, is a chaotic, dangerous place that tends to produce among its denizens an intense feeling of survival-born camaraderie).

At the top of the hierarchy is the executive chef, or chef/owner, which at elBulli is of course Ferran Adrià (Juli Soler, who runs the front of the house and who originally hired Ferran, is also an owner). Beneath him come the chefs de cuisine. In most restaurants, there is only one, and he (the vast majority even now are male) is not only the executive chef's second in command but the person who oversees the kitchen every night: if not actually cooking, he is at least there making sure that the people who *are* cooking are doing it right. At elBulli, however, there are three chefs de cuisine, each roughly equal to the others, though with his own sphere of influence: Oriol Castro, Eduard Xatruch, and Mateu Casañas. Beneath them comes a position Ferran created that replaces the sous chef of Escoffier's blueprint. Eugeni de Diego is the head of production, responsible for ensuring that all the mise en place (the phrase translates literally as "set in place" and refers to prep work, though at elBulli it is used to signify not just the work, nor the diced onions and julienned herbs produced by the work, but the entire period prior to service) is done correctly, which means he is responsible for ensuring that the stagiaires are doing their mise en place correctly.

Below Eugeni come the chefs de partie, each in charge of one of elBulli's six stations besides Pastry: Cold, Starters I, Starters II, Meat, Fish, and something called "Small Kitchen," which prepares staff meals and otherwise does a bit of everything—though in a separate, claustrophobic space squeezed between the main kitchen and the dishwashing station. Given the promiscuous nature of elBulli's cuisine, the labels attached to stations are less an indication of what actually gets cooked there than an instinctive reliance on an organizing principle that, in a normal kitchen, would be logical. (At elBulli, the fish station, for example, is responsible for the rabbit canapé; Starters I turns out the abalone, which comes not, as one might think, at the beginning of the meal but about two-thirds of the way through it. Cold Station's dishes, however, are uniformly cold.)

It is not just the brigade that finds its origins in the restaurants of late-nineteenth-century Paris and Lyon; nearly every other aspect of the modern professional kitchen's structure can be traced to France as well. At elBulli they may refer to the station as "Cold Station" (cuarto frio) rather than garde-manger, and it may be responsible for spherifications and freeze-dried meringues instead of salads and pâtés, but the connection is clear. There are other remnants of the French system as well: the cooks—stagiaires and permanent staff, all the way up to Ferran—wear blue aprons, tied around their necks, during mise en place (which goes by its French name, just as the dishwashing station is called plonge). During service, Ferran, the chefs de cuisine, and the chefs de partie switch to white aprons—a traditional distinction in the French kitchen. The stagiaires keep their blue aprons on throughout the day and night, however, lowering them from neck to waist when it comes time to start service.

Yet, for all these debts, elBulli also rejects some of the most important French traditions. First among them is the food itself. ElBulli has done away with mother sauces and the classic repertoire of dishes, and so represents the greatest rupture ever in the history of cuisine. But there are more subtle rejections as well. None of the chefs, for example, is called "chef"; if you want to address Oriol or Mateu or even Ferran himself, you call him by his first name. ("I just can't bring myself to do it," confesses Sunny. The result is that, like a recently married man urged to call his new mother-in-law "Mom," the stagiaires don't call Ferran anything.) It's as if elBulli exists in a permanent state of tension with the French heritage of modern cuisine, at times embracing its traditions wholesale, at others pointedly rejecting them.

o o o

On their first full day of training, no one dares arrive late. By 9:45 the stagiaires are lined up in their white jackets and blue aprons on the outdoor stairs that lead to the kitchen's back door. All of them clutch notebooks. Most stayed in their apartments the night before, getting to know their new roommates and trying to catch up on sleep, though a few, the Argentine Diego Corrado proudly among them, went out for drinks. ("Of course, I went out," he says the next morning, looking none the worse for wear. "We have to celebrate!") At precisely 10 A.M., Eduard Xatruch's commanding voice comes up the stairs. "*Señores*, let's begin." For the next six months, those words and that voice will signal the start of their workday.

The kitchen gleams as spotlessly as they left it yesterday, empty except for a vaguely menacing pile of carrots that sits on the long center counter, or *mesa central*. This will be the morning's main task: brunoising (chopping into fine, uniform dice) vegetables for the bolognese sauce that will comprise family meal later in the week. In this, elBulli is repeating a long-standing culinary tradition: all initiations start with the carrot. But first the stagiaires have a kitchen to learn.

Oriol and Eduard become whirling dervishes as they issue instructions for how to set up the kitchen. Carts go at the end of each counter. Trash cans go underneath, next to but not touching the legs of the counters. Rolls of paper towels go into the well beneath the counters, alternating with washcloths ("Smell them first!"). Dirty utensils go into the tray beneath each salamander; remember to carry those trays with both handles when you take them to the dishwasher. Don't walk in front of the pass, even during prep. Never throw out anything, not even carrot skins, without asking first. Tell Eugeni whenever you go to the bathroom. Smell the plastic containers before you use them, and wipe them out with a paper towel just in case. Drink only water while you're working, and then only from plastic cups—not directly from the bottle. When you move through the kitchen, walk in straight lines and turn at right angles—no meandering. Keep an offset spatula in your pocket at all times and a towel tucked into your apron string. When you wash your hands, don't dry them by flicking the water off, wipe them on your towel.

If the stagiaires find these instructions illogical or mildly infantilizing, they do not say so. They assiduously take notes when Eduard suggests they should be careful not to get crumbs everywhere while eating bread at family meal (thereby reducing cleanup time) and nod in apparent agreement with Oriol's hand-drying instructions. "I know this is ridiculous," the chef admits. "I know it's a drag. But everything we do, we have to do well. If a single piece of paper sits on the floor and no one picks it up, the whole thing, all of this, starts to falls apart."

All of this starts to fall apart: this sentiment too is French in its origins. Escoffier himself wrote of the importance of a kind of universal precision, noting that without it, with the moment's inattention that could lead to an imperfectly formed potato scale on a piece of red mullet or an insufficiently braised piece of beef, the restaurant's most important emblems—its dishes—would be imperiled. Thus, it comes as no surprise that at elBulli, there are very particular ideas about how a carrot should be cut. Eugeni demonstrates, peeling the carrot first and lining up the discarded peel in neat stacks. He trims the ends from each carrot, then slides it lengthwise over the blade of a mandoline. Once he has perfect carrot planes, he slices them into sticks and then again into the tiny cubes that brunoise requires. He pats the mound of carrots—all twenty-four pounds of them—and motions for the stagiaires to line up on either side of the center table. "It would take one person ten hours to get through all these," he says. "But with all of you, we can get it done in ten minutes."

Not exactly. Roughly two hours after they begin, Ralph, Begoña, and thirteen others are still dicing carrots into tiny cubes. Eugeni periodically passes through to inspect their work, shaking his head with dismay. "This one," he says, reaching into a plastic bin that at elBulli is called a *taper* (an abbreviation and approximate phonetic rendering of Tupperware), "has nothing to do with this one." To an outsider, it may seem silly to devote fifty hours of manpower to one element of a dish that won't even be served to the restaurant's customers. Does it really matter that each tiny carrot cube is the same size as every other if they're going to be cooked down into a sauce—and a sauce that only the staff will eat?

The reason the answer is yes pertains not only to carrots but to hand drying and tablecloth rolling (always from right to left) and the precise location on a one-liter *taper* where you paste a label. It's not that the way these things are done are necessarily the best or most logical way; it's that they are done—that attention is paid to them—at all. Ferran and Oriol and Eduard are not despots (at least not more than any other well-regarded chefs), nor are they possessed by a burning need to control every aspect of life at elBulli. Rather, they seek to create an environment in which there is a right way to do even the most menial task because they believe that same mind-set will carry over into the tasks that do matter. In other words, you take the time to chop the carrots in uniformly fine dice—even though they'll be cooked down in sauce and even though it's only staff who will be eating said sauce—because doing so helps ensure that the infused sugarcane sticks in the mojito cocktail will be precisely the same length, the drops of vinegar dew on the oyster leaf will be equidistant from one another, and the tiny lines of powdered freeze-dried shiso that adorn the *nenúfares* will all narrow away from the center and toward the rim of the plate. You do it because it reminds you, from the moment you walk down the steep hill that leads to elBulli's back door until you stuff your dirty jacket into your bag and walk back up some fourteen hours later, that you are in a place where nothing short of perfection is acceptable. (Or at least that's the idea. Those stagiaires who have worked previously in a Thomas Keller kitchen will maintain that things at elBulli fall a bit short of their standards.)

In the end, it takes the stagiaires a little over two hours to brunoise the carrots. Just before 12:40, Andrea reaches for the final one and places it on her cutting board. An almost audible sigh of relief ripples through the line: done. But before anyone can even wipe his hands, Eugeni and Luis are standing at the head of the counter with two large trays, filled to overflowing. "Now," says Eugeni. "Garlic."

o o o

A little less than four hours after the stagiaires begin, it is time for family meal. At elBulli, the staff eats together, in one seating, in the kitchen itself. As a result, the minutes before and after the meal require a nearly complete dismantling and reconstruction, as the counters that just moments before were filled with cutting boards and tubs of alginate baths are transformed into tables and then are transformed back again. Eduard and Oriol take their places at the front of the pass and begin a new set of instructions, no less exact than before. Counters are cleared completely and wiped down, floors swept, trash cans emptied. Plastic lawn chairs appear at the front of the kitchen (to the cooks, so caught up in their own tasks, their apparition must seem magical, but it is actually the servers who have dragged them in from the storage room outside) and are distributed around the counters. A glass is put at each place setting. Bottles of water and loaves of bread appear on what are no longer counters but tables, as do platters bearing parts of the meal that will be served family-style. It's all incredibly noisy and incredibly fast; for a few minutes the kitchen explodes with an activity made all the more intense after the studiously quiet atmosphere of mise en place.

But the key word is "minutes." The kitchen breakdown for family meal is supposed to take no more than five, and as Eduard keenly observes every move, one eye stays firmly on the clock. Periodically, he'll call the time, "*Señores*, you've got three minutes." In a kitchen that is always humming with purposeful movement, these moments of action seem nearly frenetic, as each stagiaire rushes to do the task she has been assigned and the chorus of *quemos* reaches a fever pitch. When the "dining room" is finally ready, the entire staff lines up at the doorway to the small kitchen to receive, one by one, the day's reward: a plate of food. As they sit this first day, Toni Moraga, one of the chefs de partie, notes their location on a map. For the rest of the season, each stagiaire will be required to sit in the same seat during family meal.

Thirty short minutes later, the chaos begins again, like a film running in reverse. Off come the bottles of water and bags of bread, up go the chairs. The tables—reconverted into counters—are wiped down again; the floors are reswept. Diego is charged with rolling up the blue tablecloth that has covered the pass during mise en place and family meal and replacing it with the gold one that signals service. He's forgotten the crucial instruction, however—tablecloths are rolled from right to left—and thus loses valuable time in unrolling the cloth and starting again. After all, this setup too is being timed. And because this is the one that will precede service, it comes with its own set of tasks. Kim and Iosu are assigned the pass and must learn to place each utensil and set of serving dishes in a particular relation to the large bull's head that adorns the center of the table. Within days, they'll be expected to have all the locations memorized, but for now they furiously take notes. The other stagiaires busy themselves with the plates, wiping down every one in the house with gin (the alcohol removes fingerprints without leaving a taste or smell). For all this, the kitchen again has five minutes, provoking an urgency more commonly associated with medical emergencies or a newspaper's election-night deadlines. When it's over and everything is set for service, Eduard convenes the group and reports with barely disguised disgust: ten minutes. The stagiaires hang their heads in failure.

Luckily, on June 11, service is still five days away. This barely controlled frenzy of breaking down and setting up has been a trial run for the real thing, slated to begin the following Tuesday. The stagiaires will spend the next several days mastering a slew of tasks, from how to clean a fetal pig's tail to how to spherify pesto to how to turn milk into a skin that can be filled and rolled. But in the middle of their days there will be this frantic sequence to master, this race against the clock. Provided, of course, that they successfully clean the rocks outside the restaurant.

o o o

As a physical structure, elBulli comes as a shock to most first-time visitors. The most cutting-edge cuisine in the world is served in a small beachside restaurant that in good light looks inviting in a gemütlich sort of way but in the wrong light can just as easily look frumpy and out of date. Except for the dramatic views of Cala Montjoi from its patio and dining room windows, there is nothing striking, or even particularly modern, about the front of the house. But outside, in the parking lot and the rugged landscape that surrounds elBulli's white stucco walls, there is, for those who pay attention, a small, unobtrusive sign of its status as the premiere avant-garde restaurant in the world. Outside, there are rocks.

ElBulli's parking lot is made of gravel. But around that gravel, and in the ample landscaped area leading to the front door, are thousands—maybe millions—of flattish slate rocks that act as ground cover, obscuring the dirt beneath with their modulated colors and pleasingly geometric shapes. But that geometry is not wholly natural; look carefully, and you'll see that the rocks—whether those that line the front window where arriving guests get a glimpse into the inner workings of the kitchen or the ones that swirl into a hill just below the parking lot—neatly overlap. And they neatly overlap because a stagiaire, on his first full day of work at elBulli, placed them there.

It's a tradition nearly as old as Ferran's tenure at the restaurant. "I remember it perfectly," says Marc Cuspinera of his first day in 1989. "I couldn't believe they were making me clean rocks." Twenty years later, Nico Bejarano can't believe it either. He and Diego are dismantling the hill, moving each rock in the mound to the side. As they do so, Andrea comes through and rakes away the pine needles that have collected over the year. Diego complains about not having gloves. Nico sighs a bit as he looks at the seemingly undiminished pile. "I'm a cook. I didn't expect to be doing this," he says grimly. In the past year, the twenty-one-year-old has done *stages* at Arzak, Martín Berasategui (also in San Şebastián), and

Comerç 24 in Barcelona, three of Spain's top restaurants. "It's not so great. All this stuff today—how to peel a carrot, how to carry a plate—it's a little tiresome." He pauses to toss a particularly large rock. "But I get it. It's true that all these details add up."

The rocks certainly add up: it takes fifty people (the kitchen stagiaires are joined by their front-of-house counterparts) more than five hours to finish the task. When it is over, most of them will look back on the chore almost fondly, recognizing in it a form of hazing that, now completed, proves they belong in the illustrious club of elBulli stagiaires. But for a few of the most reflective cooks, the rocks are a metaphor for what is to come. For some, they are evidence of an admirable quest for perfection in every aspect of the dining experience. For others, they are one more component of the restaurant's avant-garde reputation, proof that most anything—even the ground cover outside the restaurant—can be turned into an aesthetic object. And then, for a very few cooks, there is the more disconcerting conclusion: the rocks are a sign that elBulli is willing to expend the talents of some of the world's most energetic, devoted, and ambitious young chefs in tedium.

o o o

Why would anyone willingly seek out six months of often boring, physically exhausting, and utterly unpaid labor? "It's a dream," says Luis Frey, who goes by the nickname Lucho. Rangy and blond, he's been hooked on cooking since he was sixteen and worked in a local pizza joint, despite the fact that his parents would have much preferred that he go into the family mattress business. Lucho represents the most idealistic— and, it should be said, most common—rationale for signing on for the elBulli *stage*. Quite simply, he worships Ferran. As does Perfecto Rocher, an amiable Spaniard who tried for four years before finally securing this *stage* at elBulli. "I have all his books," he says. "I've been reading them since I was a kid. I think I've got his recipes memorized."

No one denies that a *stage* at elBulli will look good on a résumé, but for most of the apprentices, it wasn't only the restaurant's reputation that attracted them; it was the chance to really *know* it, and learn from it, that was most appealing. Colombian by birth, Nico gushes, by way of explanation, "I've always wanted to be here. Not just to get some recipes but for the whole spirit of the place." He taps the notebook he keeps in the pocket of his jacket. "These aren't notes, these are concepts. If I ever get my own restaurant, I'll be able to use all of their models." Even the more jaded—or better-informed—stagiaires sound a bit starstruck. "Two people who worked here told me what I was getting myself into," says Sunny. "They told me it was really hard and that I'd be bored to death. But nothing would have stopped me from coming here."

For an ambitious young chef, a *stage* at elBulli, then, is the equivalent of getting into Harvard or making the Olympic hockey team. For so esteemed an opportunity, the stagiaires are willing to pay a price—literally. In addition to the cost of getting there, which for many includes an international plane ticket, they must budget for food and any other expenses during the six months they are there. And, as with many a Harvard student, a stagiaire's parents often pay for whatever he can't. Yet even those without financial support will do what they can to get here—they just sacrifice more once they arrive. Unlike many of his fellow stagiaires, who took the opportunity of being in Europe to travel on their days off, Mike Álvarez (a Spaniard despite his American-sounding name) never leaves Roses; he can't afford even to go home to Galicia. Luke, from South Korea, has to limit the number of times he goes out with the rest of the crew for after-work drinks. And Jorge Puerta, from Venezuela, confesses to going hungry sometimes because he can't afford groceries; some weeks family meal is the only meal he eats all day.

All stagiaires have a story about the sacrifices they have made: the wives and boyfriends left behind, the jobs abandoned. But cooking is already a career that demands what most would consider extraordinary sacrifice, and for most of the cooks who come to elBulli, the restaurant's requirements seem, at least on paper, no more onerous than those of any other. That doesn't diminish the fact that their days will be long, that the work will be physically hard and emotionally stressful, that their housing conditions are cramped, or that they are far from home. But during these first days, the stagiaires are certain it will all be worth it, confident that what they learn will compensate them for the hardships they endure.

o o o

Four days until the opening, and the list of things the stagiaires don't know—from how to organize the walk-in refrigerator to how to plate the dish called *yemitas*—is practically infinite. The restaurant eases its burden by beginning the season with the previous year's menu and gradually swapping out the dishes with new inventions. But for the stagiaires, even the old dishes are new and require preparations unlike any they have undertaken before. Garlic is not just peeled but organized by clove size. Olives are not just pitted but then puréed, and the purée is passed by hand—fifteen pairs of hands, to be exact—through a flexible net sieve, squeezing all the time to extract the full amount of juice (this liquid will become the restaurant's famous spherified olives, served with the starting cocktail). Mackerel is not just cleaned and filleted but filleted in such a way that the belly comes out in a perfect, V-shaped shield. This task in particular strains the capacity of many of the stagiaires; minutes after they begin, the center table looks like an eighth-grade biology class gone bad.

Yet the mackerel is hardly the most complicated thing they will do; at elBulli, difficulty comes in numerous varieties. Some tasks are challenging because the product is new and unknown to just about everyone. None of the stagiaires, for example, has ever worked with *ortiguillas* (sea anemones) before, and learning to separate the slimy fringe from the equally slimy body is tricky. Picking up a pair of scissors, Eugeni explains a little about the product: how anemones grow in three areas of Spain, but these—from Cádiz, in the south—are best. He then demonstrates how to cut an intact circle from a creature that behaves largely like a ball of phlegm. The stagiaires attempt to follow his instructions, but most fail miserably; the apple-cheeked Sergi Palacín, one of the local culinary school recruits, ends up with a few shreds of slimy tissue that he pokes disconsolately around a plate. Eugeni demonstrates it again; the stagiaires try once more. Oriol comes over to inspect their work, shakes his head, and orders the stagiaires to leave each prepped anemone on a plate until Eugeni can check it. "We can't have any mistakes on Tuesday," he notes. "I don't care if Eugeni has to demo it a hundred times. You've got to have it down by Tuesday."

There are chores that are physically hard: because the restaurant makes its own coconut milk for its spectacular "balloon"—a dish that looks like a dinosaur egg—kilos of coconuts need to be cracked open and chopped into pieces, a job that requires a good hammer and strong biceps. Yet the coconuts pale in terms of exertion compared to the tuna marrow, which comes encased in thick, bony pieces of spine as tall as some of the stagiaires themselves. With cleavers, the cooks struggle to pare away enough bone to render the spine fragile enough to break, then carefully scoop out the gelatinous marrow inside. They are supposed to extract it in a single, bloblike piece.

The work is bloody and mildly disgusting—there are thick veins to contend with—but nothing as bad as the rabbit brains. For those, the stagiaires are confronted with several trays of neatly arranged rabbit heads, their fur and skin removed to expose the pink flesh beneath, their tiny teeth bared, their unseeing eyes all staring in the same direction. Each cook picks up a head, positions it on his cutting board, and drives the tip of a chef's knife through the center of the skull until it splits open. Picking up the half head, he now carefully spoons out the cerebellum. Provided, of course, that he hasn't accidentally driven his knife too hard into the carapace. In that case, he will have splattered the brains all over the interior of the skull. "I never got used to that one," confesses Jorge, who was once a vegetarian. "I just couldn't look at those rows of peeled bunny heads."

Almost all of the prep work requires a level of precision that is new to all but a few of the stagiaires. Anyone who has been to culinary school knows how to turn a vegetable, paring its rounded edges into flat surfaces, so that the finished product resembles something akin to an American football. The idea is that when those carrots or parsnips are plated, all the vegetables will be the same size and shape, imparting a pleasing geometric symmetry to the dish. At elBulli it is rhubarb that must be turned, only in this case it's not because one piece of rhubarb will be sitting next to another—in fact, there is only one piece per plate. The rhubarb is being turned so that it looks more or less like the *espardenya*, the sea cucumber beloved in Catalan cuisine, with which it will share a plate. For the visual effect to work, however, the rhubarb must be pared to a length of precisely six centimeters and then cut so that its ends taper gently. And that requires not only a ruler but a piece of modeling clay. In fact, the clay pops up everywhere during this first week, a splotch of bright red or blue molded to the correct size and held up as a model against which to measure a turned piece of rhubarb or a hand-piped gnocco or a baguette-shaped meringue. It is one of elBulli's minor innovations and one of its ironies: that precision in this supposed temple to technology requires not some finely calibrated machine but a substance most commonly found in kindergarten classrooms. "We use it to minimize arguments over who has the size right," says Ferran. "That's what we want. A minimum of opinions."

Precision, physical endurance, the abilities to overcome disgust and keep one's opinions to oneself: these are all key qualities in a stagiaire. But although the cooks may not realize it yet, another characteristic will be infinitely more important to their success at elBulli, and that is the mental and emotional ability to withstand the tedious. In this first week, when every task is new, it makes a certain sense to spend hours at a time squeezing olives or cracking coconuts. "You have to repeat it over and over until it becomes second nature," says Luke uncomplainingly. But there are signs, even now, of what is to come.

First thing on the morning of June 12, for example, the new cooks learn to make yubas. The group is divided in two, with half crowding around the flattop as Eugeni demonstrates. A yuba is a milk skin—the solid film that forms, as anyone who has ever made hot chocolate knows, when milk is boiled. Ferran learned the technique in Japan, and he has used it for the last few years at elBulli, turning it into the protagonist of several dishes. Later in the season, the yuba will be made of soy milk and will become one component on a plate filled with several of soy's possible iterations. But for now the kitchen will be serving skins made from cow's milk as the wrapper of a dessert called "omelette surprise."

Emma Leftick pulls a yuba from a pot of milk

(Francesc Guillamet)

Eugeni begins by pouring several cartons of organic German milk into a pot. Even this mundane task comes with methodological instructions that border on the banal: "Lower the carton into the pot and pour from there," Eugeni commands. "Otherwise, you'll splatter." Milk safely in the vessel, he turns on a flame and waits for the contents to boil. As the skin starts to form, he presses it lightly with a pastry brush to prevent air bubbles from forming. An unspecified number of minutes later, he deems the skin sufficiently solid, scoops it up with his bare hands, and carefully lifts it onto a sheet of plastic wrap. This is the trickiest step in the whole process: getting the yuba to lie flat and wrinkle-free, without tearing. If it rips, it goes into the trash. If there is a hole in it, it goes into the trash. If there is a tiny air bubble through which, once filled, its innards might leak, it goes into the trash. Each of the stagiaires

takes a turn practicing before Eugeni asks for volunteers to be in ch.
In the haste to show themselves eager for any responsibility, a slew o.
hands shoots up. Eugeni pauses for a moment to look at each face before
choosing Iosu Sainz and Miguel Alexander Pérez. The others eye them
with a mix of envy and resignation, suspecting that the selection has
been a judgment and that those not chosen have been found wanting.
But all is not what it seems at elBulli. Iosu and Miguel Alexander have
no idea what they've just volunteered for.

With each new task, the learning process is the same. Utensils
and receptacles are laid out in twin lines on the center counter. Taking
his place at the head of the table, Eugeni demonstrates the proper
technique, then hovers over the stagiaires as they attempt to replicate
his movements. If too many of them fail, he does the demo again. Once
he's sure they've got it, the entire line—fifteen stagiaires—begins on the
product in earnest. As they near its completion, Eugeni pulls away some
of the cooks and starts them on a new task, which he again begins by
demonstrating. And so it goes, through pigs' tails (blanch the tail, split
it open with a paring knife, scrape out the cartilage, lay it flat in a tray),
rabbit ears (blanch the ears, peel the skin and fur, swab a stick through
the crevices to clean out any dirt, insert a skewer to keep the ears flat, lay
in tray), and pistachios (crack, peel).

In these early days, the stagiaires are too excited by the new products
and too afraid to screw up to mind or even notice the repetition involved
in their prep work. And there are so *many* unexpected steps, so many
things to keep in mind with even the most mundane products: they
must remember to smell each oyster after they open it and hold each
pea-sized mandarin orange segment up to the light to check for seeds. If
they forget—if one oyster accidentally goes straight from hand to *taper*,
Eugeni will be there, chastising. Watching them from the sidelines,
Marc Cuspinera comments, "In three days they get enough information
to drive any sane person crazy." As he observes them struggling to keep
up, he makes a little joke: "Go on, ask them if they have any questions."

o o o

The center table plates during service (Francesc Guillamet)

With two days to go before the opening, the stagiaires finally begin to learn how to plate. From the very beginning, the pastry apprentices have worked in their own station, but by now all the rest have been divided as well, based on criteria that are neither expressed to them nor understood by them. Sunny is clearly one of the most technically skilled cooks, but he is sent to the small kitchen, which—perhaps because it is responsible for family meal, perhaps because it is so small that it is claustrophobic—is seen by many of the stagiaires as the rough equivalent of remedial math class. Meanwhile Cesare Marazzi, who puts off some of his peers with his laissez-faire attitude toward work, gets assigned *cuarto frío,* considered one of the more desirable stations because its cooks tend to work with the most avant-garde techniques and technology. Unsure of the criteria by which judgment is made, the stagiaires console themselves with the thought that none of these assignments is permanent.

But how *are* the assignments made? Language figures into the decision—the chefs don't want to put anyone into a position of even the most minor responsibility if he doesn't speak Spanish well, which is why Sunny and Emma—both of whom came through a Thomas Keller kitchen—get sent to Small Kitchen. But beyond that, the new assignments are based on largely intuitive judgments. Having watched the stagiaires do little more than clean proteins and pare vegetables—and having never seen most of them even turn on a stove—the staff still feels confident about its ability to judge its new apprentices. "You can definitely see differences among them," says Luis, the affable chef de partie of Starters I. "Everyone has lots of energy, but some are more nervous, depending on their experience. You can see who pulls to one side or another, who uses the knife well, who's faster, who works clean, or who just barely wipes a cloth over the counter, who is aware of what's going on around them." Aitor Zabala, the chef de partie of Cold Station, doesn't get to choose his own crew, but he understands how they were selected. "We've been watching them—how they do basic things like chop," he says. "Cold Station is its own little world, so I need people who aren't too young and who can take responsibility for themselves. They have to be good." He pauses for a minute. "But they can't be too good. The very best go someplace else."

The very best go, in fact, to the chefs de partie in the main kitchen. Marc sees Nico, Txema, and Roger as among the strongest cooks, so the three of them are assigned as assistants to Luis on Starters I, Anthony Masas on Meat, and Sergio Barrosa on Fish. Because this assignment frees them from the center table during part of mise en place (which, even on the fifth day of work, is quickly becoming drearily repetitive), it is highly coveted. The fact that during service an assistant may occasionally be called on to actually cook—and not just plate—makes it all the more so. But of all the stagiaires, it is Andrea who wins what everyone agrees is the best job. Three days into her *stage*, Oriol taps her as his "creativity" assistant. The assignment means that she will have to come in earlier than the other stagiaires and that the very first thing she will be required to do in the morning is spray for flies, but she will also be quite literally at Oriol's right hand as he invents and tests new recipes. She, more than anyone else, will witness what elBulli is all about.

The remainder—about fifteen of the stagiaires—stay at the center table, where, during service, they will be responsible for plating any dishes the chefs de partie and their assistants can't do themselves. Which is why, on the morning of June 14, Oriol begins the laborious work of teaching the stagiaires not only what the forty or so plates currently on the menu should look like but how to make them look that way. They start with the gnocchi—a dish that looks like the traditional Italian pasta made from potatoes but is in fact made from spherified polenta so that its texture is lighter and its interior almost liquid. Sauced lightly with coffee, hazelnut oil, and Parmesan cream and dressed with strips of yuba, the gnocchi are finally garnished with a sprinkling of coffee beans and capers.

Oriol shapes a few pieces of modeling clay into "gnocchi," then starts assigning tasks. Luke brings over the plates; José Luis takes them to the salamander to heat, then returns them to the center table. Pablo places six gnocchi on the plate, grouping them in pairs so that they form a triangle; Laia drizzles a tablespoon of Parmesan cream over each. Antonio follows with ground coffee beans, carefully applying them in a line. Diego places three capers in the middle of the triangle; Mike lays on two pieces of yuba. Jorge spoons a bit of saffron-infused cream on top of the two strips of yuba. Last comes Roger with a pipette, squeezing a few drops of hazelnut oil onto the bottom of the dish. This would all be confusing enough if the plates were passing one by one on a conveyer belt, but they are not. Indeed, they are stationary; it is the cooks who are moving. Oriol teaches them to rotate clockwise around the table so that, ideally, they won't crash into one another. But in the heat of the moment, with everyone watching and Oriol there calling out "C'mon, c'mon," the action looks more like a scrimmage than a plating, and the dishes reflect the chaos. Oriol spends a good five minutes delineating mistakes: the yuba is touching the gnocchi, the capers are touching the yuba, the coffee beans are not equidistant from one another. "Anytime you make a mistake, we're going to send the plate back. And let's say that plate is part of a four-top and you've got other tables behind you. We send one plate back, we're going to throw everything off. You'll be totally fucked."

They try again. This time Oriol calls, "Three gnocchi," and for a moment, the stagiaires all freeze, like deer caught in headlights. Toni Moraga has to intervene: he quickly tells Luke to get some plates and the other apprentices fall into place. At last, the finished product get Oriol's approval. They move on to the next dish, an asparagus canapé wrapped in an obulato—a tissue-thin, clear paper made from potato starch that will be heavily featured in the 2009 menu. It's delicate enough that several attempts are ruined simply by the sweaty grip of a nervous stagiaire. Next comes the omelette surprise. For it, yogurt air—yogurt that has been turned into an ethereal mousse by shooting it through a siphon—is piped onto a yuba, which is then rolled up and dusted with sugar. The sugar, in turn, is caramelized with a hand torch, and the whole omelette is garnished with tiny flowers. One after another, new dishes are added to the roster, until finally Oriol is imitating service, calling for three gnocchi, two canapés, two omelettes at once. The cries of *"Quemo!"* grow louder and more insistent as the entire kitchen leaps into motion. José Luis breaks into a trot as he goes to fetch more plates. Eugeni calls him on it immediately, reminding him of yet another rule: no running in the kitchen.

o o o

On June 15, a gnawing anxiety wakes Eduard Xatruch at dawn. Though he's been working at elBulli for the past twelve years, he seems never to have relaxed into the job. In large part, that's because so much of the burden of running the day-to-day operations of the restaurant depends upon him. He may share a title with Oriol Castro, but the two have divided their labors neatly, and Eduard makes sure that, when it comes to the mechanics of the kitchen, everything runs smoothly. And thus, every year right before the restaurant opens, he is awakened by this worry: Will they form a machine?

At elBulli there are many metaphors for how the kitchen should work. Oriol tends to refer to its ideal state as a *piña*—pineapple—which is common Spanish slang for something that is tightly united. Ferran calls what goes on behind the pass a ballet—a series of moves that flows like choreographed dance. But for Eduard, the most practical of the three—and in many ways the one with the greatest pressure on him—a well-run kitchen hums like a machine.

One day before the restaurant opens, Eduard knows his machine isn't running smoothly. The other chefs will say, with perhaps just a bit too much enthusiasm, that everything is going fine, that the *chicos* are working hard, that it will all fall into place, that it always does. But Eduard notices everything that goes wrong. As he prepares to purée olives, Gaël sets up the Thermomix in the wrong place. Anthony leaves a stack of trays jutting over the edge of the counter, where anyone could knock them over. Unable to rid himself of the vocabulary of his former job, Txema keeps saying *"Voy"* ("Coming through") as he rounds a corner, despite the fact that Eugeni corrects him repeatedly: *"Quemo,* Txema, *quemo."* Eduard catches two stagiaires failing to smell their oysters as they shuck them—a failure that could condemn the restaurant to food poisoning charges should bad shellfish make its way to the diners. Oriol looks over the turned rhubarb, finds a problem with the ends—they don't look sea cucumber–ish enough—and dumps them in the trash, telling Eugeni to demo them again. Family meal setup and breakdown times have been pared but are still not where they should be. Even simple communication remains a problem. Pablo Pavón, the chef de partie of Small Kitchen, sends Emma to Cold Station to get some yuzu (an Asian citrus fruit), and Aitor, who is busy shaping meringue rolls, responds that he'll bring them to her. She nods a bit too earnestly, starts to walk away, then thinks better of it and goes back. *"No entiendo,"* she admits sheepishly.

But the greatest threat to Eduard's machine is a lack of concentration. Much of the stagiaires' work may look mindless, but it requires intense focus if the proper effect is to be achieved. Nothing seems simpler, for example, than cutting black strands of codium seaweed (the cooks use scissors to snip its branches at their base to get tiny Vs), but one quick joke with another cook, even a glance up at the clock, could easily result in a cut that is more Y than V. For Eduard, the embodiment of discipline, that possibility is unacceptable. Every task requires total focus, yet with one day to go, all he can see is the lack of it. There is a pit in the squeezed olives, a seed in a mandarin section. Miguel Alexander's sweeping after family meal leaves whole spots of the floor untouched; it remains anyone's guess whether Diego will remember to unroll the tablecloths in the proper direction. During prep, Sergi suddenly grabs his chest and doubles over in pain. Eduard and Oriol rush to his side, fearing the young cook has suffered a heart attack. But no: Sergi has snagged his nipple ring on the inside of his jacket. Oriol finds it funny, but Eduard is not amused. "The time for mistakes was three days ago," he says with a quiet firmness that silences not only Sergi's nervous giggles but everyone else's too. "There's no more time for mistakes."

The stagiaires finish the last day before opening around midnight. Fourteen hours earlier, they had watched a film entitled *A Day at elBulli*, a documentary about the day they would themselves be living in a few short hours. It was a strange experience, watching the people they know as their new bosses—Ferran, Oriol, Eduard, Mateu—interact with people they had never met but whose jobs they would be performing. For some it was exhilarating, seeing each dazzling creation come out of the kitchen to be received with utter delight by the diners. For others it was almost religiously comforting, a suggestion in its faithful re-creation of the minutes between the time when Eduard first came downstairs and turned on the lights to the one when the exhausted waiters turned them off again, that they were part of something bigger, more important, than the simple process of putting food on a plate. But for almost all of the stagiaires, it was also deeply enervating. "It made me realize that there's no room for mistakes," says Andrea. "That video totally freaked me out."

Seated outside on the stone bench near the dressing room, the formal training period behind them, a handful of stagiaires smoke cigarettes and tries to imagine what the following day will bring. Daniel Ryan, who comes from Baltimore by way of Alinea and Alain Ducasse, echoes Andrea's sentiment. "Ferran Adrià knows that it's the first day, he knows that we're going to make mistakes. But for the client who has been anticipating this meal all year, there's no room for that. It really ups the pressure." Ralph, who has worked only in small restaurants before and is still getting used to the crush of people in the elBulli kitchen, freely admits that he is nervous. "I haven't learned the plates yet," he says, fiddling with the buttons on his jacket. "I don't know what I have to do." His countryman, Gaël, nods miserably in agreement. "At least you have plates. I still haven't figured out where I'm supposed to stand."

But others are looking forward to the start of service. Sunny confesses to a bit of relief at having the training period behind him. "Look, it's hard enough to train two people, let alone thirty-two, so I can't complain. But I'm ready for a little more excitement." Kim nods her head in agreement. "I'm ready too," she says. "I want to see what it's all about." It is Luke Jang, however, who puts the anticipation most eloquently, despite his imperfect Spanish and a Korean upbringing that one would not normally associate with intimate knowledge of American popular culture. Untying his apron, he smiles broadly. "It's like being a kid and knowing you get to go to Disneyland the next day. I feel like I'm going to Disneyland."

o o o

So much of what happens at elBulli is the result of years, if not decades, of honing and practice. Much of what the stagiaires experience as new and exciting—which is basically everything from how stations are organized to the fact that no one ever uses butter to make a sauce—has been arrived at through extensive testing, year after year, one variable altered at a time and then another. That history is what makes the permanent staff at elBulli so valuable to Ferran—they, as much as he, are its institutional memory. Marc, the chefs de cuisine, and the maître d's all have more than a decade under their belts, and so, on opening night, even though they themselves haven't worked a service in six months, they step seamlessly into their roles, remembering how to time orders, how to plate certain dishes, how to greet diners, and how to clean the dining room and kitchen without ever having to stop to think about it. Like semiretired ballplayers called back for one last game, knowledge is imprinted not only in their brains but in their bodies—they have physical memories of how to carry out each task. Ferran's creativity—the ability to totally reinvent his menu each year—rests in part on this stable collective memory, the confidence that, though the menu will change, everything else will be exactly as it should be.

That said, 2009 promised some unusual upheavals. Although rumors had run every year that this season would be elBulli's last, they became significantly louder earlier in 2009, when the restaurant was named best in the world for the fifth time. Now that he had affirmed his position so resoundingly, the thinking ran, how could Ferran risk losing that status? Yet no restaurant is great forever. So strong was the speculation that Marc even made a joke about it at the stagiaires' first meeting. Promising that anyone who successfully completed the *stage* could come back the following year to work and observe for a week or two, he smiled slyly. "That is, if we're still around."

Ferran was also coming off an ugly public battle with Santi Santamaria, a fellow three-star chef, who had criticized him openly not only for veering from any recognizably national tradition of cooking but for actually endangering his clients' health with the additives he uses to achieve many of his dishes. It was the first time that the normal fraternal feeling of Spain's top cooks had fractured publicly, and Ferran was both hurt and annoyed by the charges. The critics were ready to pounce: Would the greatest chef in the world change his style of cooking in response? In the past few years, many of them suggested, he had been moving away from technological innovation and was emphasizing ingredients in new ways. Would that trend continue, in an effort to prove that he didn't need the scientific trickery that Santamaria had accused him of exploiting? Or would he roar back with more wizardry than ever?

But the biggest change was the season itself. For the past twenty-two years, elBulli had opened only in spring and summer, seating its first customers sometime in April and its last in September. The season has a certain inherent logic: elBulli is, after all, located in a beach town. But for the first time, Ferran had decided to shake up that logic; in 2009 the restaurant wouldn't open until June and would run until the end of December. The new season would mean all sorts of changes: new purveyors would have to be found, for example, and guests wouldn't only leave the restaurant and descend the mountainside in pitch blackness; it would be dark on the way up too.

Pressed for a reason for the change, Ferran would say something about wanting to take advantage of autumn's products—the mushrooms and squashes and game with which he doesn't usually get to work. As far back as 2004, he had noted in one of his books that he thought it would be "fun" to open in winter instead of summer. But spend enough time with him, and you might start to feel that he did it out of sheer impishness, a desire to change something simply because it could be changed.

o o o

By the time most of the stagiaires arrive at 1 P.M. on June 16, Iosu and Miguel Alexander have been working for hours. The assignment that so cheered them when they first received it—making yubas—has quickly become drudgery, one that requires them to turn up two hours earlier than anyone else in order to finish in time. Each yuba takes roughly fifteen minutes to make, and they have to prepare seventy. Bleary-eyed in the morning light, they stare into their pots of boiling milk.

The others don't look much peppier. When Eduard calls the staff meeting at precisely 1 P.M., the stagiaires file in one by one to take their places around the kitchen's edge, their nervousness and fatigue palpable. All the stagiaires in José Luis's apartment stayed up studying late into the night, going over the elements of plates they had worked on, pressing one another for details about the ones they hadn't seen. They got about four hours of sleep. Kim, agitated in equal amounts by her desire to perform well and the heat in her sweltering apartment, didn't sleep at all. Even Oriol admits to feeling a little nervous.

Which is why Ferran begins the morning meeting by trying to calm everyone. "Tonight people will come from all over the world to eat our cooking. For them, it is a very big deal. For them, they expect tonight to be the best meal, even the best day, of their year." He pauses to look around at his new crew, whose faces have drained of all color at this reminder. "But don't worry. The world won't end this week, no matter what happens in this restaurant. Relax. Have a good time."

With those words, Ferran hands the meeting over to Oriol and Eduard. Although elBulli prepares an individual fixed menu for each table from among the roughly fifty dishes it has on hand at any time, enough new plates are introduced that the chefs routinely use the morning meeting to draw attention to any anomalies. Tonight, for example, a few lucky tables will get to try the new sugarcane cocktails, and Oriol details how many of those plates have been "sold" in order to alert the responsible stations to add their preparation to mise en place. Eduard mentions special tables: in this case, Rafael Ansón, the head of the Royal Spanish Gastronomic Academy, is coming with his family. There will also be a table of nine, which promises to complicate service. The rest of the meeting is given over to more mundane matters, such as the facts that the dressing area is too messy and some stagiaires haven't been turning out the lights when they leave the staff bathroom. There is also a problem with spoons: they keep disappearing. Although it is only the chefs de partie who taste, and thus who regularly use spoons, they frequently forget to put them back into the water-filled bins on the stove top, where they are supposed to stand at the ready; instead, the spoons end up in the bin with dirty dishes. Or something like that— the truth is that no one really seems to know where all the spoons are going. In any case, it's a problem, and Oriol is about to assign a stagiaire the task of making sure there are always spoons available, when Ferran, who has been flipping through papers at the kitchen table he uses as a desk, raises his head and interrupts. "There aren't enough spoons?" he demands. "Well, there's an easy solution for that. Why doesn't each of us put our names on a spoon? With tape and a marker." Oriol and Eduard exchange a look that could be mild horror. "No, no, no," Ferran talks over their apparent skepticism. "This is good. This way you can keep it with you, and everyone will know it is yours." It's a trick that Ferran has already adopted for writing instruments, which once had a tendency to disappear from his desk. Now he writes only with a lurid Barça souvenir pencil whose end is capped with a child's oversized eraser. Everyone in the restaurant knows who that pencil belongs to, and no one would dare touch it. But spoons are a different story. The chefs de partie look around nervously, as if to say, Are you really going to make us worry about where our spoons are? Eduard looks no happier at the idea but remains quiet, contemplating, perhaps, the idea of walking around all day with a dirty utensil in his pocket. Ferran starts rummaging through a drawer for tape.

In a kitchen where no one ever strolls but instead moves with a walk so purposeful that it always threatens to break into a full-scale run, mise en place is even more urgent today than before. The stagiaires trim anemone fringe, shuck oysters, crack coconuts, and squeeze olives with new fluidity and answer every request or command with robust oídos— the only human sound, in fact, in the otherwise deathly quiet kitchen. When Eugeni points to a small puddle of water on the floor, Luke drops to his knees with such rapidity to mop it up that he looks as if he's been shot. All is not perfect—Eduard has to demo the rhubarb again—but there is a synchronicity to the activity that wasn't there before.

This synchronicity is perhaps most evident when the delivery truck arrives from the Boqueria market at midafternoon and the stagiaires line up outside to unload it. Earlier in the week, the process bore a significant resemblance to a Three Stooges routine, with apprentices running into one another as they climbed and descended the stairs that led from the unloading area to the kitchen door. Eduard would pull an item from the truck, place it in the waiting cook's arms, and issue an instruction ("Peanuts: storeroom. Xantham gum: storeroom. Blood sausage: walk-in. Yuzus: Mateu"), but because most stagiaires weren't familiar with either the item in question or the place it was to be delivered, there was quite a lot of bumbling, and more than a few urgent whispers between them (*Where* did he say this goes?). This time, however, everyone knows more or less where everything belongs, and the movement up and down the stairs is ordered and fluid, like a machine.

But there are still new things to learn. In Pastry, Mateu spends the first part of the morning teaching Mizuho Nakamura—or Miso, as he and the other Spanish chefs insist on calling her—how to use the heat lamp to mold three-dimensional leaves made from candied mango dusted with freeze-dried basil powder. In the main kitchen, Oriol is still testing the new mojito—sugarcane sticks soaked in rum and mint, that the diner sucks rather than drinks—that he plans to serve that night. And throughout the day Ferran is there, tasting, questioning. Sometimes, seated at his table, with e-mails awaiting response and trial menus spread around him, he waits for Oriol to come over and dab sauce on his outstretched hand or place a plate before him. At others, he will meander over to the flattop, and dip his spoon—the spoon now inked with FERRAN in big red letters—into a pot. At around five in the afternoon, he looks over at the center table as they peel the skins from sticky cloves of black garlic and says to no one in particular, "It feels like you've been here forever, right? Don't forget, you still have eight more hours to go."

Still, it's a rush to the finish. Iosu and Miguel Alexander finally plate their last yuba around 5:30. Twenty-five minutes later, Oriol is still tinkering with his sugarcane cocktails. He looks up at the clock and says, "Crap." Today the crew will eat half an hour earlier than it normally does, to make sure everything is properly set up by the time the first customer arrives, but that means they've had less time to finish mise en place. As the last products go back into the walk-in and counters are cleared, the stagiaires are moving with frantic speed. *Quemo, quemo, quemo:* chairs slam into place around the tables and water bottles are set down even before tubs of pared ham fat can be cleared. *Quemo, quemo:* platters of salad go onto the table along with loaves of bread. A long-standing friend of the house, the owner of a local bar, has dropped off several large boxes of pastry to mark the occasion, and those go onto the bar, as do pears that the staff will pick up for dessert. The activity is so intense that a writer visiting that day feels compelled to press himself against the wall in order to avoid being run over. Through it all, Eduard watches their movements and the clock. He won't allow himself to smile, but the lack of criticism tells the stagiaires they've got at least this part of the timing down. Or almost. Suddenly Oriol grabs a chair to stand on, and pulls down the clock. "I just realized that it's not synchronized with the one in the small kitchen." He rushes to align the two, just as the staff is filing in for dinner. *"Quemo,"* he says. *"Quemo, quemo."*

The stagiaires bolt down a meal of salad, ribs, and the pastries. Most then throw back espressos (though, given the adrenaline level in the room, it would seem that few need the caffeine) before going outside to take in a bit of fresh air. In the precious minutes before they are called back, they chat nervously. Katie will be on the pass in Pastry, which is also responsible for the first snacks that go out. She seeks reassurance from the others. "I know Mateu will take care of everything," she says, referring to her chef de cuisine, "but I have no idea what to expect." Before anyone has a chance to console her, however, the half-hour dinner break is over. The stagiaires lower their bibs and retie their aprons around their waists. Then, in total silence, they descend into the kitchen to begin cleaning plates. Ferran is already there, simultaneously buttoning a clean jacket over his bare chest and sucking back a Germanic herbal digestif from one of those small bottles you get on airplanes; the digestif, he says, calms his stomach after tasting so many different dishes throughout the day. He removes the papers from his table in the kitchen and straightens the cushions on the chairs. "It's a sign that the show is about to begin," he says, then looks up through the plate glass window at the overcast sky. It has been threatening to rain all day, and in a kitchen where so many of the dishes contain fragile, freeze-dried elements, humidity is the worst enemy. It's hard to tell from his gaze whether Ferran is beseeching the gods for mercy or challenging them, but the question quickly becomes irrelevant as Luis's voice booms through the kitchen. "There are people outside." The door to the restaurant opens, and as the clocks in both the main and small kitchens hit 7:30, Ferran says, "Okay, *señores*, let's begin."

o o o

At elBulli, all diners are ushered into the kitchen before sitting down to eat. Led by one of the multilingual maître d's, they are brought directly to Ferran, who is always standing at the pass, ready to welcome them. Given the awe in which many of his customers hold him, the routine would feel like a papal visit if it weren't for the warmth with which Ferran greets them and the busy industriousness going on all around him. Later in the season, the stagiaires won't notice this part, not even when famous chefs such as Wolfgang Puck come to dine. But on this first night, as the first clients—an Australian couple who have dressed up for the occasion—are led into the kitchen, the cooks stop for a split second and gape. Eduard's voice quickly breaks the trance. No sooner are the first couple on their way out of the kitchen then he calls, "Two coníferas," ordering the new pine-and-yogurt cocktail that comes with a side of pine shoots to munch on. From Pastry comes the response. *"Oído!"*

The second table, a family of four, is led into the kitchen. On normal nights, Eduard expedites while Ferran observes how the kitchen is working, monitors the plates as they go out, and continues tasting new recipes. But tonight is no ordinary night, and on this occasion, Ferran does the expediting himself. As each new table is led into the kitchen, he moves gracefully out in front to greet them and pose for pictures, while Eduard slides into place at the pass and seamlessly continues expediting.

Glancing out the window, Ferran notices that the rain he has feared all day has begun. He makes sure that Mateu, who works with many of the products that must remain dry and crisp, knows about the weather. *"Oído,* Mateu?" he asks. *"Oído,"* replies Mateu with a sigh. An overweight American walks into the kitchen with a slim woman, whom he introduces to Ferran as "my new wife." It is fifteen minutes past opening, and there are now three tables seated in the restaurant. Eduard orders two of the new sugarcane cocktails from Small Kitchen, where he gets a chorus of distant *oídos* in reply. A minute later he calls out, "Start two menus," which is the signal to the kitchen that a table has finished its snacks and cocktails and moved on to the main part of the meal. By now, the stagiaires have finished cleaning plates and stand ready to spring into action as black-clad waiters stream by the front of the kitchen with silver trays. The restaurant has been open for only twenty minutes.

Ferran calls for four chicharrones (which are normally fried pigskin but in this case are made from the skin of chicken feet) and four avellantos (a fragile cake made from crunchy amaranth grains and ground, freeze-dried hazelnut skin, barely pressed together). There is enough work for only three or four stagiaires, but twice that many crowd around the plates. The noise begins to grow, and Ferran hisses, *"Señores, silencio!"* He calls the next plate to one of the chefs de partie, "Antonio, four Peking," only to get two confused *oídos* in response. There are two chefs named Antonio (as well as a stagiaire), though neither goes precisely by that name—one calls himself Anthony, the other Toni. There is a moment of chaos as Ferran tries to figure out who should be preparing the order, but he doesn't have time to resolve it because another group has just walked into the kitchen, and they too want a picture with him.

The chefs figure it out themselves (Peking come from Toni in Starters II), though everyone's nerves are on edge: as Pablo goes to plate the delicate crêpes that Toni has prepared, his hand shakes. Ferran has enough time at the pass to call two more orders: a Parmesan "crystal" to Mateu in Pastry and four bizcochos to Aitor in Cold Station (bizcochos are his brother Albert's spectacular invention—an airy but substantive sponge cake made from miso and black sesame paste, aerated in the siphon and then baked in a microwave). As each tray is readied to go out, Eugeni, Eduard, Oriol, and Marc (who has come in specially for the night) stand nearby, watching intently. One sends back a chicharrón that has been fried too long, another catches a plate with fingerprints on it. The noise level rises again, as cooks rush through the kitchen with cries of *"Quemo! Quemo!"* and again Ferran, raising his own voice now, silences them.

By 8:50 P.M., when the last table shows up (it is Ansón, the Gastronomy Academy president, who always comes to dine on the first night of the season), the kitchen has descended into apparent chaos. It is only now that the stagiaires have grasped an essential point of elBulli: during service, no one will be calmly telling them to put this element here, plate that component there. Instead, they have to listen to all the orders as they are called, figure out what station they'll be coming from, remember what goes on which dishes, then, worst of all, fight off their fellow stagiaires for a place at the plate. They have been taught to move around the plates in an orderly, clockwise fashion, carefully putting "their" element on the dish before stepping aside to allow the next stagiaire through with the following item. But what actually happens during this first service looks like a rugby match, and a bloody one at that. Stagiaires with small cups of herbs elbow others with pipettes of oil out of the way in order to get to the plate, while still others, momentarily bereft of anything to do, crowd around trying to watch. At one point Eugeni physically pushes Sergi out of the way because the stagiaire is taking up too much space gawking as nine of his companions try to plate.

The food going out becomes more complicated as well. At the start of a menu, most of the dishes are dry snacks, prepared earlier in the day, that need only to be placed on their appropriate receptacle. But by this point in service, stagiaires have to remember techniques. Aitor corrects Ralph because he is messing up the mochi—slippery balls of Gorgonzola foam that have an unnerving tendency to behave like mercury. He is supposed to dribble each ball back and forth on a paper napkin four times, to ensure that no liquid makes it onto the plate, but his mochi are landing with tiny pools of water around them. Emma is constantly running between the small kitchen, where the grilled strawberries that accompany the mochi are prepped, and the salamanders on opposite sides of the main kitchen, where they are heated before serving. The baby cuttlefish have to be seared on the plancha; the asparagus canapés lifted onto their plates with perfectly dry hands; the pigs' tails garnished with exactly three sprigs of microgreens.

A server hurriedly picks up a tray, and in the brusqueness of the movement an orange segment falls from the plate to the floor. She looks around to see if anyone has noticed and, not seeing anyone, continues on her way—after all, there are a lot more segments on the plate. But just before she reaches the edge of the dining room, Xus González, one of the maître d's, calls her back; he has been watching the whole time. "What are you doing?" he demands before sending her back to the pass. Aitor can't bring himself to look at her as he replates.

The orders keep coming. "Do you have two cuttlefish working?" *"Oído!"* "Two beans." *"Oído!"* "Two olives and four airs." *"NO OÍDO!"* comes Mateu's frantic reply. Andrea goes to plate two asparagus canapés but, finding no more of the correct plates on the pass, throws out her arms in despair. Tempers start to fray. Ferran yells at the chefs de partie: "You have to look at the tickets!" Eduard yells at Sergio: "You have to listen!" Eugeni yells at Gaël: "You have to follow the chain of command!" Then it is Ferran again, clapping his hands and yelling for silence. Pol Perelló, one of the longtime maître d's, walks into the kitchen and says with a wry smile, "It's as if I went to sleep for eight months and just woke up. Nothing's changed."

In the midst of this chaos, Oriol has been quietly preparing a few plates. One of the most interesting products he and Ferran discovered in Japan during the months while the restaurant was closed was the obulato—the same clear sheet of potato-starch-turned-paper that cradles the asparagus canapé. It's a remarkable product—adaptable to any size or shape, it can act as a seemingly invisible base for supporting most any product that isn't too wet. All day, he's been testing a dish in which the obulato is folded into a cone, filled with a pine nut praliné, sealed with a laminating machine, then cut into a small, neat triangle. Now, at last, he has the dish down. He gives one to Ferran to try, and the two agree they're ready to send out—a special plate for Ansón, who will be the first customer to taste them. Oriol lays three triangles on each of four plates, along with small bowls of broth to dip them into. As a server picks up the tray, he tells her to instruct the clients to pop the triangles into their mouth quickly after dipping—otherwise they'll dissolve. She nods her understanding and is halfway out the kitchen before she turns back. "But what do I call them?" she asks. Ferran and Oriol look at each other: clearly, they've forgotten to name the dish. "Call them ravioli," Ferran answers without missing a beat. "Pine nut ravioli."

At 10 P.M., Cold Station is in the weeds—or in the purée, as they say in Spanish. Its dishes, the restaurant's most complicated, have to be timed perfectly to prevent them from melting. Ferran calls the first set of lulos, made with the tart pulp of a South American fruit, and Lucho comes running with the plate's garnish: shavings of frozen foie gras. To ensure that the fatty liver stays icy, Aitor pours a bucket of liquid nitrogen over the plates, and for a moment smoke billows over the pass and out onto the main floor, momentarily transforming the kitchen into the set of a horror movie. But the plates aren't finished—Jacobo Astray is still adding garnishes—and Ferran hurries over. He yells at Aitor, "What are you doing putting on the foie before the lulos are ready?" Aitor sends the foie shavings back to the freezer and starts the plates again. But he is only halfway through before Ferran is ordering nine yemitas, an Asian-inspired dish made with spherified egg yolks. Aitor throws down nine plates, and the entire station starts to work on a single order: Ralph squeezing out the yolks with a syringe, Jacobo spooning on the yogurt gelée, Lucho adding a few drops of thickened tea, Aitor sprinkling toasted sesame seeds. It's taking them too long, and Oriol runs over and jumps into the fray, "C'mon, c'mon, c'mon," he urges, grabbing the powdered shiso (a minty herb) and dusting it on himself. Aitor grabs the syringe out of Ralph's hand and starts squeezing yolks; Marc comes over to wipe down the edges of plates. Finally the dishes go out. But by then, of course, there are more lulos to plate.

At 10:45, Laia and Emma start rolling the first omelette surprise, a pre-dessert. Thirty minutes later, the first chocolate box goes out, a sign that one table, at least, has finished its meal. But eleven others are still working, and some still have a lot of menu to get through. Eugeni plates nine asparagus canapés. One isn't right; he tosses it disgustedly aside and demands another, as urgent as a surgeon calling for a clamp. Roger drops a plate, and the noise of the crash brings the entire kitchen to a momentary standstill before Oriol is on him, chastising him for his clumsiness. By now the nine-top has reached its omelette surprises, and twelve stagiaires are at the center table, nine of them rolling yuba around the yogurt foam that three others spray from siphons. Ferran comes over to watch and is displeased with what he finds. He lays into Eduard for not ensuring that the stagiaires have mastered the technique. Eduard studiously avoids looking at him. But at 12:30, just as the main kitchen has finished with all its plates (Cold Station and Pastry are still hard at work), he calls an emergency training session. Luis looks at the clock, looks at Eduard to see if he is serious, and shakes his head. For the next half hour, the stagiaires, with thirteen hours of mise en place and service behind them, practice rolling milk skins. No one says a word the entire time.

Finally they are allowed to break down the kitchen. Each grabs a bucket of soapy water and attacks a different part: stove, floor, counter, walls. With those chores done, Oriol sends them outside to hose down the unloading area and take out the trash. While the stagiaires clean, the chefs confer about the night. Eduard says, "Well, that's one day down. Only 195 to go." Asked if he thought there were any serious mistakes on this first night, Ferran says, "For the customers, no, nothing they would have noticed. But for us, absolutely. Just wait until tomorrow's meeting."

Tomorrow's meeting is about ten hours away, and by now only the pastry cooks are still turning out plates. Most of the stagiaires are outside, anxiously awaiting word that they can change and go home. Finally Oriol comes upstairs. In anticipation of getting the all-clear, Diego begins untying his apron. But alas: Small Kitchen needs help breaking things down, and the walk-in is a mess. As they descend back into the kitchen and their final chores of the night, a by-now familiar sound floats up the staircase. The voices issuing it are tired, even exhausted, but the sound is no less constant than before. *Quemo. Quemo, quemo.*

two

July, or **Achievement**

"Jam," Mateu says. "I need you to make jam."

Katie Button nods enthusiastically, envisioning a morning spent stirring pots of fragrant berries on the stove top. It is several days into the season, and finally, she thinks, she will get to do the kind of cooking she likes. Tall and coltish, with long, honey blond hair that she tames with bobby pins while she's working, Katie is the least experienced professional in elBulli's pastry kitchen and, except for the kids who are still in culinary school, the least experienced stagiaire in the entire restaurant. But jam is something she knows how to make. Since she was a child, her mother has run a catering business, and the twenty-six-year-old spent much of her adolescence and young adulthood helping her mom prepare sauces and roll out doughs. It was simple but delicious food, made with care and the freshest ingredients, and it's what Katie loves best.

Mateu explains that he's going to teach her to make the jam that pools under the dessert called Ices. The first step, as always, is to gather the ingredients. Katie nods appreciatively and begins to head to the walk-in where produce is stored when Mateu stops her.

"Go to the *almacén* and get two canisters of lyo-*melocotón* and one of lyo-*fresa*."

"*Almacén?*" Katie asks. The word has not yet come up in the textbook she is using to teach herself Spanish.

Mateu points in the general direction of the storeroom. "Okay?"

"Okay!" she responds, momentarily forgetting in her enthusiasm to use *oído*. The "lyo" part she has learned; the word is short for *liofilizado*, elBulli-speak for "freeze-dried." But she is still processing all the words in the sentence. "*Melocotón?*"

Mateu cups his hands together in the shape of a medium-sized round fruit, realizes the futility of that, and points to his eye. "Just read the label."

Katie disappears and comes back with two canisters of freeze-dried peaches and one of strawberries. Mateu is waiting for her. "Now get a *báscula*."

"*Báscula?*"

Remarkably, Mateu never loses patience. He grabs a scale and shows her the proper ratio of strawberries to peaches. Katie carefully jots down the proportions in her notebook, then weighs them out herself, checking repeatedly to make sure she has them right. As she empties the canisters, she remembers to put the lids inside them, just as she has been taught. She goes to get a bowl, smells it, wipes its interior, and pours the freeze-dried fruit into it. Only now she realizes she's missing something. She goes back to the dish station, fetches another bowl, smells it, wipes its interior, and finally pours a small dose of amaretto into it. She weighs the container with the liqueur in it, removes it from the scale, and is about to add it to the fruit when she stops herself: *Was that right?* Back on the scale the amaretto goes. She weighs it again and this time pours off a little. Satisfied, she finally adds it to the fruit, reconstituting it. It has taken her a lot of time and multiple trips to the dish station, but at last she has it: jam.

Mateu comes by to check the results. "*Muy bien*, Katie," he says encouragingly. She beams.

Katie Button

(Francesc Guillamet)

o o o

By early July, the stagiaires' nerves have calmed, leaving in their place a ravenous desire for information. Most of them don't have college degrees—"I wasn't very good in school" is a common refrain—and what they want to study, they want to study in a kitchen. Now that their more pressing worries have been resolved (*Will we get through service? Are we as good as last year's crop of stagiaires? Am I as good? Will I ever learn my way around a fucking sea anemone?*), they have an almost palpable hunger for more: more techniques, more access to Ferran, more challenging tasks, more tricks, more knowledge. The stagiaires have learned all the mise en place required for the opening menu and have more or less mastered the tasks that, only two weeks ago, befuddled many of them. Everyone is an expert at shucking oysters; they all know their way around a rabbit ear. In fact, they've become so skilled at their jobs that most no longer have to come in at noon to ensure they have enough time to finish their prep; morning meeting now starts at 2 P.M. or, on very good days, 2:30. Iosu and Miguel Alexander still have to arrive early to start their yubas, but even they have picked up speed and usually finish the day's milk skins by 4 P.M. or so. Eduard and Eugeni are still on top of people, still correcting—Gaël for forgetting to put a cloth under his cutting board one day, Sergi for still mauling the sea anemones. ("That's really ugly," Eduard says in response to one particularly butchered specimen. "Do you not get that this is a minimalist dish?") Oriol still has to remind people about the proper method of hand washing. And according to Ferran, the kitchen is still too noisy during service; people are putting plates down too hard, it should be completely silent except for the orders being called and the *oídos* issued in response. But the criticism is a little less frequent, and some things, such as the setup for family meal—now perfectly timed—garner no criticism at all. Service is also smoother; most of the stagiaires have figured out a way to stake a claim to certain components of certain plates. If plating seems no less like a scrimmage, at least it is a scrimmage in which each cook knows the plays and his proper position. Outside work, the stagiaires have managed to relax a bit: they've had a few days off and time away from the kitchen to make friends (Roger and Laia—whose lanky hair is dyed a shade of reddish pink not generally seen outside the tropics—have even started dating). And everyone has learned his or her way around the town of Roses. Like generations of elBulli cooks before them, the stagiaires now stop for coffee and pastries in the morning at Sant Pau and gather for drinks after service at L'Hort. And with all of that out of the way, they have suddenly, startlingly, found themselves with time to think. As they stand at the center table, bent over the task at hand, it sometimes seems as if a collective thought balloon has opened over their heads: *What's next?*

Not everyone is thriving. In fact, three of the stagiaires have already left the restaurant. Pablo, suffering from health problems, didn't want to leave, but one call from Marc to Pablo's parents convinced them it might not be wise for their son to be on his feet for fourteen hours a day, and he went home. Cesare was a more protracted case. Despite his assignment to the coveted Cold Station, the Italian's disenchantment with elBulli was evident in both the smirks with which he occasionally received direction and his attitude—an imperfectly spherified pesto square here, an unwiped plate there—toward work. Still, he gave no advance warning. At the morning meeting on the Tuesday after the first two days off, he simply wasn't there. But even that departure wasn't as shocking as Perfecto Rocher's. Not only had the thirty-year-old applied for an elBulli *stage* four years in a row before finally getting in but his American girlfriend had moved to Barcelona for the season so that they could see each other during his days off. Although he had been assigned to the small kitchen, he seemed thoroughly content with the work and remained as enthusiastic as ever about the restaurant. When he left, he told Marc it was for financial reasons—a car payment had something to do with it—and hinted that his girlfriend had played a role in his decision. But the truth was that he had been offered a job opening Julian Serrano's new restaurant in Las Vegas and his chef needed him right away. "I really loved being at elBulli," he says. "Leaving like that left a bad taste in my mouth." A few days later, two new stagiaires had taken Perfecto's and Cesare's places.

However particular the details, the departures were motivated by some common tensions. At the start of the season, both Perfecto and Cesare were excited to be at elBulli, thrilled to have the chance to learn from a restaurant each greatly admired. But in the world of professional cooking, learning requires you to subsume yourself and your ego in the undifferentiated mass that labors at the bottom of the kitchen hierarchy. "Humility," Oriol Castro answers when asked what makes a good stagiaire, and it takes only a glance at the center table to see what he means: you have to be willing to be a cog in the machine and take your lessons where they come. In Cesare's case, whatever he learned—and he did pick up new techniques, though not, he says, to the extent he had hoped—didn't compensate for the ego-crushing drudgery of the work and the uncomfortable position of being on the bottom rung. Perfecto, on the other hand, succumbed to the other enemy of this kind of education: ambition. He might have spent many years longing to immerse himself in elBulli, but, given the opportunity to break away from the brigade and assume control of his own kitchen, he leapt at the chance.

Most of the stagiaires feel some version of this tension. However much Ferran may refer to elBulli as a classroom, the education the restaurant offers differs significantly from that of a university or even a culinary school. The kitchen, after all, does not reward individualism; instead it requires a near-total submission to the brigade. The paradox for an aspiring cook is that the characteristics of a good apprentice (humility, an ability to swallow your ego) are antithetical to those that will one day make her a great chef (ambition, a strong sense of self). Thus all of the stagiaires face the same dilemma: How do they prove themselves apt, humble students while simultaneously standing out from the mass they are meant to meld into? With few options for resolving that conflict, most of them alight on the same tactic, which is not merely to comply with the rules but to surpass them. It's not enough to show up on time each morning; many of them arrive thirty or forty-five minutes early, even if it means they will do nothing but change into their uniforms and sit outside on the bench. (Eventually so many will come so early that they will annoy Ferran, who likes having the quiet morning hours to think.) And instead of merely moving briskly in the kitchen, almost all of them move with the exaggerated speed and intensity of a novice firefighter gearing up for his first three-alarm call. Racing through the kitchen as if a trip to the dishwasher were a minor emergency, chopping garlic as if the global supply might dry up at any moment, they seem veritably *propelled* by their determination to demonstrate how hard they are working. The irony, of course, is that everyone else is moving with the same determined vigor and in the end, no one stands out at all.

o o o

Katie hadn't always wanted to be a chef. For most of her life, she was drawn to science; like her father, she was enchanted by things like chemical reactions and the life cycle of insects. As a child growing up in South Carolina, she received a new chemistry set every year for Christmas, and although she was a strong all-around student, she excelled especially in science. By high school, she already mapped out her path: Ivy League college, graduate degree at a prestigious institution, then a career as a researcher at one of the country's premiere laboratories. It almost all came true. After graduating from Cornell, she got her master's degree at Paris's École Centrale and was one of three students in the world to receive a joint doctoral fellowship in biomedical engineering from the National Institutes of Health in the United States and Sweden's Karolinska Institute. At twenty-four, she was preparing to divide her time between Baltimore and Stockholm, where she would research apoptosis and the effects of aging on the brain. It was all in keeping with her pattern of striving: the best grades, the best schools, the best job. "Prestige, approval, they were always my thing," she says now. "I could count on them."

Scientist that she was, Katie didn't count on a crisis of faith. But then, for a month during the summer of 2007, before she began her PhD program, she went to Zambia to build houses with Habitat for Humanity. There she found herself fulfilled by work that produced such clear and immediate results. She also met and became involved with a man who worked in humanitarian causes; suddenly a lifetime in the lab didn't seem as appealing. "It helped put things into perspective. I didn't care about money or prestige anymore. I wanted to become Mother Teresa, join the Peace Corps, spend my life in Africa," she says. "But I was also very confused. I felt totally lost."

She returned to the United States and spent the rest of the summer traveling as she tried to figure out what to do with her life. She didn't feel prepared to go back to Africa, but she couldn't shake the apprehension she felt whenever she thought about graduate school. As August ended, she moved to the Washington, D.C., area, where the NIH is located, but her sense of dread only grew. "It was going to take me seven years to finish my PhD, and I just wasn't sure about it." A few days before the semester began, she realized she wasn't ready to make the commitment. In one of the darkest moments of her life, the girl who had always pushed herself to be the best decided to give up her fellowship. Guilt consumed her as she called her schools to inform them of her decision: she couldn't forget that they had chosen her from among hundreds of applicants. But that was nothing compared to telling her parents. "I had always done everything right. I never rebelled," she explains. "So when I did this, they really freaked out."

Her father was especially disappointed by the decision. Ted Button had spent most of his life working as a pilot, but he had always longed to be a chemist. It was he who had nudged his daughter from an early age into science and bought her those Christmas chemistry sets. When Katie had begun college, he had started subscribing to *Nature*, the prestigious scientific journal, so that he could keep up with what she was learning. "He would read an article that interested him and then call me up to point it out to me," says Katie. "When I came home, we would go into the living room, just the two of us, and have these 'science talks.'"

Yet for all the guilt and confusion, Katie also felt immediately relieved by her decision. Now she just needed to come up with something else to do. Until that moment, her path had always been clear to her, and she had ticked off achieved objectives like items on a grocery list. It was a shock, then, to find herself, at age twenty-four, unemployed, living in a new place, and with absolutely no idea of what she wanted to do with her life. She took a job waiting tables at Café Atlántico in Washington, D.C., because it was a restaurant she had heard of, and now that she had surrendered her cushy fellowship, she needed the money. But underneath that immediate need lay another motivation, hidden and barely admitted, not even to herself. "I think I unconsciously picked serving because it was a way to be connected to food," Katie says. "And food was the thing I had always loved."

o o o

No period within elBulli's transition to its new menu is more intense than the ten-day stretch that begins on July 7. Normally, the restaurant is open Tuesday through Saturday, with two days off each week. But once each month, the restaurant stays open for ten days in a row. On the first day of 2009's first ten-day sequence, the stagiaires take their regular places around the edges of the kitchen for morning meeting, their arms crossed confidently across their chests, now that they no longer have to frantically write down everything said to them. Oriol and Eduard go through the usual list: the tasks imperfectly completed the day before, the plates sold for that night's service. But just before they are about to break, Ferran issues a reminder both exciting and daunting: "*Señores*, remember: at the end of these ten days, we'll have the new menu virtually in place."

For diners—even those who have been there before—elBulli's emphasis on constant reinvention means that each of the thirty-five or so courses they eat will be new to them. The restaurant maintains a database of its clients, so that when one makes a return visit, it can call up exactly what he or she ate during previous meals. Each day, Lluís García, the director of the front of the house and one of the most gracious professionals in the business, prints up a list of that night's reservations. To the right of each name he types any aversions or allergies. (The number of the latter has grown exponentially in the last few years, and the chefs occasionally find themselves struggling to cater to diners who claim allergies to seemingly innocuous but omnipresent ingredients such as garlic or lemon. Offal—regardless of the animal it comes from—also threatens the health of a remarkably high number of diners.) In the same column, Lluís notes the date on which the client last dined at the restaurant; Eduard Xatruch will use that information to draw up the table's menu for the night. If no one in a group has ever been to elBulli before, the table may get a dish or two from an earlier year—the spherified olives, for example, have made repeat appearances since their debut. But otherwise, every single bite a diner puts in her mouth will be new. At elBulli, there is no such thing as returning for a favorite dish.

For the stagiaires, the emphasis on reinvention means that no sooner have they mastered 2008's menu than they must begin learning new dishes. It is true that some of the new season's plates have been served from the very first night. Almost everyone, for example, is now getting Ansón's pine nut ravioli, which means that two stagiaires now fold, fill, and seal two hundred triangles a day. The triangles are no longer called ravioli, however; after a brief, forgettable period as "Cold Fondue," the dish now goes by the name Shabu Shabu, a play on the Japanese hot pot, in which slices of thinly sliced raw meat are dipped into boiling broth. The mojitos and caipirinhas made from infused sugarcane that went out to a lucky few on June 16 are also on nearly every menu, where they confound the waitstaff, who must come up with an acceptably polite way of explaining to diners how to consume them. ("'Suck it' just doesn't sound right," notes maître d' Pol Perelló.) The stagiaires don't like the *cañas*—as the cocktails are called—any better. It's one of the axioms of elBulli's cuisine that the dishes that seem simplest often demand the most taxing labor. In this case, the cocktail, which is little more than a few sticks of sugarcane steeped in rum, lime, and mint, requires a couple of people with handsaws to cut the tough cane into manageable pieces, two more with cleavers to pare away the bark, and anywhere from two to eight more cooks to trim the cane first into flat planks and then into precisely measured sticks. The task provides Eugeni with entirely new sources of criticism: the people doing the sawing often forget to wear the protective chain glove he requires, and those doing the cutting often fail to get the sticks exactly seven centimeters long. It drives Sunny, the South Korea–born stagiaire from Minnesota, crazy, too: he hates what he perceives as the laziness of those who can't be bothered to measure the sugarcane sticks, the waste produced by the parers who don't take care to remove as little flesh as possible along with the bark, and the inefficiency of the saw-and-glove combination. It would be much faster, he thinks, to simply hack the cane into pieces with a chef's knife. "Sometimes I want to say to him, 'Eugeni, let me do all the *cañas* by myself,'" Sunny confesses. "I'd get them done faster."

On July 7, the first of the ten-day stretch, 38 of an eventual 120 or so dishes have been made final; by July 16, that number will have risen to nearly 80. The kitchen struggles to keep up. One day the *mesa central* has replaced its oysters with cockles; the next it suddenly has to learn to clean the kidneys of baby goats. One morning, about halfway through the week-and-a-half-long period, Eduard brings out the by now familiar tray of rabbit heads, only this time the skulls are still attached to the shoulders. He picks up a truncated carcass, pries apart the rabbit's mouth, and uses a pair of tweezers to pull out its tongue. From now on, the stagiaires will be pulling rabbit tongues; the size of a sage leaf, they will be deep-fried and set next to the fried brain on the rabbit-ear canapé.

Perhaps the most labor-intensive new dish the stagiaires must master is the rose. Sometime during the course of the previous year, Ferran got the idea that he wanted to make a dish using rose petals. The trick was finding ones that were edible; many varieties, he discovered, have an unfortunate effect on the gastrointestinal tract. Finally, Eduard, who is also in charge of sourcing, located digestible, organic roses in Ecuador and arranged for their shipment. They arrived in thick bundles, their long stems topped with fat white buds. In his earliest tests, Oriol began by plucking the petals and laying them out on a plate with a drizzle of oil: a take on carpaccio, the Italian dish composed of thin slices of raw, dressed beef. It wasn't right: the flowers were too bitter. He tried cooking them briefly in boiling water, and, although an imperfect method, it provided the spark that would allow the dish eventually to come together. Oriol lay the boiled petals on the plate, then dressed them with lemon juice, olive oil, and salt. Ferran tasted a petal and smiled. "Tell me that doesn't taste like artichoke," he said.

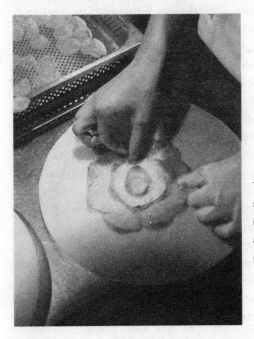

To plate the artichoke rose, a stagiaire places cooked petals in concentric circles, forming a flower.

(Francesc Guillamet)

Thus the artichoke rose was born. Over the next few weeks, the dish is honed. The chefs learn that they need to cook the petals three times, blanching them in ice water in between scaldings, to rid them of bitterness. They also learn that a final pass through a pressure cooker gives the petals a more pleasing texture. Eventually the finished plate will be drizzled with both artichoke and rose oils, to play up the flavors of both references the dish makes. But the essentials remain the same: the petals are laid in concentric circles so that, to the unsuspecting diner (over the course of the season, the dish stumps several visiting chefs, including David Chang and Juan Mari Arzak), the plate looks like a rose made from thinly sliced artichoke leaves. In fact, however, it is a rose made from roses made to look like artichoke leaves. Ferran is thrilled with it. Watching an early iteration go out one night, he nods his head knowingly. "This is going to be an incredible year," he says.

What is less incredible, at least from the stagiaires' point of view, is the work involved in making the artichoke rose. First the flowers have to be removed from their stems and the petals individually separated. Early on, Emma is assigned the task of cooking them; she spends a couple of hours each day over pots of boiling water, lowering the fragile petals in and out. "It's incredibly boring," she comments wryly, her face damp from the steam. "But my skin has never looked better." Once the petals are in their final ice bath, the tubs are brought over to the center table, where the stagiaires reach into the frigid water, lift out the petals one by one, uncurl them, and press them flat ("Remember! No wrinkles!" commands Eugeni) on a slotted sheet to dry. Or almost flat: the petals actually have to be laid with their bases lifted up a tiny bit to form a raised point; the effect is important for the final plating. And that plating, which usually begins right after the dishes have been wiped down following family meal, requires another sixty minutes or so of work. For the first part of service, while most of the dishes are coming out of Pastry or Cold Station, eight or ten stagiaires on the center table carefully lift a petal from its draining rack, unfurl it once again, press all but its tip to the plate, and gradually form one circle, then another inside it, and a third inside that. A single rose can take a stagiaire as long as ten minutes to compose.

o o o

When Katie was eighteen, her mother briefly gave up her catering business. "I was really mad at her," she recalls one night after work, her long hair pulled into a ponytail, her chef's jacket replaced with a blue hoodie. "Finally I was going to have the time during the summer to work for her, and she just gave it up, without asking me." When it came to food, there were some things that Katie and her mom didn't talk about. As a teenager, Katie always preferred *Gourmet* to the fashion magazines that her friends read. She would make both her parents birthday cakes each year—German chocolate cake for her mom; Boston cream for her dad—and Thanksgiving, with all its cooking, was always her favorite holiday. But despite her mother's example, no one mentioned cooking as a possible career. Katie was happiest in the kitchen, yet throughout her childhood and adolescence and even young adulthood, she thought of it as a refuge from real life, not life itself.

But what a refuge it was. The year she lived in Paris was one of the most memorable of her life, and not because of the work she was doing at the École Centrale. She might have spent her days conducting research, but like Julia Child and generations of enamored Americans before her, what truly excited Katie was the food—the cheese shops, produce markets, charcuteries, bakeries, and restaurants, all offering seductive enticements. It was so inspiring that one day she bought a cookbook, determined to teach herself to make puff pastry, the ethereal dough that, through nothing more than a skillful layering of butter and flour, rises spectacularly to several times its uncooked height. "The only problem is that I lived in a horrible studio apartment with literally no counter space," she recalls. "And you need a counter to make puff pastry." She went out and bought herself a roll of duct tape and a large bottle of bleach. "I scrubbed the floor ten times with the bleach and then marked off a square with the tape," she says. "And that became the counter for my puff pastry. I made my first puff pastry on the floor."

A short while later, she made it again. By then she had moved into her boyfriend's apartment on rue Mouffetard and had fallen in love with the famous open-air market there. She bought a sea bream from the fishmonger and had him clean and fillet it for her ("I wasn't quite ready to do that myself," she admits). Then she took it home, stuffed the fish with julienned vegetables, and wrapped it in the puff pastry she could now prepare on a proper countertop. She fashioned the pastry so that it looked like a fish, scoring the tail and adding little fins: a classic preparation. When it came out of the oven, she had never been more proud of herself. "It tasted bland as hell," she says. "But it looked *gorgeous*."

That year for Christmas, there were no chemistry sets. Her mother bought her Child's *Mastering the Art of French Cooking*, and her new sister-in-law (one of her half brothers had married) gave her *The Cordon Bleu Cookbook*. "I see now that that's where my true interests were," Katie says. "It just took a while for my professional ambitions to catch up."

o o o

Restaurants go through their own learning processes, one that forces them to ask the same question that the stagiaires ask themselves: In an ever more crowded field, how do we stand out? It is almost impossible to believe now, when elBulli is the most innovative, unusual restaurant in the world, but in the beginning, the only thing that distinguished it was its location. When Hans and Marketta Schilling bought a piece of land in 1961 on the sparkling, isolated Cala Montjoi, they had no greater ambition than to find a way to stay in the coastal paradise they had just discovered. Which is why, logically enough, the German couple opened a mini–golf course. Being in Spain, they quickly realized that they couldn't offer a form of recreation without simultaneously offering a place to have a drink and perhaps a snack. Thus to the artificial green of their new golf course they added a covered beachside bar—what Spaniards call a *chiringuito*—where they served beer and sandwiches. Over time, the golf side of the equation diminished (it was never exactly a moneymaker) and the service aspect increased, until finally the Schillings decided to transform their chiringuito into a proper restaurant. Centered around a fireplace that still stands today, the restaurant (which, in a nod to

Marketta's beloved bulldogs—called *bulli* in French slang—became first Bulli Bar and later Restaurante El Bulli) in the mid-1960s specialized in simple grilled meats and fish. Gradually, though, it grew more ambitious, thanks in part to Hans's travels and his love of fine dining. A pair of German cooks improved the offerings until, in 1975, Hans and Marketta hired Jean-Louis Neichel, a Strasbourg-born chef who had worked in several of France's most important restaurants. Neichel pulled El Bulli's menu toward France, and despite the fact that it was located at the end of a seven-kilometer unpaved path and had no phone line (customers requested reservations through the mail), the restaurant earned its first Michelin star the following year.

Neichel stayed until 1980, the same year that Juli Soler, then a young, unproven restaurateur with a marked penchant for rock and roll (thirty years later, he remains just as enamored: when David Gilmour, the lead guitarist and singer for Pink Floyd, requested a last-minute reservation, Juli fit him in, then excitedly conducted his predinner kitchen tour himself), became El Bulli's general manager. Within a short period, he had promoted one of the cooks, Jean-Paul Vinay, to chef. Vinay was from Lyon, and his cooking bore the clear stamp of the nouvelle cuisine that is his hometown's hallmark. He took advantage of the excellent local products to improve El Bulli's offerings, but his dishes were hardly innovative; his New Year's Eve menu for 1983 started with duck liver in aspic and culminated in a lamb saddle *en crépinette*—wrapped in pig caul. Lobster consommé, sole ballottine, stuffed rabbit with a leek gratin: these were the components of El Bulli's regular menu. Yet they were well executed enough to earn Vinay the restaurant's second star. It might not have had a particularly exciting menu, but by the time Ferran Adrià, age twenty-one, arrived in 1983 for his own month-long *stage*, the restaurant was already ambitious.

o o o

At Café Atlántico, Katie discovered she was good at serving. One of several Washington, D.C., locales owned by José Andrés, the restaurant is considered one of the city's best. It's a fun, high-energy place that specializes in updated Caribbean cuisine but includes within its core a separate space, called minibar, that serves unusually inventive tapas—a cotton candy foie gras, a beet "tumbleweed"—that wouldn't be out of place at elBulli itself. To get the job, Katie had to pass a written exam. "There were parts on wine and service that I just did so-so on," she recalls. "But I *aced* the food part. The manager couldn't believe it: 'You know what chanterelles are? You know what a gastrique is?' I hadn't had any formal training, but I knew about food."

The transition from prestigious research scientist to waitress still had the power to embarrass her when she was forced to admit it to people who had known her in the past. Yet Katie couldn't deny that she got pleasure from her new job. "I liked talking to people about food," she says. "When you give them good service, they really appreciate it." Another factor, however, made the restaurant a good place for her: about one month after she started, three staff members from elBulli, which had just closed for the 2007 season, came to help out at Café Atlántico. Two of them, Aitor Zabala and Luis Arrufat, were chefs, but one, Felix Meana, took over as a manager in the front of the house. Within a month, he and Katie were dating, and not long after that, he encouraged her to apply for a serving *stage* at elBulli so that they could stay together when he returned to Roses.

Although Adrià's restaurant maintains a full-time front-of-house staff made up of eight people, it also brings in another eight or so servers each season to help with the intensive labor of getting diners their food and otherwise making the elBulli experience exceptional. Like the kitchen stagiaires, front-of-house interns aren't paid, and most of them come straight from their studies in hospitality schools: they may be working for free, but at least they're getting course credit. Katie was out of school and had no use for credit. But she didn't have any other plans either, and six months in Spain seemed as good an opportunity as any. At the very least, she reasoned, she'd emerge better at her job. Or maybe she chose it because she hadn't completely broken her aspirational habits: instead of taking advantage of the best fellowship at the best school, she would work at the best restaurant. In any case, she got José Andrés to write her a letter of recommendation, and a few weeks later, she received word that she had been accepted into elBulli's 2008 season. It was a decision that would change her life, in more ways than she imagined.

Serving at elBulli was a totally different experience from serving at Café Atlántico. For one thing, there were no menus; the diners ate what the kitchen decided they would eat. The lack of choice made the work of waiting tables considerably easier in some ways: no one ever depended on her for a recommendation, nor did a diner angrily send a plate back when it didn't live up to his expectations. At elBulli, her job was mainly to control the timing with which each new course appeared, to run the dishes out to the tables, and, depending on the dish, to apply a last-minute garnish. She was also responsible, at least with the English-speaking tables, for explaining how a dish was to be eaten, a task that, at elBulli, is not always as straightforward as it sounds. The best part about the job was that she got to facilitate what for most diners was a unique and thrilling experience. It was not unusual to look around the dining room at elBulli and see people laughing out loud at the morsel they had just put into their mouth, and Katie—like much of the restaurant's waitstaff—considered it a privilege to be part of such a remarkable, consuming experience. It didn't hurt that she rarely had to deal with bad customers; the boorish behavior and annoyed complaints that are the lot of most waiters throughout the world, regardless of the quality of the restaurant, are practically nonexistent at elBulli. The only customers Katie didn't like, in fact, were the ones who were indifferent to the experience. "Occasionally you'd get a two-top where you could tell the man was really into food and really excited to be there," she recalls. "But his date didn't know anything about the place and was freaked out by having to eat so much."

Katie, meanwhile, was feeling the opposite of indifference. Night after night, as she would set down, say, a Styrofoam ice cream container and then explain to the delighted table that they were to sprinkle the packet of rose-colored muesli on the frozen Parmesan air inside, she found herself increasingly moved by the power of food to amaze, enchant, and provoke. Gradually a plan formed in her mind. Maybe, she thought, she could make this a permanent part of her life. And maybe she didn't have to limit herself to serving the food—maybe she could actually *make* the dishes that so delighted people. She would have to start over again, of course, in order to learn to cook professionally, but at least she would be learning about the thing she most enjoyed in the world. And maybe it wouldn't mean going back for more schooling, which she wanted to avoid. Maybe she could learn on the job. And not just any job. Maybe she could learn at elBulli itself.

The fact that Katie—female, smart, highly educated, overachieving—would consider a career in the kitchen is indicative of just how much the profession has changed. Although there have been a handful of celebrity chefs for at least as long as there have been restaurants—and even earlier, if you count the reputation of some of the men who cooked in aristocratic houses—the work itself has long been seen as menial, almost servile. Throughout the nineteenth and twentieth centuries, there were attempts in France to raise the status of the chef to that of artisan or even professional, but as late as the 1960s, Jacques Pépin could see they had not amounted to much. As he considered whether to take a job as White House chef for the Kennedys or as head experimental chef for the chain Howard Johnson's, he was guided by a clear vision of what cooking meant. "My training as a chef had taught me that being a chef—no matter where," he later wrote, "was a blue-collar job. Period."

It was, in other words, a job that someone like Katie or, for that matter, Mario Batali, Dan Barber, Daniel Patterson—all of them the products of upper-middle-class parents who sent their kids to college—would never have considered had they been planning their futures in the 1960s. It would take another twenty or thirty years before cooking became an acceptable, even admirable, profession in the public eye. Of all the aspects of the food revolution, this may be the most dramatic: by endowing restaurant cooking with respect, prestige, and a measure of glamour, it has drastically broadened and improved the pool of people willing to take on the labor. "Thirty years ago, most people who worked in restaurant kitchens had either just gotten out of the army or were on their way to jail," says Batali. "Now you get all these people who went to college, then found their passion in cooking. The level is suddenly much higher because the people cooking are a lot smarter."

Katie, certainly, was smart about how she went about entering the field. To meet her desire for public approbation, she would train in the best restaurant in the world. And to satisfy her scientific frame of mind, she decided, she would focus on pastry. More exacting and less intuitive than savory cooking, pastry met her need for precision; the pleasure she imagined it would give her reminded her of the delight she found in the elegant equations she had studied in college. "I like to follow a recipe," she admitted. "I know there are people who say, 'Oh, if you use recipes it shows you don't really know how to cook.' But a recipe gives you consistency. You always know what the finished product will be like."

So it would be a career in pastry, and it would begin at elBulli. Now she just had to convince Albert Adrià, Ferran's younger brother and the head of both the restaurant's pastry division and its laboratory in Barcelona, to take her on. It wasn't easy: of all the stations at elBulli, Pastry demands the most experience, both because its products are the restaurant's most delicate and because the team is small and works independently of the rest of the kitchen. The stagiaires accepted into Pastry always came with professional experience—often a great deal of it. Katie had no professional experience at all, which is why Albert politely but firmly put her off for months. But one night toward the end of the 2008 season, she went to run a plate of *nenúfares*, then stopped, realizing something was wrong. A complicated pre-dessert made up of a dozen or so elements floating in a small pond of herbal tea, the dish— whose name translates as "water lilies"—was missing the tiny streak of minuscule amaranth grains that formed one of the many garnishes. Katie took it back to the pass and, in the process, changed Albert's mind. "So we know you're paying attention," he said approvingly. "If you go back home and learn something about pastry, we'll take you. You're in."

Katie returned to the United States and, as she had promised, took a *stage* that would teach her the basics of pastry. In fact, she found work with Johnny Iuzzini, then one of the country's hottest pastry chefs, at Jean-Georges Vongerichten's flagship restaurant, one of only five restaurants in New York at the time judged worthy of four stars by *The New York Times*. She stayed there for six months, then took a paid job as a line cook at the splashy new restaurant that her former boss José Andrés was opening in Los Angeles. Felix was waiting for her there; he was The Bazaar's new general manager. She would spend the next four and a half months running garde-manger at what turned out to be one of L.A.'s most exciting restaurants—another feather in her cap. In its first year, The Bazaar, would earn four stars from the *Los Angeles Times*, the paper's highest ranking. At last, she thought, she was ready for elBulli.

o o o

Among the many things that distinguish a professional from a home cook is this: a professional coughs into his elbow. Not his cupped hand—that tends to be occupied—and not, of course, into the open air, where food is almost always exposed. Instead, he raises his elbow to shoulder level, like a wing, turns his head into it, and coughs there. The experienced stagiaires at elBulli arrive at the restaurant knowing this, but the young ones, those still in culinary school, have to pick it up. You can watch them learning these little things, hungrily acquiring the actions and phrases that will identify them—if only to one another—as cooks. Knife skills and a well-developed palate may be critical for the professional, but the true culture of the kitchen lies in subtle signs and rules that have little to do with food itself. Your apron is tied low, for example, right above your hips; tie it around your waist, and you'll invariably be informed that you look like a grandmother. You register no sign of pain when you stick your hands into boiling liquid or flip a piece of seared meat in a smoking pan. When dining out, at least in restaurants with obvious ambition or skill, you smell your food before you eat it, sticking your face myopically close to the plate and inhaling deeply, as if the meat or fish before you were a fine wine.

Once Ferran had to learn these things, as well. When he took his first restaurant job at age eighteen, at a seaside hotel south of Barcelona, he had no experience or particular interest in cooking. Like most young Spanish men at the time (and, let's be honest, most today), he ate what his mother cooked for the family's meals—which meant, since he still lived at home, that he likely had never even fried an egg for himself. But when he dropped out of school and needed to earn money for a planned vacation in Ibiza, his father got him a job in the kitchen of an old friend, Miquel Moy. Ferran spent a few months as a dishwasher, but gradually, with the chef's encouragement, began picking up cooking skills. It was Moy, in fact, who made the fateful decision to give Ferran a copy of a nearly century-old cookbook called *El Práctico*, written by two Argentines, that covers with almost encyclopedic comprehensiveness the classic recipes of several cuisines. Ferran, who has startlingly good recall and whose mind has always tended toward the encyclopedic, started memorizing.

As he studied, he spent the next two years moving from one Catalan restaurant to another. None of the food Ferran cooked in these places was exceptional, but the training, along with what he read, gave him enough knowledge and skill that, when he was drafted into the navy in 1982 (the dictator Franco may have been dead, but military service in Spain remained compulsory until 2001), he quickly won a position as a cook in the admiral's kitchen. There he met Fermi Puig, a fellow Catalan, who the year before had begun working in a small French restaurant on the Catalan coast called El Bulli. Fermi urged Ferran—who at the time still went by the Spanish version of his name, Fernando—to take a *stage* there during his summer leave. A few months later, both he and Fermi were discharged from the military, and by the spring of 1984, the two friends had taken full-time positions at El Bulli as chefs de partie— Ferran for meat, Fermi for fish. It would be Ferran's first real immersion in the world of the classic French cuisine. It was not, however, his first brush with the kitchen's subculture.

In his hugely popular *Kitchen Confidential*, the New York chef Anthony Bourdain exposed what he called "the underbelly" of professional cooking. When the book came out, the restaurant-going public found both shocking and deeply, deeply alluring its stories of drug-fueled debauchery; of cooks getting revenge on annoying customers by spitting (or worse) in their food; of practical jokes that centered around well-placed severed "fingers"; of chefs driven into violent rages by an improperly fried potato. Bourdain may not have been cooking haute cuisine, and he may have alienated some colleagues who had spent the better part of their careers trying to elevate the status of the chef, but he also shed light on the profound, almost mystical, respect for craft that motivates most of those who have succeeded in the field. The pages of his book are full of descriptions of people who "could stay up all night snorting coke and drinking Long Island iced teas, getting into trouble of the most lurid kind, and still show up the next morning and knock out a thousand meals."

With that portrayal of the testosterone-fueled, joke-playing, waitress-shagging, trash-talking, coke-snorting world of the professional cook, Bourdain made the chef an almost irresistibly appealing, romanticized figure—a pirate, to use his own metaphor—dedicated in equal amounts to hard work and hard play. Without a doubt, the book helped draw legions of aspiring young chefs into the profession. But though Bourdain may have been the first (entire cadres of chefs have since written memoirs, and each one—even those who are women—seems intent on proving his or her bad-boy creds) to expose the excesses of the kitchen to a broad public, he was hardly the first to experience them.

In his autobiography, Marco Pierre White notes, for example, that when he wasn't perfecting his cooking skills, he was so driven by his pursuit of casual sex that, by the time he opened Harvey's in 1987, he had already earned the nickname "The Jagger of the Aga." The genteel Jacques Pépin, in his memoir, recalls the hazing that new Parisian cooks were subjected to in the late 1940s: their chefs would send them from one restaurant to another with an order to retrieve a (mythical) chicken-deboning machine. In *Down and Out in Paris and London*, his classic tale of trying to get by in 1920s Europe, George Orwell too describes a uniquely aggressive environment, where fights among the staff were not only constant but necessary for maintaining the breakneck pace of service. "It was for this reason that during the rush hour the whole staff raged and cursed like demons," he writes. "At those times, there was scarcely a verb in the hotel except *foutre*." Traveling backward through history, past Escoffier and Marie-Antoine Carême, we might find M. Boulanger, the owner of the world's purportedly first restaurant, hurling pots at the *commis*, cussing out the dishwasher, and getting thoroughly tanked after work.

Surely that aspect of the job helps explain some of Ferran's initial attraction to the profession. After all, he took that first position in the kitchen at the Hotel Playafels only because he wanted to earn enough money to spend the summer partying in Ibiza. And once he started working at El Bulli, his dedication to having a good time didn't stop. Stories about those first few years—when clients were few and the staff was sleeping in campers outside the restaurant—are legend. His biographer Colman Andrews describes Ferran as "crawling on the floor" the first time he went to a club with his future business partner Juli Soler and cites Fermi Puig's depiction of the rather hectic schedule the cooks maintained: "We'd work until midnight or so—assuming we had customers—and then we'd all go to the discos in Roses to meet Swedish girls." In those days, the staff, including Ferran, went out for drinks most nights after work, often returning home only an hour before it was time to hit the markets or be back in the kitchen. "Once we even got thrown out of the hotel we were staying at for an event," he recalls with a chuckle. "Just like the Rolling Stones."

As it helped attract new numbers to the profession with its tales of debauchery and devotion, Bourdain's book also, ironically, endangered the very thing he described, the kitchen as pirate ship. As Francis Lam explains in an essay he wrote for *Salon* to commemorate *Kitchen Confidential*'s tenth anniversary, the book had the unexpected effect of making "civilians" want to delve even further into the chef mystique Bourdain describes. Henceforth they wanted to *know* their chefs and the fascinating extremes of their lives. In an effort to meet that desire— and no doubt flattered by the attention—chefs began to spend more time in the dining room talking with customers and transgressed the ancient frontier that is the swinging door by inviting favored diners into the kitchen. They also brought the kitchen to the diners, creating the open kitchens so popular in the first decade of the 2000s, which some Spanish critics, with their weird habit of naming trends in vaguely nonsensical English, call "showcooking." That openness, in turn, led to greater professionalization (that is, fewer pirates) in the kitchen. "It turns out," wrote Lam, "that no one wants to see dinner being made by a bunch of dudes snorting rails of coke."

The highest-end restaurants may never have succumbed to the bad-boy culture that Bourdain describes—at least not during work hours. But elBulli's evolution to a more serious, organized kitchen coincided with the growth in its own ambitions. By all accounts, Ferran stopped going out for nightly binges about the same time that he became sole chef de cuisine. And although others on the staff would maintain the tradition for years to come—longtimers still look on the late 1980s and early '90s as a kind of golden age of elBulli hedonism—the kitchen gradually became increasingly serious. A lot of that had to do with the expanding staff: there's a lot less room for flexibility in a kitchen of twenty-five people than there is in one of seven. As elBulli went after its third Michelin star, and later, as Ferran struggled to keep up with the flood of media attention and the ever-climbing expectations of his diners, the kitchen's freewheeling, "hippie"—as some detractors called it—atmosphere gave way to an ever-more-regimented environment. Drinking on the job became a firing offense. More than one incident of lateness was grounds for firing. Even practical jokes were barred. Ferran might still be welcoming new stagiaires with the phrase "Maximum seriousness, in order to have a good time," but it was clear that the weight now lay on the first part of the equation.

Today's stagiaires cling to the barest remnants of that former age. They may still imbibe prodigiously but on "school nights" tend to limit themselves to a few quiet drinks at L'Hort after work—the clubs and all-night benders are confined to days off. They do smoke; even many of the stagiaires from the United States, where the practice is generally frowned upon, rush outside at the start of family meal, taking advantage of the time it takes for everyone else to line up for food, to suck down their first cigarette in five hours. Indeed, cooking is one of those last bastions where smokers far outnumber nonsmokers. And, like any battle-scarred veteran, they will in certain moments proudly compare burn and knife scars, each mark a sign of valor. But these days elBulli is much more like the regimented navy of Ferran's training than any pirate ship. That may be a loss for the Bourdains of the world, but it has been a gain for Katie. Without that change, she would never have aspired to become a chef.

o o o

When she showed up at elBulli on June 10, Katie was nervous, even though in many ways she was in a better position than other stagiaires. For one thing, her boyfriend, Felix, owned an apartment in Roses, which meant that, although she'd be living alone (Felix had stayed in Los Angeles), she wouldn't have to live in the restaurant's group housing. She would have a little privacy, a small break between her work life and her home life. She found a ready-made family in Felix's mother and siblings, who invited her for meals on her days off and would drive her to Figueres when she needed to get her visa extended. She also already knew elBulli from her full season's experience: how intense Ferran could be during service, how fast to move during the setup for family meal, how irritating all those *quemos* could be. She even knew about the rocks.

Yet for all her knowledge, she didn't have the background that got her new peers their positions in Pastry. Luca and César Bermúdez had years of experience between them; Mizuho had worked in some of the top restaurants in Paris. Even Daniel, who had worked Pastry only once before, had several years experience in some of the best kitchens in the United States. Before she started, she would tell herself that being in a position above her skill level wasn't such a bad thing—it could force her to get up to speed more quickly. But once she was in the kitchen, even working with Mizuho on something as simple as hulling strawberries reminded her of the distance between herself and everyone else. "I'm watching her and thinking 'Oh, man, how does she do that?'" Katie admits. "I wouldn't call it competition, exactly, but it did make me wish I worked faster."

Katie had one other thing going for her: her boss. Tall and lean, with dark hair and the high cheekbones of a cologne model, Mateu Casañas had joined elBulli as a stagiaire in 1997, the year after the restaurant had earned its third Michelin star. Just nineteen at the time, he'd had only six months' culinary experience working in his family's restaurant in Roses, a job he had taken when he dropped out of college that same year. One night he met Juli Soler at a bar, and the two men got to talking. Maybe it was the drinks, or maybe it was Juli's disarmingly goofy demeanor, but Mateu found himself opening up a bit and confessing that he was at a loss about what to do next with his life; he thought he might want to cook, but he wasn't sure. Juli invited him to come up to the restaurant and meet Ferran, which is how Mateu became a member of the select group that would spend their entire career with the restaurant. "I'm one of the ones who was born at elBulli," he says, only half joking.

Mateu Casañas, chef de cuisine
of Pastry (Francesc Guillamet)

As a stagiaire and then a chef de partie, Mateu moved through all of the savory kitchen's stations. He was about to become chef de cuisine when Ferran reminded him that the one place he didn't have experience was with pastry; would he like to try? In the interest of well-roundedness, Mateu signed on in 1998 as pastry cook. By then Albert had been in charge of the section (a position he had held since joining elBulli in 1984, just one year after Ferran himself) for more than a decade, and under him elBulli's sweets had become as provocative and exciting as anything turned out in the main kitchen. For the next decade, the two worked side by side. By 2008, Albert had both published a gorgeous coffee-table book called *Natura* and was running a wildly successful tapas bar, called Inopia, that he had opened a year earlier in Barcelona. All of which helps explain why that year was his last at elBulli. In 2009, Mateu was on his own for the first time.

Maybe it was innate talent, or maybe it was fatherhood—he has two young children—but somewhere along the line, Mateu learned to teach. He is always careful to explain what he is doing and always clear about his expectations of the six stagiaires who work under him. He knows that explaining *why* something is done a certain way is much more effective than simply telling someone *to* do it. Thus, each time he comes across first Katie, then Mizuho, then Daniel grating lemon with the Microplane and setting aside the zest, he offers the same gentle correction: if you do it directly into the bowl you're working with, rather than letting it sit, you'll capture more of the essential oils that impart flavor. He also has the crucial ability to tailor his lessons to his students' needs. After working in several restaurants in France, Mizuho, for example, knows her way around a pastry kitchen, but she doesn't know Spanish. Mateu has acquired a vast, expansive vocabulary of articulate gestures designed to communicate quantities and techniques for apprentices with little Spanish. For Daniel, who calms his anxieties about being caught unprepared by stockpiling extra supplies of Silpats and pastry brushes at his station, Mateu grants a kind of tolerance that he wouldn't necessarily extend to the other cooks. With César, who is both the most experienced of Pastry's stagiaires and the moodiest, Mateu has learned whenever possible to withhold his criticism, to grant a wide berth. With Katie, he knows to start at the beginning and take nothing for granted. And by beginning, he means absolute basics. "First thing every morning, before you even say hello," he says to her on the first day, "I want you to come in, put down two cutting boards with towels underneath, and put out measuring cups." In Mateu, Katie has found the perfect mentor.

Which is not to say that he isn't critical. One day, Mateu taught Katie to enrobe croquants—the word normally refers to a hard candy made from sugar and nuts but at elBulli can refer to any (in this case honey) caramelized substance—in chocolate. It didn't look difficult: put candy on fork, dip in chocolate, let drain. But Katie's croquants came out misshapen and lumpy; worse still, she couldn't figure out what she was doing wrong. Eventually, she realized that Mateu was tapping the dipping fork, hard, on the edge of the bowl to get rid of the excess. But by the time she fixed the problem, he had already come to a conclusion about her enrobing abilities. Trying to be nice, Mateu told her the job was probably too much for one person to handle; in the future, they would do the enrobing together. Katie's shoulders slumped a little when he left. "Well, that was humiliating," she said. Her croquants went into the trash.

o o o

Among the things one does not learn at elBulli are these: how to make a béchamel sauce; how to compose a salad; how to break down a pig or chicken or sea bass; how to make a velouté; how to clarify a stock; how to press a terrine; how to prepare a pâte au beurre or pâte sucré or pâte à choux. In other words, one learns none of the basics of classical French cooking. Of course, none of the stagiaires has come to elBulli for that kind of education; if they had wanted it, they would be *staging* with Georges Blanc in Vonnas, France, or at the Maison Pic in Valence. They would be *staging*, in other words, at the same places Ferran did.

Ferran spent only a few weeks at each (he still has the 1985 letter from Georges Blanc that testifies that he has successfully completed a *stage* and is now "free from all obligations"). But between those brief stints, Ferran acquired close training in classical cuisine through his own avid reading and because, when he began working there, El Bulli was essentially a French restaurant (admittedly one that specialized in nouvelle cuisine, but still: French). One of that cuisine's distinguishing characteristics is that it relies on a comprehensive taxonomy developed by Escoffier. There are five "mother" sauces that any chef must master; all others stem from that original quintuplet. Roasting builds on the cook's knowledge of larding, perfect sole Florentine requires the ability to make a perfect fish fumet. Before he ever began to experiment, in other words, Ferran immersed himself in haute cuisine's deep roots.

Does it matter that an elBulli stagiaire today does not necessarily have the benefit of that kind of training? Ferran himself seems of two minds, at times arguing that "You can't make a great béchamel foam without knowing how to make a great béchamel" and at others questioning why the ability to make a great béchamel should be considered inherently more important than the ability to make a great spherified olive. As a group, the stagiaires themselves are similarly divided, with some convinced that there is no longer any need to study the classics ("Why should I?" asked Mike. "I know I'm never going to cook that way") and others longing for a more comprehensive kind of training.

However revolutionary the cuisine at elBulli may be, it does not form a system. It is a philosophy, an approach to cooking that can be applied to a limitless variety of ingredients, but it is hardly a codified curriculum. Spherification does not build on an earlier recipe; its variations depend only on the kind of gellifier added, not on any progression of technique. The Pacojet is a tool that opens the door to any number of new textures, but you do not need to have first learned how to use a blender in order to operate it. Ferran has stated that one of his projects for the two years elBulli will be closed is to create a comprehensive encyclopedia of all the techniques developed, and maybe that will expose a kind of structure heretofore hidden. But in the meantime, there is a piecemeal quality to an elBulli education, a sense that what they learn or don't learn is arbitrary, that leaves some of the stagiaires longing for something more authoritative.

Some, but not all. There is only one subject that unites all the stagiaires in complaint and that is tasting. One of the basic tenets of professional cooking is that you can't learn what distinguishes an extraordinary dish from a merely good one without putting it in your mouth. It is a lesson drilled into a young cook's head. At the Culinary Institute of America, new students are issued a supply of tasting spoons along with their toques and textbooks, and it's a common joke that they will gain fifteen or so pounds their freshman year because they will be sampling so much. Jean-Georges Vongerichten famously keeps packets of plastic spoons at each station.

Yet at elBulli there is no tasting, at least not among the stagiaires. Ferran and Oriol routinely taste a complete dish as they are developing it; Eduard and Mateu often do so as well. The chefs de partie get that chance only when a mistake so grave is made during service that it prevents an entire plate from going out—in that case, the plate will be shuttled back behind the pass and quickly scarfed down by the spoonful. Otherwise, they are confined to tasting individual components—a spoonful of sauce here, a ball of spherified currant juice there—to check for proper seasoning. The stagiaires, however, don't even get to do that. As Eugeni reminds them every time he catches a cook trying surreptitiously to pop a mandarin orange segment into her mouth, there is no eating on the line.

Ferran defends the policy with an appeal to logistics: forty-five people in the kitchen, more than fifty dishes in circulation at any time. "Impossible," he says, shaking his head. "Think of how much it would cost. Think of how much time it would take." But for the stagiaires, it is one of the great disappointments of their time at elBulli. After all, it is almost impossible to deduce what, say, a rabbit brain with sea anemone tastes like if you have never tried either ingredient—let alone understand how they work in combination. Even a dish as simple as the *estanque* defies easy comprehension. Frozen water, mint powder, brown sugar—the stagiaires know what all those things taste like. But until you crack the surface with your spoon, crush the thin sheet of ice against your tongue, and feel your breath turn cold from the mint and your teeth crunch against the sugar crystals, it's impossible to comprehend the dish, with its conjurings of ice skating on frozen lakes and Christmas Day. (Trying a bite of an *estanque* deemed too flawed— its surface wasn't perfectly smooth—to go out one night, Nico put it this way: "It's all in the crack.") The stagiaires satisfy their curiosity by sneaking spoonfuls of porcini broth and discretely popping spherified lychees into their mouths, and occasionally using a detour to the freezer to beg for a chocolate or two from someone in Pastry. Luca even occasionally goes around collecting on one spoon all the elements that go into a finished dish, in the hope of getting a sense of how its flavors work in combination. The fact that they will never know the taste of the dishes they spend so much time crafting galls them. "How can you learn anything?" complains Gaël. "It's like trying to play the violin wearing mittens."

o o o

What she lacks in skill, Katie makes up for in determination. She never complains and would never dream of showing up late, even if it means leaving behind the other stagiaires she regularly drives to work. Her jacket is always clean, her pocket always contains pen and notebook. She keeps lists of her tasks, so that when Mateu asks what she has to do after she has finished painting the liquid batter for the yogurt croquants over snowflake stencils, she can pull out the notebook and make sure she has the right answer. She tends not to go out much after work, preferring a good nine hours of sleep to the beers at L'Hort that other stagiaires favor. And before she gets into bed each night, she studies Spanish for half an hour. Katie, in other words, is the quintessential good girl.

A good girl with grit. Later in the season, when they know her better, the other stagiaires will tease Katie about her controlling impulses. But they won't be telling her anything she doesn't already know. Even at Jean-Georges—her first time working in a professional kitchen—she had a tendency to take charge. "Once we were trying to get out bonbons at an event," she recalls, "and I was delegating tasks. Another intern got really mad at me. She started yelling at me, 'Stop telling me what to do! You're the same as me!'"

There is chagrin in Katie's voice as she recounts the tale, but a bit of steel as well: she knows that she isn't the same as the other stagiaires. In her, many of the personality traits that distinguish a good apprentice are intensified. She likes organization and structure and never chafes against the hierarchy of the kitchen. "I think we work best when Mateu is telling us exactly what to do," she says. "Otherwise we're just running around with our heads cut off." The most criticism she has ever lobbed at her superior was to admit, with a bit of a smile, that sometimes she doesn't understand why Mateu makes them prepare quite so much ice cream ahead of time. She works hard, despite the fact that Pastry has the longest hours in the kitchen. And perhaps more than any other apprentice, Katie is driven by the sense that getting by is not enough. For all her desire for clear lines and properly defined roles, she feels an intense pressure to excel. She may be far from the laboratory, but she hasn't lost the part of her personality that got her into the kitchen. Which is why just a few weeks into her *stage*, she decides that the fastest route to success is through elBulli's own path to excellence: creativity. She decides to create her own dish, the bell jar.

From the beginning of the season, the chefs, including Ferran himself, have encouraged the stagiaires to think creatively. Oriol and Mateu have even suggested that, should one of the apprentices come up with a good idea for a new dish, the kitchen will try it out, to see if it might be worth developing. Katie takes them at their word and for nearly a week stays up late at night, sketching ideas, filling in ingredients. Finally, she is ready to present her dish. During one morning meeting, she raises her hand and asks to speak. Mateu tells her it's a busy day and that she should wait for tomorrow; he repeats the same message the following day. After a few rounds of that, impatience gets the better of her, and one morning Katie simply starts blurting out her idea, describing it as quickly as she can so that no one has a chance to cut her off. She thrusts a sketch into Mateu's hands and is rewarded with his interest. "Okay, Katie," he says. "Let's try it tonight."

The inspiration for Katie's dessert came from the potato-starch obulato. Pastry had been testing large sheets of it, drying them in a low oven so that they became crisp and fragile. But Katie wanted to drape the obulato before it hardened, so that it took the form of a transparent bell, which she would then place over a terrarium-like scene. She got the idea from the collection of bell jars her mother kept in New York; instead of plants, hers would top a dessert. Inside, would be a floating island, made from meringue, cast in a pool of cold elderflower soup, topped with goat cheese ice cream and perhaps some caramelized walnut powder. All the elements would conform to the same monochromatic scheme except for a single flower, made from chocolate, that would stand out on top. The "jar" would go over the entire concoction, waiting for the diner to crack it open with a spoon, shattering sweetened obulato pieces into the dessert below. Or at least that was the idea. When Katie finally gets to test the dish, the obulato doesn't shatter so much as tear. Still, Mateu shows it to Oriol, and for a gratifying few minutes, the two hunch over the dish, discussing its potential. Too soon, however, Oriol raises his head and gently suggests that the dessert is a little too representational for elBulli; they like things more abstract. Katie nods her understanding, but she looks as though she's been punched. It hadn't really occurred to her that, after trying so hard, she could fail.

That very week, though, Mateu begins working on a new snack, called the pañuelo. He takes an immense obulato, the size of a coffee-table book, coats it in a dried corn caramel and bakes it, then; while it is still hot, lightly drapes it into rippling folds. When it dries, he serves it upright, like a massive, stiff curtain. Mateu tells Katie that her bell jar served as the inspiration for the pañuelo. It should have been pleasing news, but Katie doesn't feel consoled. Instead, she worries that the chefs are condescending to her. "What, just because you shaped the obulato while hot?" she asks. "Otherwise, it has nothing to do with my bell jar." For the rest of the season, as the kitchen keeps experimenting with the pañuelo, she blushes a bit every time someone makes reference to her contribution. (Her discomfort is made all the worse when she finally learns what *pañuelo* means: "handkerchief" or "tissue." "And they coat it in something yellow?" she asks incredulously. She wants to suggest that perhaps the name is not the most felicitous, but by then, the dish has been going out for weeks. By the end of the season there will be a chocolate pañuelo as well.) But for the next five months, the bell jar incident gnaws at Katie. Maybe she just isn't used to failure, or maybe she is frustrated that all her extra work—all that effort to make herself stand out—didn't amount to more. Or maybe she's aware of just how high the stakes are for her.

Among the stagiaires, Katie is one of the few who arrived at elBulli knowing exactly what she will be doing when the season ends. In January, she and Felix will move to North Carolina, along with Katie's parents, and together they will open a restaurant. Katie will be executive chef, despite the fact that she's never held any position higher than garde-manger. Two months into her *stage* at elBulli, she has proven that she can work hard, make smart choices, and push herself farther than almost anyone else. What she still doesn't know, simply because hasn't had the chance to find out, is whether she is any good at everything else that goes into the making of a decent chef: managing staff, watching costs, and, most important, creating new dishes. Katie takes the bell jar rejection hard because she worries that it foreshadows what's to come. Are her skills strong enough? Is she creative enough? Is she even a good enough cook? One night after work, seated in Si Us Plau, the same bar where she and the other stagiaires began their first day, she confesses she isn't sure. "I know that I'm not ready for this. Not old enough. Not experienced enough." She pauses to take a sip of her beer before posing a question that Ferran could have asked himself as he took the helm of elBulli in 1987. "But if someone hands you the chance to live your dream when you're twenty-six, are you really going to turn it down?"

three]

August, or **Discipleship**

If you were to dine at elBulli, you would arrive in Roses fairly early in the day. With no luxury hotels to speak of and an excess of shops selling bad pizza and cheap sandals, the town tends to attract tourists who don't quite see the point in spending 230 euros per person on dinner. So, like most elBulli diners, you have likely made Roses a one-night stop. Maybe you have driven up from Barcelona and arrived just in time for a light lunch of grilled fish at Rafa's and an afternoon siesta. Or maybe the excitement has kept you awake. After all, you have probably waited years for this opportunity, so that when you finally got the e-mail from Lluís García informing you that elBulli would have a table for you, you felt a little as if you'd won the lottery. Which helps explain the fluttery feeling in your stomach as, sometime after 7 P.M., you begin the drive up the unmarked road that leads to the restaurant.

If it is your first time, you will likely drive a mile or so before you start to worry that you have made a wrong turn. The lack of signage, the tortuous, potholed road, the complete absence of guardrails standing between you and the craggy cliffs—can this really be the way? The scenery will distract you for a while—mountainside jutting down to aquamarine water, scruffy pines glowing in the fading light—but a couple more miles on, you'll be convinced that you're lost. Are you going to be late for the one reservation you most want in the world? Will they save your spot? There are few places to turn around on the twisting road, and so you continue, fretfully, until finally the road begins to descend and you spy some white buildings in a bend up ahead. One bears the restaurant's name, but it is so modest that you may find yourself thinking, "Is this really it?"

Should you arrive before 7:30, the gate to the restaurant parking lot will still be locked, and you'll have to wait outside with the other clients who didn't want to be a minute late for their meal. Inside, Oriol Castro will be holding a last-minute meeting with the dining room staff, explaining the night's new dishes, asking if there were any problems with any courses the night before. Not until Oriol ends the meeting, as he always does, by wishing the staff a *buen servicio* will one waiter walk outside and up the hill to unlock the gates. You'll cross the parking lot, never noticing the carefully placed rocks because you are so excited to finally be walking through the narrow wooden door with its homely little plaque of a bulldog. But if you look to the right, just before you cross the threshold, you'll realize that you can see into the gleaming kitchen. It feels like you are spying on Willy Wonka.

Inside the restaurant, one of the maître d's will greet you warmly in your own language. He'll ask if you'd like to start the meal with cocktails on the veranda, and you will of course say yes, since the view there, down to Cala Montjoi's beach, is so inviting. You'll sit at one of the heavy wooden tables, trying not to be too obvious as you steal glances around you: the other diners, the dishes coming out at other tables, the bustle of the staff. Within minutes, though, a waiter sets your first course in front of you: a cocktail (or freshly squeezed juice, if you don't drink alcohol) unlike any you have tried before. Regardless of what the "drink" comprises, there will be something about it that is amusing or delightful: a honey-dipped pine shoot to chew while you sip the pine-flavored concoction in your glass, the shock of opposite sensations as you down your hot-and-cold gin and tonic. Then, the snacks will start appearing, in groups of two or three, each one on its own specially designed plate: pristine disks that look like elaborately decorated candies from a Parisian *confiserie* but taste of salty sesame; crisp, translucent rectangles of raspberry punched up with wasabi's heat; a thin cracker that tastes purely and intensely of the juiciest tomato you've ever eaten.

Along with the excitement, a bit of anxiety usually accompanies a meal at elBulli. You've heard so much about this restaurant and for so long, how can it ever begin to live up to its reputation? The question of what exactly you will be putting in your mouth also disarms you: at elBulli you have no choice in the menu. Although you may have specified ahead of time that you don't like liver or are allergic to shellfish, the list of products the restaurant uses is so far-reaching and unusual that you will, inevitably, end up eating things you have never seen before, let alone thought to rule out. As you finish your time on the patio and are led into the dining room by the maître d', the first source of anxiety begins to recede; the snacks have convinced you that elBulli really may be everything you've heard it is. But the second source—the mystery of it all—has only grown.

You are seated. Instead of the sleek, design-conscious interior you expected for so renowned an avant-garde restaurant, you are led to a red velvet, cushioned banquette and a table covered in thick white linens. There are no minimalist rocks or spiky floral compositions on the table; a single red rose in a glass vase forms the only centerpiece. The white stucco walls are hung with oil paintings that would not look out of place at a red-sauce joint in New Jersey. The tile floors show their age. Seated there amid the faded pillows and tchotchkes, attended by a staff that sincerely seems to have your well-being at heart, it's hard to believe that anyone is going to make you eat anything scary. And then one of the first "tapi-platos" comes out (tapi-platos are how the restaurant refers to its "main" courses—the tapas-sized dishes that come after the snacks and before the pre-desserts), and it's a hideous, shaggy black mass that resembles volcanic rock but has the feel of a damp sponge.

The waiter tells you to eat it in two bites. You look at your dining companion nervously, then look around the room. No one else seems to be suffering. In fact, they seem almost joyfully happy with what they are eating. At the table next to you, a woman is actually laughing between bites. And so you put the ugly, shaggy, squishy thing in your mouth and tentatively chew. It turns out to be delicious: slightly sweet, with the toasty flavor of black sesame and a delightful texture somewhere between layer cake and sea sponge. It reminds you of something, though you can't quite say what.

This, then, is what dinner at elBulli is like: a recurring cycle of emotions. Excitement, mystification, delight, nostalgia, and then, with each brief interval between courses, the resurgence of anticipation and a bit of fear. Thirty or so times, a waiter will appear tableside with calm, almost compassionate instructions for how to eat the thing in front of you. Thirty or so times, you will surrender to the next course and, usually (though not always; if everything were exquisitely pleasurable, the meal would lose the tension that Adrià seeks), find yourself delighted by whatever surprising flavors and textures it contains. And so it goes, through fried chicken cartilage and pressed cotton candy paper and sherry-tinged baby goat kidneys and sea anemones and truffles and rabbit brains and lychee-filled shellfish for dessert. Finally it is midnight. You move back to the veranda for coffee, and the server delivers a large, marvelous box, a treasure chest of chocolates. You start opening drawers, some obvious, some secret, to find a different, exquisite candy in each compartment: in one, a tiny piece of coral dusted red, in another a fresh mint leaf coated in dark chocolate. The tension of the night dissolves in one last burst of pure, childlike pleasure, as you realize that elBulli really *is* as good as they say. You pay the bill, which suddenly seems a lot more reasonable than it did when it was only an abstraction, and depart amid a chorus of warm good-byes from the staff. Somehow, even though it is now pitch-black, the drive back down to Roses seems less precarious than before. You think it may have been the most thrilling meal of your life.

No matter how exciting the concoctions on each plate and the elaborate theater that accompanies the serving of them, the one moment that many diners at elBulli recall as the most memorable has nothing to do with the food. As each party enters the restaurant, but before it is seated on the patio, Pol or Luís or David López demurely suggests that perhaps the group would like to see the kitchen and greet the chef? First-time guests are usually surprised but flattered by the offer, wondering modestly if perhaps the staff has detected some level of sophistication or other special quality that warrants such an invitation. In any case, no one ever refuses. The maître d' nods his approval and leads you past the massive stone fireplace that was once where the restaurant grilled its meats. As you step into the kitchen, he turns, points to the metal strip bolted to the floor, and issues a mild warning to watch your step. You pass the humidor and the coffee station, but you don't notice any of it, because there, up ahead, is Ferran Adrià.

The view from the kitchen as Ferran greets diners
(Francesc Guillamet)

Most likely his back is to you, for even at this late hour, he is still testing new dishes with Oriol. He stands at the front of the kitchen—maybe waiting observantly at the pass, maybe pacing near the bar, and, upon hearing you enter, turns, smiles, and welcomes you to the restaurant. He nods graciously when you ask if you can take a photo and pulls you toward the restaurant's famous sculpture of a bull's head, midway down the pass. You hand off your camera to whomever led you into the kitchen and stand there, beaming, as if Ferran Adrià were your best friend in the world (if you are in fact, a friend, he will pose with his arms around you. If not, he will cross them in front of his chest). Then, when the camera has flashed and Luís or Pol or David is gently urging you along, you turn and, just for a moment, try to catch a glimpse of what it is that the thirty or so cooks behind the pass are doing as they prepare this long-awaited meal.

Now switch the frame. You are standing shoulder to shoulder with thirteen other cooks, laying cold rose petals on a plate. You've been standing there, with only one thirty-minute break, for the past six hours. You are not allowed to talk to anyone else on the line, so any jokes or wisecracks are issued in whispers. You have been chastised before for not focusing, so for the most part you keep your eyes on the plate in front of you. But it's impossible to ignore the flash of bulbs as the cameras go off, one every few minutes for about an hour and a half, from in front of the pass. You steal looks at the clients, posing there with Ferran, dressed in their formal evening wear or their jeans and sandals. Even from a distance you can see that their faces fairly shine with anticipation. You wonder what their meal will be like. After all, you wouldn't know: neither you nor any of the other forty people you work with has actually eaten at elBulli. And thus you don't know that the servers will take the matcha tea powder you set out when you're plating the shrimp and whisk it with the straw brush until it turns into a bright green broth whose slightly bitter herbaceousness will play nicely off the sweetness of the crustacean. You don't know what it's like for a server to pour the bowl of foie gras ribbons, frozen with liquid nitrogen, over the plate of lulos, so that smoke billows over the table in clouds and the tartness of the fruit is mellowed by the richness of the liver as it melts. You don't know what it's like to have a magic box of chocolates placed before you and open drawer after drawer to find only more. You know only what it's like to fill that box, piping one perfect mint leaf after another with melted chocolate for elBulli's take on an after-dinner mint.

This is the great paradox of elBulli: that the most exciting dining experience in the world depends on the most extreme absence of excitement. It depends on the rigor, the discipline, and, to be honest, the utter boredom of the men and women who are standing in those two straight lines, laying cold rose petals on plates. Like all great restaurants, elBulli's dazzle rests in large part on the willingness of its apprentices, in the name of education, to do the dreary work no one else wants to do—and to do it for free. It's just that here the equation—learning for drudgery, learning *through* drudgery—is different.

o o o

If Luke is able to bear the sometimes crushing routine of mise en place better than many of the stagiaires, he has the South Korean army to thank. His real name is Myungsun Jang, but at elBulli he goes by "Luke" because, he has learned from experience, the latter is far easier for Europeans to pronounce. Like all young Korean men, he was obliged to enter the military and enlisted at age twenty-two. Stationed at a secret location in the mountains, he spent the grueling first four weeks in basic training, learning to fire a rifle, going on twenty-kilometer marches with a sixty-five-pound pack, and picking up a few chemical warfare tricks. Prohibited from keeping any personal possessions, he had to send his civilian clothing home as soon as he received his uniform; in a familiar ritual for Korean women, Luke's mother cried when she received his. Physical punishment was common—although officers are prohibited from beating their underlings, they have other means of discipline at their disposal: assigning laps, piling a soldier with extra weight during marches, forcing him to assume the *wonsan pokgyeok* position—sort of like downward-facing dog but with his body weight supported by his head rather than his arms. It was not unheard of for new recruits to die— "accidentally," Luke points out—during training. But the combination of extreme physical labor and utter submission to discipline fostered a tolerance for difficulty that would serve Luke well later in his life. When basic training was over and his squad was distributed to bases throughout the country for the remaining twenty-nine months of their service, Luke found that, unlike some of his unlucky companions who had been sent to the border with North Korea, he was reassigned to a kitchen. Of all the positions in the army, it was the job he most wanted.

Food had always been important in his family, and some of Luke's best memories are of holidays spent with his cousins at his grandfather's cottage in the mountains, where the main event was a massive feast grilled over an open flame. His energetic mother, a housewife turned entrepreneur, was a good cook—"and fast," which in Luke's world is the highest possible praise. His father, who had left a university career teaching language for a better-paying office job, loved to eat. "Whenever there was good news, we would have a feast or go to a restaurant," Luke recalls. "Even when we were poor, it was always very important to go out to eat." By the time he was twelve, both his parents were working full-time, and it fell to young Luke to prepare family meals. Nothing fancy, usually rice or soup, but it was during those times, he says, when he was alone in the kitchen and waiting for his parents to come home, that he decided he wanted to be a chef. When he turned seventeen, he took his first job, working at a small Chinese restaurant in Seoul.

A position as army cook, then, was the best possible outcome of his conscription. He still had to turn out for morning drills and periodically had to demonstrate his weapons-readiness, but unlike his comrades, many of whom spent time patrolling the barren border of the demilitarized zone that divides South Korea from its enemies to the north, Luke at least got to spend his day chopping cabbage and cleaning chickens. He had been doing that for a little less than a year when he heard about a culinary contest with divisions for both military and civilian cooks. He asked his commanding officer for permission to enter and found himself a few months later at a hotel kitchen in Seoul, having entered—Luke is nothing if not driven—both divisions. He took gold in the public competition for his lamb with mustard sauce and crisp nuts and silver in the military one for his steamed sea bream with pumpkin and white kimchi. The latter tormented him for a while—how could he have come in *second*?—but there was another prize awaiting him that almost made up for the shortcoming.

Back at the military base, the general heard about Luke's win and contacted the young man because he was looking for a new cook to prepare meals for him and his wife. The general had spent eight years in the United States and was far more worldly than the average Korean officer. Luke was immediately drawn to him and yearned for the job, but he knew it would require more sophisticated skills than those he employed in the mess hall. In the days leading up to his audition with the general, he forced himself to go over techniques and flavor combinations in his head. Finally it was time: Luke went to the general's house, where, in a nod to those eight years in America, a carved pumpkin marked the holiday being celebrated halfway around the world. The officer showed Luke the kitchen and explained where all the utensils were. Then he handed him a whole octopus. "Make something with that," he said.

Luke had never cooked octopus before. Still, he had watched his mother prepare it enough times that he knew the basics. He turned it inside out, removed the innards from the head, then simmered it for nearly two hours to make sure it was tender. At that point he could have done the typical thing: stir-fry it with chilies and mushrooms to make *nakji bokeum*. But Luke wanted to show that he could do more than the traditional dishes, more than was expected. So he cut off the tentacles, sliced them as thin as carpaccio, then drizzled the slices with a sauce made from soy and yuzu. It was simple but elegant, and the general couldn't stop talking about how well the flavors melded. Luke got the job.

Overnight, what is usually the most difficult period of a young man's life became the most exciting for Luke. He moved out of the barracks and into the general's house, and although he would have to turn up for preparedness exercises every three months, he was suddenly free of the daily drills and workouts—to say nothing of the drudgery of preparing kimchi for hundreds of hungry soldiers every day. He still woke at 6 A.M. but in order to prepare the general's breakfast, not for calisthenics. He shopped, planned menus, and tended the little vegetable garden behind the general's house. Early each afternoon, he began preparations for that night's dinner, which, because the general and his wife liked to entertain, was usually fairly elaborate. The two treated him like a son, and between

Luke Jang
(Francesc Guillamet)

their encouragement, the practice, and the time the work gave him to dream, Luke came up with a plan for his future. He loved the cuisine of his homeland, but he wanted to know more. "Korean food is great," he says, "but it's still pretty traditional, even backwards. I wouldn't have been able to learn anything new if I stayed there." To become the sort of chef he wanted to be, Luke would have to travel.

o o o

"I hate August." Ferran stands impatiently at the top of the driveway that leads down to the kitchen and tries to cross the road to his house. For the past two months, he has been slipping out of the kitchen at 5 P.M. for an hour's worth of exercise in his garden. ("Can't you tell?" he asks. "I've lost six kilos!") But now a line of cars snakes its way to and from the beach, making it difficult to cross—especially because many of them pull over abruptly to allow their passengers to spill out and pose with the restaurant sign or, when they see the man on the side of the road, the chef himself. "I find people in my yard sometimes, halfway up the hill to my house," he says, dashing across as several cars honk in recognition. You'd have thought a busload of tourists in Beverly Hills had just spied Brad Pitt picking up his newspaper.

There are a lot of reasons why August is Adrià's least favorite month. For one, the heat and humidity—so treacherous to the crackly pink sugar that is pulled, flamelike, around a raspberry, so threatening to those crisp corn *pañuelos* inspired by Katie—are at their highest. The weather is especially an issue for pastry, and Mateu is on his stagiaires constantly for not closing quickly enough the door to the tiny, chilled petit fours room, where chocolates and other delicacies vulnerable to temperature and humidity are stored. One night, just before service, he realizes that the mint leaves for the After Eights have turned brown in the heat, and a moment's panic surges through the team as they rush to pull the imperfect leaves from their drawers in the chocolate box. Remarkably, the kitchen itself doesn't feel uncomfortably warm—the ventilation system, at least in summer, is so expert that elBulli is possibly the only restaurant in the world where the cooks don't end the night bathed in sweat. The only real clue to the season is hair, which lies a bit lanker than usual. Gaël and Luke have even abandoned their now-futile hair gel.

But temperature and its cosmetic effects aside, the real reason Ferran hates August is for the people it draws. Roses may not have much in the way of historic monuments or charming streets, but it does have a beach, and in August, when nearly all of Spain and France is on vacation, about half of each country's population seems to be lying on the town's white sands. The unmarked road up to Cala Montjoi becomes clogged with cars seeking a less trammeled piece of beach. Accidents can stop traffic for hours when a gawking sightseer drives off a particularly impressive curve.

Summer vacation also means a higher percentage of diners who aren't exactly at elBulli for the artistic experience. "They come because they've heard it's the most famous restaurant in the world, and they want to say they've been here or they want to check it off their list," Ferran says. "Not because they truly appreciate what we do here." And it's true—in August, the restaurant does fill with a larger number of sunburned clients given to criticism and misunderstanding, including one unfortunate sod who gets himself so drunk at dinner that he throws up at the table. The situation is disheartening enough to Ferran that for several years now, he has dreamed of closing the restaurant altogether in August, a perhaps less-than-sound business decision, considering that it is the most popular month for reservation requests. But Adrià says he doesn't care about that—he'd shut down on Saturday nights too if he had his way. The only thing that prevents him, he says, are the stagiaires. "What would they do for the whole month of August? We couldn't just send them home."

The stagiaires themselves don't really notice that August is different from any other month. True, the bars where they hang out at night are a lot more crowded, and they have to leave earlier in the morning to get to work on time because of the traffic. But the restaurant's clientele? Those supposedly less sophisticated customers who fill the dining room each August? That they don't notice at all. It's one of the things that makes the experience of working at elBulli different from that of almost any other restaurant: there are no particularly bad services. Nor, for that matter, are there particularly good ones. All the services are more or less the same.

That's because elBulli controls almost all the variables. It starts with its own staff; by hiring so many people and establishing such an elaborate system of control there is little room for the kind of personal errors that can upset an entire service. Asked for the worst mistake a stagiaire has ever committed, Ferran has to search far back in memory. "Well, there was that time in the late eighties, early nineties," he recounts. "We had told a stagiaire to make a fish stock and, when it was done, to strain it. So the stagiaire did what he was told, and a little while later, I went over to get it. He handed me a bunch of boiled fish bones. I said, 'Where's the stock?' And he pointed to the bones—he had drained them, just as he was told, and thrown away the rest." René Redzepi, who did a *stage* at elBulli in 1999, recalls a more simple mistake with horror. "It was a big table—an eight- or ten-top," he says. "And they were on the duck course. They had been plated and the waiters had started to take some of them out, when Lalo, who was expediting [Eduard "Lalo" Bosch, who today works in elBulli's administration was chef de cuisine from 1996 to 2001] realized one duck was missing." The chef called to the meat station for one more, but for some reason—I still don't know how this happened—there wasn't any more. We were out of duck." René shakes his head, still cringing at the memory. "Lalo went crazy, screaming that we should all remember this day because it was the worst day in elBulli's history." The idea that falling one dish short—a routine event in most restaurants—could constitute the worst night in history is telling; elBulli make so few mistakes that an ordinary one takes on disproportionate significance.

Without an à la carte menu, there is no doubt about which dishes will sell and which will not; the kitchen has eradicated that mysterious alchemy by which every table on a given night decides to order the lamb chops and none the pasta. Mise en place is strictly controlled, with each task accounted for on a daily chart that prevents any station from ever running out of a preparation during service. The cooks can also rest assured that no diner is going to send back a dish because it's not cooked to his liking or isn't what she expected—those criteria don't even figure into the elBulli universe. There are no delivery men who flake out at the last minute: elBulli has a dedicated shopper, José Maria, who travels daily to the markets in Roses and, for more exotic products, twice each week to the Boqueria market in Barcelona. A party doesn't reserve for four people but show up with six. Almost no one cancels a reservation at the last minute—and if they do, the restaurant always has someone to take their place. The only thing that can throw off the kitchen is timing: if eight tables show up at once (the restaurant groups reservations into three or four time slots, separated by half an hour each, but, this being Spain, not everyone is exactly prompt) or if someone decides, halfway through his meal, to get up for a leisurely smoke on the patio. Otherwise, every service is remarkably similar to every other one.

In other restaurants, the distinction between good and bad services fuels the brigade's motivation. Like long-distance runners, cooks talk about "the zone," that adrenaline- and seratonin-fueled state in which everyone is working perfectly, orders are coming out on time, and the whole night goes by in a kind of athletic dance. Daniel Ryan misses the feeling. The twenty-eight-year-old stagiaire from Baltimore worked for a while at Alain Ducasse's restaurant in New York, where—as in most kitchens—each cook had his own station, did his own mise en place, and took care of his own orders one at a time. "With that kind of cooking you get into a groove," Daniel says almost wistfully. "At elBulli, it's different; everything is done in big projects. So the groove, the kind of ecstasy you feel turning out a hundred covers, is missing." The ecstasy-fueled services make the bad ones worthwhile. But even the bad ones—the ones where you can't stop overcooking your meat, or somebody burns himself, or you run out of sea bass, or everyone is in the weeds, the purée, the shits (choose your metaphor)—serve their purpose, providing yet another war story to be recounted in hilarious detail over drinks late at night. Even more than the zone, the weeds unite the members of the brigade, making them feel that they have endured something together, and bringing them closer as a result.

Without the unifying highs and lows, elBulli's crew is perhaps a little more susceptible than normal to petty fractures. Certainly by August, cracks have begun to appear, a frazzling of nerves that seems the result of too much time spent in one another's presence. At home, Andrea fights with Laia, one of her three roommates, over things such as who is responsible for the clutter in their room. She chalks the tension up to overexposure more than any core conflict. "I'm kind of tired of being with the same people," she says. "I wish I didn't have to see so much of them." Katie feels the same way. She's been staying home at night and visiting Felix's family on days off, rather than spending more time with the people at work. "You know, I just don't have the desire to make the effort. I'd rather have a social life with people outside the restaurant." Nor are the tensions confined to extracurricular hours. Laia fights with José Luis at work over who does what. "He's lazy," she says simply. "She's bossy," he retorts. Mizuho complains about what she sees as rudeness and a kind of competition among the stagiaires as one person gets stressed out and starts ordering others around. Lorenzo resents Luke for telling him he's not focused enough; Luke resents Lorenzo for letting down the rest of the team. When it comes to plating, those full-on rushes when six or eight cooks struggle simultaneously to finish a dish, there's a bit more pushing than strictly necessary.

With little else to occupy their minds, the stagiaires transform the minor occurrences of personal life into the objects of full-blown intrigue. Is Emma, the auburn-haired Canadian stagiaire, going out with Aitor, the tattooed chef de partie in charge of *cuarto frio*? They tend to sit together when everyone is out at night. But how can they possibly communicate, seeing as Aitor speaks little English and Emma's Spanish barely exists? Maybe, the stagiaires snicker, they have another way of communicating. Did you notice that Eugeni tries to keep them apart in the kitchen? Is that because he knows something and is concerned that a burgeoning romance will distract them from work? Or is it because he is hoping to have his own shot with Emma? Emma, whose predilection for girlish dresses belies her backbone, hates the gossip swirling around her. One night she decides to put an end to it. "Yeah, we're sleeping together," she announces to her fellow cooks. "Is that a problem?" The next day she moves in with Aitor.

That episode, and a pressure cooker that explodes one night during service, constitute the two highlights of the month. Otherwise, a kind of torpor has set in: as the novelty of the kitchen and menu wear off, it begins to dawn on the stagiaires, with noticeably sobering effect, that this is all there is. A handful, it is true, have rotated into new stations, but not nearly as many nor as quickly as most had expected. At one meeting Diego—always quick with a raised hand—asks with a touch of frustration if others are going to be assigned to creativity or *cuarto frio*. Eduard assures him that there will be changes in the future. But with nothing more concrete than that, many of the stagiaires begin to fear that they will spend the next four months doing exactly the same thing that they are doing now.

o o o

Fifteen thousand dollars is how much Luke figured he would need to embark on his itinerant culinary education. If he were going to do it right—and his many months in the military had taught him the value of doing things right—he would need a lot more money than the measly army stipend he had been putting away each month. He called a friend in Australia who ran a beef-packing plant and asked if he had any jobs. The friend invited Luke to come work in the local slaughterhouse. The bloody, backbreaking work paid well and offered Luke a chance to learn English. As he was saving up the necessary funds, however, tragedy struck: his father was diagnosed with cancer. Luke made it back to Seoul just in time to be with his dad when he died. He spent the next three months at home with his mother, but his destiny, he felt, wouldn't wait. One night he told his mother he had to leave again. "This is really important to me, Mom," he said as she cried. But she said she understood, and Luke went back to the slaughterhouse. A few months later, he had at last accumulated his $15,000. It was time to start spending it.

The curriculum that Luke had designed for himself didn't involve classes in flavor profiling or *stages* in prestigious kitchens; it was much more simple than that. He would go to the best restaurants in the world and eat. On paper it sounded sybaritic, but Luke approached the task with the utmost seriousness. In order to save money for meals, he would hitchhike as much as possible and camp instead of staying in hotels. And in order to truly understand what each restaurant was trying to accomplish, he would make a point of trying to talk with the chef every place he ate. He gave himself ten months before his money ran out.

His first meal was at Tetsuya's, Tetsuya Wakuda's famed Japanese-French restaurant in Sydney, Australia. Climbing its austere steps, he was awed by the hushed intimacy inside and the plate-glass wall in the dining room that looked out onto a lovely garden—no place his family had taken him had ever been as exquisite as this. He was surprised, however, to find that the tasting menu wasn't as diverse as he had expected—vanilla ice cream made an appearance three times, as did raw fish (although, considering Wakuda's Japanese heritage, this latter was not, perhaps, surprising). And although Luke got to see the kitchen,

Wakuda himself was too busy at the time to speak with him. All in all, it was an inauspicious launch.

Still, he had begun. From Australia Luke went first to the Philippines and from there to Vietnam and Thailand. India was a favorite stop, and he especially loved the tandoori dishes at New Delhi's opulent Bukhara restaurant. From there he made it to Turkey, which he loved even more for its hospitality; instead of arresting him for sleeping in the rough, one policeman in a small town outside Istanbul took him to dinner at a café, then invited him home to stay with his family for three days. In Germany he traveled to the elegant Die Schwarzwaldstube; in Italy to Gambero Rosso. He was, quite possibly, the only backpacker in the history of the Eurail Pass to keep a neatly folded suit and tie in his rucksack. Before each meal, he would unpack his jacket and slacks, hang them near a hot shower to get out the wrinkles, and dress properly for the evening.

What was Luke searching for? At home in Seoul, he had read everything he could on chefs he admired, but he soon found that eating widely provided a depth of knowledge that no book could match. Still, it was more than just a mental catalogue of textures and flavors that he was after. In each restaurant, he asked to speak with the chef, and almost always, the chef obliged. "I was a paying customer," explains Luke, with one of his trademark shy smiles. "They had to be nice to me." He would probe each chef for his philosophy, ask for his recommendations for training. And always he would end with the same question: "What is the most important thing for a chef?" He was searching, in other words, for a mentor—or maybe more than a mentor. He was looking for someone to whom he could dedicate himself wholly, just as he had dedicated himself to the general. He was looking to make himself a disciple.

It wasn't until Luke reached Spain that he found the right opportunity. He had first read about elBulli when he was in the military, and even though he found the photo that accompanied the article a little off-putting (Ferran, he thought, looked gruff standing in his favorite cross-armed position), he was thrilled by what he learned about Ferran's passion, his energy, his will to reinvent both cuisine and himself. That inkling—that this chef, above all others, was worth traveling to—perhaps explains why Luke was so determined to overcome the hardships he encountered when he tried to reach elBulli. He arrived in Roses with little problem but, once there, had no means of getting to the restaurant itself—he could hardly afford the 25 euros that a taxi would cost, and there was no other transportation available. So he walked. Seven kilometers, uphill. It was a hot summer day, and the trek took Luke a couple of hours, but finally, he was standing there, by the restaurant's discreet entrance. An entrance that, it being Sunday, was firmly locked. ElBulli was closed.

He walked back down to Roses. The next day, he tried again: seven kilometers up in the blazing sun. Again he found the gate locked and no one around. He walked back down to town. Up the following day and back down again—Luke didn't realize it, but the restaurant was on one of its monthly four-day breaks. All told, he would climb the mountain to Cala Montjoi and descend back to Roses about ten times before he finally got in. Not, it should be said, to eat—elBulli could hardly come up with a reservation for this scraggly wanderer who turned up on its doorstep, no matter how impassioned he might be. He did, however, get the chance to meet Ferran. Standing face to face with him gave Luke goose bumps, but he managed to get out his crucial question: What is the most important thing for a chef? "Don't copy," said Ferran. That was it.

Luke didn't know it, but Ferran himself had received that piece of advice years before, from the wickedly talented, if mercurial, Jacques Maximin. As part of a group of Spanish chefs invited on an eating tour of the Côte d'Azur, Adrià had attended a demonstration where the chef of the Negresco reportedly answered a question about creativity with the same words. It struck the young Korean as the most interesting thing he had heard in his travels so far, and he was moved by the passion with which Ferran delivered the words. Still, he kept moving. After elBulli, Luke traveled to France, where he ate at Michel Bras's restaurant in Laguiole and Pierre Gagnaire's in Paris (it was on a train to Paris that he met the French couple who gave him the name Luke, since Myungsun taxed their pronunciation capabilities). He kept moving, eating at Heston Blumenthal's cutting-edge Fat Duck in Bray, England, and Thomas

Keller's flagships in both New York (Per Se) and Napa Valley (The French Laundry). The only place he didn't get to on his list was Grant Achatz's Alinea, because he ran out of money before he could buy a ticket to Chicago. Ten months to the day after that first meal at Tetsuya's, he was back in Seoul.

And he was miserable. Now that he had seen the gastronomic world, Korea felt more backward than ever when it came to cuisine. "There wasn't a Pacojet in the whole country!" he laments, referring to a device, common in European and American professional kitchens, that makes ice creams and other frozen purées without significant quantities of sugar. And he couldn't get Ferran's words out of his head. The more he thought about it, the more he realized that this one simple idea— don't copy—represented a complete revolution in cuisine. Luke had read a lot of culinary history, and he knew that professional cooking was founded on a set of recipes that a talented chef might hone, polish, even reimagine to fit his own vision. But Ferran had overturned all that. He didn't start with someone else's recipe and tinker with it. Ferran started only with himself, with his own ideas. "That takes so much passion," Luke says. "And courage."

Having found his master, Luke was ready to wholly dedicate himself to the task of discipleship. He had no money and no job offer. His mother, who had understood his desire to travel the first time but had missed him terribly in his absence, wanted him at home. Yet Luke felt he had no choice. Ten days after he returned to Korea, he left again for Europe. This time, he decided, he would do a *stage* at elBulli.

o o o

Cooking is one of the few professions that still allows for discipleship. True to its artisanal roots, it has a long history of mentorship—you learn to cook by watching an expert do it. The deep roots of that tradition is part of its appeal. As an apprentice with Michel Guérard, Daniel Boulud was reassured to learn that his mentor had had his own mentor. It reminded him, he writes, "of the jazz legend Fats Waller playing organ and doing his own *stage* with an organist in Paris, who in turn had studied with a student of Franz Liszt." Finding a mentor means plugging into a long chain of greatness in the hope of finding your place within it. It can give a young cook a sense of direction and purpose.

Any good discipleship demands rigor, and indeed, training to be a cook requires a physical exertion and mental steeliness that would not be uncommon in, say, one of those aspiring yogis who must learn not only to hold the lotus position for hours but to stick needles through his cheek while he does it. Much of any culinary apprenticeship consists of training to withstand its twin demons: exhaustion and tedium. It's why most every chef in the world can tell horror stories about the hardships of her time at the bottom of the kitchen hierarchy. When Boulud did his first apprenticeship with Gerard Nandron in Lyon, he spent so much time washing lettuce, his arms plunged deep in water, that he earned the nickname "the Beaver" (his assistant suggests that Boulud was not wholly distressed to learn years later that in English the word has another meaning). Dan Barber recalls having to shuck three hundred oysters every morning at Michel Rostang in Paris, according to a precisely designed procedure. First, the twenty-four-year-old stagiaire had to wash each oyster by dunking it exactly three times in ice-cold water—though not, it must be clear, water that actually contained ice. Then, he was taught, he had to hold the oyster in his right hand and, with a dull paring knife in his left, open the shell by going under the belly, being careful not to nick the flesh. ("Which was ridiculous," Barber points out, "since no one was going to see it. This was for oyster ravioli.") He had to make sure that he held the oyster upright—not the most natural position but one that ensured that the juices ran directly into a container below. And since Rostang permitted his cooks only two towels a day, Barber also had to make sure that his didn't get too dirty or wet from the oyster liquor since that would mean his allotment was rendered useless for the rest of the day. "But that was the point," Barber recalls. "If you washed them right, your towel didn't get dirty when you held it. And because you opened them upright, all the juice went into a container and was saved to finish a shellfish sauce, instead of soaking in a towel." It was a model, Barber found, that could be applied to other preparations as well. Tomatoes, for example, also had to be dunked three times—though this time in boiling water—in order to be skinned and then again held upright as the peel removed without nicking the flesh, so that the juice would fall neatly into a bowl, to be used later for vinaigrette.

In other words, there was not only a purpose to every step, no matter how seemingly absurd, but a building block in each—something that served as the foundation for something else, a lesson a young cook might carry with him, might employ, for the rest of his career. But what happens if the tasks you repeat each day of your apprenticeship are not ones you will be able to use elsewhere? What happens, for example, if you have to make Montjoi lentils?

Spaniards adore what they call *cocina de cuchara*, or "spoon cuisine," a reference to traditional stews soupy enough to make forks impractical. Each region has its own variation—red beans with ham, white beans with blood sausage, chickpeas with cod—but lentils have somehow defied the boundaries of regional identity to become a national dish, available in restaurants throughout every part of Spain. Including, as of August 2009, one in a small corner of the Catalan coast.

ElBulli's version is more delicate than most. A bit of translucent broth, a dusting of spice, and, at the bottom of the clear glass bowl, a small heap of tiny olive green legumes. Only they aren't, of course, actual legumes. "Montjoi lentils" are made from a batter of melted clarified butter and sesame paste that is the exact color of a Puy lentil. Squeezed through the narrow tip of a syringe into a bowl of ice water, the batter seizes, transforming each drop of liquid into a small, elliptical sphere. As long as it stays cold, you have a "lentil" (by itself, it tastes mostly of sesame, but once it is submerged in the lentil-flavored broth, with ham oil dotted on top, the taste is reminiscent, if not an exact match, of the beloved bean stew). It's a brilliant dish—delicious and playful at the same time. And the playfulness is layered.

This is a standard elBulli trick: to serve something that resembles what it is called but is not, in fact, made of it. In this case, there is the "lentil" that looks and tastes like a lentil but is not a lentil. But there is also a self-referential quality to the dish. The knowledgeable diner who understands Adrià's signature techniques tends to sit down to the bowl of Montjoi lentils and assume—indeed, may even pontificate to his dining companions—that the tiny disks at the bottom of the bowl are spherifications. Maybe made from lentil purée, maybe made from some other substance altogether, but definitely mixed with calcium carbonate and run through the alginate bath. The joke is that this isn't an elBulli trick at all. There are no additives in the Montjoi lentils, and they are not spherified. There is nothing to them, in fact, besides butter and sesame and the natural reaction that occurs when a liquid fat encounters cold water. (For serving, the lentils are strained from the ice bath in which they float.) The diner's expectations are twice dashed. Montjoi lentils are elBulli's idea of an inside joke.

But for the stagiaires who make them, the lentils are not the least bit funny. Each bowl contains precisely thirteen grams, which comes out to several dozen lentils, and since the dish appears on almost every menu, the stagiaires must push approximately two thousand drops of lentil batter through their syringes into ice water each day. Divided by eight or so people, that's 250 lentils per stagiaire. And although the technique is ridiculously simple (put lentil batter into syringe, push plunger), a lot can go wrong. Push too hard, and you'll get a stream instead of a drop; even the slightest excess of pressure results in globules that look more like tiny bullets than legumes. The batter also tends to firm up if it spends too long in the syringe, making it hard to expel properly, so a stagiaire may have to carry hers over to the flattop to warm it a bit. And as Lucho points out, the worst thing about the lentils is that because you're working from a huge, full bowl of batter, you can always see exactly how much remains, and it always seems to be more than you had hoped. It takes the stagiaires more than an hour to finish a day's batch.

If, in its double entendre, the Montjoi lentils perfectly represent the diner's experience at elBulli, so too do they capture what it means to be a stagiaire in the restaurant's kitchen. For one, it is a remarkable, genre-bending dish that depends, for its dazzle, on a cheap, ample supply of labor. In a normal kitchen, with far fewer staff, it would be nearly impossible to dedicate the time and effort of even one cook to reproducing such a painstaking component. But at elBulli, there is labor to spare—in fact, it is precisely so that the kitchen can produce dishes like the lentils that the restaurant takes on so many stagiaires. This dish also represents what, for the apprentices, is the very worst of the elBulli experience. The lentils take *forever* to prepare, causing hands and arms to cramp from holding the syringe in the right position for that much time. The process is incredibly boring—drip, drip, drip, like some kind of culinary water torture—but holds just enough potential complication that they can't completely space out. Worst of all, the preparation seems so futile. It's not just that they are boring themselves silly for a single dish but that the dish—the technique it requires, the unique blend of exactitude and mindlessness—doesn't really have any applications beyond the lentils themselves. Even if another restaurant wanted to adapt the technique to new ingredients, where would it get the manpower to make the dish?

At one point, watching Emma steam herself over a boiling pot, Ferran says, with just a touch of pride, that what they do at elBulli is create specialists. Pointing to her, he emphasizes his point: Emma is now the "world expert in roses—no one knows more about cooking roses than she does. Not even me." Given that Emma is likely the only person in the world to spend hours each day plucking, blanching, and straining edible petals, he is probably right. But what, exactly, is the value of this esoteric knowledge?

Perhaps that's the wrong question. Many chefs hold that the most important thing a stagiaire learns is never a single technique or even a collection of them but the self-discipline to carry out each one perfectly, every time. Yet for someone like Luke, who spent more than two years in the South Korean army, who worked in an Australian slaughterhouse to fund his ambition, and who has spent the better part of a year sleeping outdoors on the ground and walking long distances so that he will have enough money for the three-star meals that are his self-created education, that answer doesn't satisfy either. He had mastered self-discipline long before he arrived at elBulli. Now he wanted guidance.

o o o

When Luke returned to elBulli in the summer of 2008, there were just two months left in the season. He had not contacted the restaurant beforehand and thus did not have a *stage* arranged there. In fact, no one knew he was coming. He just hiked those same seven kilometers uphill and asked, in nearly nonexistent Spanish, to work. Marc Cuspinera was at the restaurant the day Luke arrived, and he explained to him, patiently, that elBulli has a system for selecting its stagiaires, that the selection process is quite competitive, and that there simply wasn't room in the kitchen for him at that time. Luke was undeterred. He went outside and set up his tent and sleeping bag on the hillside across from the restaurant, close enough to Ferran's house that Ferran's wife, Isabel, joked that Luke was camping in her garden. A couple days later, he went back to the restaurant and asked again; again he was refused. By now Isabel, who had at first been a little startled to see this lanky Korean lurking near the house, had grown accustomed to his presence. She began to exert gentle pressure on her husband. "He's really very nice," she told Ferran. "And he certainly is dedicated." After three weeks of camping and constant pressure, Luke was finally allowed in. He would spend the next eight weeks doing the most dreary of center table's tasks, but he didn't mind; he understood that he had come late and was just glad to have found a place. Nor did it bother him that he had practically no contact with his chosen mentor; he knew it would take time for him to earn Ferran's trust, and for the time being, he was thrilled simply to be in the great man's presence. Luke worked as hard as he could and then, with the end of the 2008 season upon him, signed up for another *stage* the following year.

In the interim, he couldn't afford to leave Spain, so he took a *stage* in Andoni Luis Aduriz's two-starred Michelin restaurant Mugaritz, just outside San Sebastián. Aduriz had trained under Adrià and is today one of the most innovative, accomplished chefs in Spain, so Luke knew he would learn a great deal from him. But mostly he was just passing time until June 2009, when elBulli would open again and he could return for the full season.

Luke in his assigned seat at Ferran's side during family meal

(Francesc Guillamet)

When at last it began, there was no happier stagiaire than Luke. Even as the apprentices cleaned the rocks on the first day, he was absolutely ebullient. "This is my passion," he said, grinning broadly as he lifted one stone after the next. That passion was obvious not only in the joyful smile he kept at the ready but in the vigor with which he worked. Taller than anyone else in the kitchen even before a copious amount of gel gave his jet black hair a few extra centimeters, he already stood out. But his sense of urgency distinguished him even more. Whether he was crossing the kitchen in a sort of superhero glide that allowed him to traverse the distance between one station and another in a single step or scrubbing down the flattop with a motion so intense it seemed bionic, Luke moved with an efficiency that would have been flamboyant if that weren't a contradiction in terms. His *quemo* was sharper, his sweeping more rapid, his plate polishing more fervent than anyone else's; the only thing for which he was consistently criticized was running in the kitchen. He was the most physically eloquent of the stagiaires, channeling his body's kinetic energy so that it silently but forcefully conveyed the message *I am working really hard.* Sometimes, when he spied coworkers slacking off, that message transformed itself into a subtle reproach: *I am working harder than anybody else.*

In the early days of the season, the chefs used him as a model, not only because he was the only stagiaire who had actually worked in the kitchen before but because his work ethic was so impeccable. They called on him to stack the plates that needed to be wiped down before service because he already knew which plates were used for which courses. He was assigned a broom for the post–family meal cleanup because Eduard already knew he could rely on him to leave a floor utterly free of crumbs. Luke did the tasks uncomplainingly, with a ferocity that bordered on the manic, because it was the only way, he said, that he would learn. The fact that he already knew how to do the jobs, having learned them the previous season, did not seem to occur to him.

Nowhere was his complete submission to the work clearer than with spherification. A process that uses algae-based gellifiers and calcium carbonate to turn liquids into semisolid globules, spherification is one of the signature techniques of elBulli. It requires the cook to drop a spoonful of some kind of runny substance—red currant purée, say, or pesto or olive oil—first into an alginate bath and then, when a transparent skin has formed on the outside that will allow the product to keep its rounded shape while remaining liquid on the inside, into a tub of water for rinsing, and finally into another for storing. The entire process is exacting: at one point Aitor chastised a stagiaire for crowding his spheres—"It should look like a lake," he said. "Not a swimming pool." But the most time-consuming part of the chore is the transfer between baths. The cook is supposed to scoop up each spherification with a slotted spoon, drain off the excess liquid, and slide it into the new tub. At this point in the process, it is not unusual to see a stagiaire pause during the draining and stare off into space. Once he gets over the gee-whiz factor of the technique, the actual task is deathly boring, and it can be hard to maintain focus.

Not for Luke, however. He had a trick. Like a señorita opening her fan, he flicked his wrist gracefully with every movement. Even hours into the numbing routine—dip, scoop, dip—he would add that little flourish, time after time, as he transferred the globule from one bath to another. The flick was so consistent that it seemed mechanized and so delicate that it looked affected, but it served a purpose. In fact, it allowed him to get the spherifying liquid off the sphere in a single motion, without having to wait for it to drain. That way, Luke finished his spherifications sooner than anyone else.

Watching him race through his tasks, the chefs would smile at one another and shake their heads, as if even they couldn't believe how hard Luke worked. But for Luke, nothing about what he did was funny. Learning required the utmost dedication and focus, and he would not tolerate a moment's lapse in himself or, for that matter, in anyone else. Many of the stagiaires tried to pass the time they spent doing mise en place at the center table by carrying on whispered conversations with each other or daydreaming; Sunny would go over hikes he had taken recently, while Antonio Romero entertained himself by thinking about the bars he and his friends had hit on their day off. But Luke remained centered on the task at hand. "The only thing I think in my head while I am working," he said, "is 'faster, faster, faster.'"

o o o

Eugeni de Diego hears those words in his head, too. Thin and anxious-looking, he is elBulli's "chef of production" (a position roughly equivalent to sous chef in other restaurants), which means he is in charge of mise en place. It is up to him to ensure that the major tasks are finished each day by the time the crew sits down for staff meal, which he also oversees. He has the closest relationship with the stagiaires and the most inherently antagonistic—constantly watching, constantly correcting. It is he to whom Miguel Alexander presents the roughly three cups of julienned lemon peel it took the center table nearly an hour to complete and he who, unhappy with the unevenness of the pieces, unceremoniously dumps them on the table, hands Miguel Alexander a pair of tweezers, and sets him to work pulling out the imperfect ones. Sometimes it seems to the stagiaires that he goes after them simply to assert his authority. One day he criticizes Emma for coming back from the walk-in empty-handed, but a short while later, when she walks into the kitchen straining slightly under the weight of a crate of water, he snaps at her again. "I don't want to see anyone carry too much," he says in front of the entire kitchen before softening his tone a bit. "You'll hurt your back. If something is really heavy, get two people."

Most of the stagiaires, in fact, have a Eugeni story—about a bit of criticism they feel is unfair or the time that he took credit for something that they had done. "Once I saw him say to someone else, 'I can do five of those in the time you do one,'" recalls one. "He always has to prove he's better than anyone else." Or there was the time an avellanto—a fragile cake made from amaranth seeds—was accidentally plated wrong: "He blamed me for it, when he was the one who had done it," says another.

Yet Eugeni is in a difficult position at elBulli. "His job is more of a pain than anyone else's," Ferran recognizes. "He has to be like a schoolteacher to them all the time." In other words, he not only instructs and monitors the stagiaires but is expected to assert his authority over them and, to a lesser extent, the line cooks, even though he himself is just twenty-five years old. At the beginning of the season, Eugeni had asked Marc how he should talk to stagiaires; Marc told him to speak to them the way he likes to be spoken to. "If you yell at them, they'll listen to you the first time and do what you want. They may even do it the second time. But if you keep yelling, they're not going to want to work for you." At the time it seemed like sage advice, but as the season advances, Eugeni has found the words hard to live by. He is still struggling to figure out his own role in the restaurant's hierarchy.

It is a tricky business. For all their bad-boy affectations, cooks tend to display a marked respect for hierarchy—or at least the upper echelons of it. Most any chef will tell you that a well-functioning restaurant is impossible without a well-run brigade, that without the militaristic order in which everyone knows his or her place at all times, the task of turning out fifty or two hundred meals each night quickly descends into chaos. And there is little doubt that the top-down chain of command that characterizes most restaurants helps the guys—and again, most are men—in the highest positions maintain a kind of order that serves their interests. The more remarkable social dynamic is that, as long as the chefs are skilled, the people further down the chain tend to embrace the hierarchy just as fervently as their superiors. You'd be hard pressed to find the enthusiasm with which a young cook will reply, "Yes, chef" today in once-hierarchical areas such as medicine or academia. With a deference that occasionally veers on self-abasement, most of the stagiaires don't just complete a task, they jump to it with an alacrity. They stand aside to let their chefs pass in front of them and would never think of interrupting one engaged in conversation, no matter how pressing the emergency.

But this respect, while automatically given, can be retracted if judged unwarranted. As Momofuku chef David Chang writes, the title "chef" can, if delivered with the right intonation, be derogatory. "What a joke, what a meaningless term it is these days: a fool in a black chef's jacket who has no fucking clue about anything. But when you work in a kitchen, your boss is your chef, and you call him or her that." At elBulli no one calls anyone "chef," but that doesn't mean they aren't evaluating. Nor does it mean that they don't miss the signifier. On their days off, the stagiaires will frequently get together to cook, and as one asks another to help with a task, the helper will often respond, *"Oui, chef."* It's a joke, of course, but something more as well; a chance to say the longed-for words and in so doing acknowledge the tradition you belong to and your place in it. For all that outsiders may think of the professional kitchen as a place of noisy, unbridled frenzy—a vision reinforced, no doubt, by those quick peeks through the window on the way from dining room to bathroom—most of its denizens like structure, even crave it. "I like the hierarchy," Katie says, "Because I always know exactly where I am."

At elBulli, hierarchy works in strange ways. The use of first names implies accessibility, and in fact, Oriol, Eduard, and Mateu do tend to be approachable in ways that chefs de cuisine in other restaurants often aren't. "I've never been so afraid of someone as I was of Chef [Jonathan] Benno," Kim Floresca says of her chef de cuisine at Per Se, even now—eighteen months after she left the restaurant—referring to him by his honorific. "But here I joke around with Oriol all the time." It's not unusual for Oriol to place a paternal hand on a stagiaire's shoulder as he answers a question or checks a preparation. Mateu receives high praise from most of his stagiaires for his patient willingness to answer their endless slew of questions. And even Eduard, whose personality is the sternest of the three, inspires a sense of collegiality that is unusual among the people who generally bear the brunt of his criticism. "I like Eduard a lot," says Diego. "I know he's got this authoritarian way about him, but that's just a role. No one else puts himself in it, so he has to. But when you talk to him one-on-one, he's a really nice guy."

Yet the sense of accessibility has its limits. Despite the first-name basis, hierarchy at elBulli is reinforced in gestures both formal and subtle. The chefs de cuisine, for example, tend not to socialize with the stagiaires. When they step outside the kitchen for cigarettes during break, they remain standing while everyone else sits. Eduard encourages questions, but only to a point. "We're not going to eat you if you ask us something," he says at one morning meeting. "But we're not going to like it either if you ask us the same thing six times." The chefs can go where they want in the kitchen, but no stagiaire can walk in front of the pass, unless she has been sent there for a specific purpose, such as to sweep. A stagiaire in charge of, say, cooking a rose petal, must take one every day to a chef to taste and either approve or dismiss, just as a chef de partie preparing a stock, no matter how many times he has done so, must daily take a spoonful of it to his superior for approval. The chefs de cuisine and, of course, Ferran himself do not have to line up to be served for family meal; instead of waiting at the back entrance, they come in through the front and are served first. Even their table—the center one— is set first and always with the best-looking salad or an extra loaf of bread.

Language reinforces the hierarchy. Ferran, Juli, the chefs de cuisine, and all the permanent front-of-house staff are Catalan, which means that they were born and raised in a region of Spain with a distinct language and culture, and a politics that tends to support greater autonomy from the central Spanish government. None of elBulli's staff is a particularly vocal Catalan nationalist (elBulli has become too much an emblem of

Spain itself for the higher-ups to allow that), and in the fall of 2009, when many towns throughout the region, including Roses, hold a nonbinding referendum on independence from Spain, none of them votes. But from their wholesale and virulent embrace of the Barça football team to the prevalence of dishes such as *escalivada* (marinated roasted vegetables) and *escudella* (chickpea stew) at family meal, elBulli's permanent staff clearly embraces Catalan culture. And that means that although they speak native Spanish, they prefer Catalan, the Romance language indigenous to the region. Though "prefer" may not be the right word; it implies a choice, and in fact Catalan seems to pour out of their mouths naturally whenever they are in one another's presence. It's what they immediately lapse into when they're shooting the shit during break, and it's what they unthinkingly use to communicate among themselves at work. Oriol and Eduard may conduct the morning meetings with the entire staff in Spanish, but should one of them need to consult the other on a particular question, he will slip into Catalan. No doubt this practice helps shield their discussion from prying ears, but it is not pure obstruction; after all, some of the stagiaires are Catalan too and can understand everything being said. But those same cooks, should they need to speak to Eduard or Oriol, do so in Spanish. At elBulli there are two tiers of language, and Catalan, at least in the kitchen (in the dining room, the servers are all Catalan and thus use the language regardless of rank), is reserved for the chefs.

The respect for rank reaches all the way to the top. So utterly in control of their own realms, Eduard, Oriol, and Mateu nonetheless defer completely to Ferran. One day during mise, one of the people who works occasionally in the elBulli office in Barcelona appears in the kitchen with a laptop and sets himself up at the table, ensconcing himself in one of the two free seats (the other two are piled with that day's allotment of mail, gifts, and press clippings) to type up Oriol's notes on the new dishes. For the first few hours he works alone, but finally he needs Oriol's help: in several cases he can't make out the chef's handwriting. Oriol hovers over the typist's left shoulder, where he accidentally knocks the cord that is charging the man's computer out of the socket. The typist plugs the computer back in and pulls out the chair beside him, suggesting it would be easier if Oriol took a seat. Oriol lightly refuses, saying he prefers to stand. The typist moves on to another recipe, and the two begin to make their way down the list of illegible ingredients when Oriol leans in and again knocks out the plug. "Dammit," the man snaps. "Would you please just sit down?" Oriol shakes him off. They get a little further, and the whole sequence happens again. "Look, if you don't sit, we can't do this!" the typist exclaims, exasperated. Oriol smiles nervously, then excuses himself, suddenly remembering a sauce left on the stove top.

The chair he refuses to take is Ferran's. Sometimes Oriol sits there first thing in the morning, before Ferran arrives, as he goes through his notes from the previous day. But this encounter occurs in the afternoon, and although Ferran is occupied elsewhere with a television interview, he is still in the house. As long as he is at elBulli, no one else sits in his chair.

This exaggerated deference is another way in which cooking promotes discipleship, and at elBulli few of the stagiaires are bothered by it. In fact, they *expect* their chefs to have privileges; they *want* them to be different. After all, those same privileges may someday await them when they are chef, and the chance to receive your plate of lentils before anyone else seems like fair reward for all those years of scut work. Most of them too respect the idea of the imperious chef. They accept that an integral part of a great restaurant is the great man—the genius, they like to say—at the top. They know that running a great restaurant carries with it a sometimes crippling amount of stress and pressure. They understand that that pressure will sometimes lead their chefs to behave poorly, to snap, to shout, to act like prima donnas. And for the most part, they understand, even embrace, this part of the territory, because if their chef is a great man, then it means they are affiliated with greatness. It's the thing that Eduard and Oriol and Mateu say over and over again when asked, as they inevitably are, if they don't mind that their names aren't on the menu. No, they respond, I know what it means to work here. I know what I have been a part of.

Still, there are limits to the stagiaires' acceptance. Ferran doesn't like to shout, and in fact, elBulli has none of the angry, testosterone-filled energy of, say, a Gordon Ramsay kitchen. At the beginning of the season he promised that there would be no insults or other forms of verbal abuse in his restaurant, and he reiterates the thought throughout the season. "If there's screaming in a restaurant, it's because control has been lost," he says. "And that doesn't happen here." Except when it does. Mistakes are sometimes made; things occasionally don't go as smoothly as one would like. At those times—and they are admittedly few—Ferran does shout. He just doesn't shout at the person directly responsible for the error.

One night, for example, an eight-top comes in a little past 8:30 P.M. It is still light out, so the group first sits on the patio, taking in the view of Cala Montjoi's aquamarine waters while they start their meal. Ever since the late 1990s, elBulli has opened meals with cocktails and "snacks" because, says Ferran, "it always seemed ridiculous to me that you would go to a fine dining restaurant and have to wait half an hour before they gave you any food beside a piece of bread." In this case, the first cocktail, the conífera, is set before them without a hitch. But then the table does something the staff hates: it orders a bottle of wine. In most restaurants, this action is heartily welcomed: a table that starts so early with a bottle is likely to continue with another and thus drive up the check. But at elBulli, a bottle of wine at this stage of the meal threatens to throw off everyone's timing. And indeed, that's exactly what happens: a sommelier stops the sequence of dishes while he brings and pours the wine, but then, critically, the server forgets to restart it. Fifteen, maybe twenty minutes pass, until suddenly Ferran realizes something is wrong. He charges over to the pass, rifles through the tickets, and begins shouting at Eduard. "That table has been seated for half an hour and they still don't have all their snacks!" he yells. "It makes no sense! Are you not paying attention? Don't you know how important rhythm is to the experience here?" At this point, he switches to Catalan and continues berating Eduard; the words "disaster" and "stupid" float through the linguistic morass. Eduard remains preternaturally calm, his eyes firmly fixed on the tickets in front of him, and continues to call out orders. Ferran switches back to Spanish. "Are you listening to me?" he demands, before harrumphing into a chair and thumbing angrily through the reservation book. He had planned to do his own complete menu tasting that night, to see how things fit together, but in the upheaval, that does not happen. Eduard asks if they should hold on to his planned menu so they can do the tasting tomorrow; Ferran cannot bring himself to look the chef in the eyes and only nods a stony yes. "That was nothing," Eduard says at the end of the night, when Ferran has gone home. "That was anger 'lite.'" Throughout it all, Ferran never once raised his voice, or even spoke, to the waiter responsible for the mistake.

A few weeks later, this pattern of reprimand repeats itself. A new stagiaire, Frederico Ribeiro from Portugal, has joined the crew. On his first day, he seems enthusiastic, but on this, his second morning, he doesn't appear at staff meeting. No one knows what happened to him; his roommates testify that he seemed fine that morning but admit that they haven't had a chance to get to know him. Finally, about an hour or so after the kitchen starts mise, Lluís walks downstairs from his office and whispers to Eduard that the restaurant has received a call: Frederico took one of the curves on the road up to the restaurant too quickly and hit an oncoming car. No one is hurt, but he is stuck about a mile from elBulli, waiting for the police to show up.

Eduard tells Ferran what he had learned, and within seconds, Ferran is yelling at Mateu, who, needless to say, had nothing to do with the accident, and nothing to do with Frederico's absence. But along with Marc, he is in charge of the stagiaires, especially on the days when Marc isn't in the restaurant. Why, Ferran wants to know, didn't Frederico have Mateu's cell phone number? What if he hadn't thought to call information and get the reservation line? Why had they had to wait all this time to find out what had happened? Hadn't Mateu impressed on the stagiaires the need for communication? It didn't matter that it was only Frederico's second day. Didn't he realize that they were responsible for the stagiaires' well-being? What if something more serious had happened? And again: why the hell didn't Frederico have Mateu's number? Mateu, like Eduard before him, freezes in the blast of Ferran's anger, a hiker hoping that if he remains still enough the large grizzly bear he has just stumbled across won't notice him.

Most cooks are accustomed to being yelled at. It's an inherent part of restaurant culture, a reflexive response to the intense stress and physical discomfort of working in a kitchen. But anger is not just an uncontrollable reflex, it's also a tool: it keeps people focused. As one otherwise mild-mannered New York chef says in reference to the staff he regularly screams at, "You need their fear. Otherwise it all goes to shit." As a result, most cooks excuse the anger, seeing in it at least a sign of virtue if not actually virtue itself. Paras Shah, a cook who has worked in David Chang's notoriously volatile Momofuku kitchens and whose own colorful vocabulary is hardly constrained, explains his chef's outbursts like this: "It's because he's a perfectionist. If he gets mad, it's because I'm not doing something perfectly. And it has to be perfect." Which is why Shah has no doubt that, once he has his own restaurant, he'll yell just as much as Chang ever did. Like abused children who grow up to abuse their own, cooks learn to scream from their superiors.

At elBulli, there are a few stagiaires, such as César Bermúdez in Pastry, who are unhappy with any display of anger; at thirty-two, he has worked most of his career in culinary schools and is unaccustomed to the rough-and-tumble of service. Still, he did work for a while at Carme Ruscalleda's three-star restaurant Sant Pau, and there, he says, no one ever screamed. "When an order came up, it was always, 'Could you please take this?' She would never have permitted anyone to yell at anyone." César is the exception, though; most of the stagiaires have experience being yelled at. Andrea, who came to elBulli from noma, recalls that Chef Redzepi's temper tantrums were legendary. "René used to get in your face and scream at you if a piece of leek wasn't set at exactly the right angle," she says. "That wasn't so great." It turns out, however, that having their chefs take the fall for them isn't so great either. The apprentices are unaccustomed to seeing their superiors chewed out, and in some ways, those outbursts bother the stagiaires more than if they themselves were the object of them. They rationalize the anger in the same way—after he witnesses Ferran raging for a solid half hour at Eduard for an undercooked suckling pig's tail that has to be sent back, the quiet Chilean stagiaire Juan Pablo Mellado explains the explosion as proof that "for Ferran, everything needs to be perfect all the time." But that doesn't assuage Juan Pablo's discomfort, or that of the other stagiaires, when Eduard, Oriol, and Mateu are reprimanded in front of them. They tend to go rigid, dropping their eyes as if to block out the scene, like children witnessing their parents fighting. At the very least, they say, they wish Ferran would do his chewing out in private. What seems to Ferran like the proper use of the chain of command ("It makes things work more smoothly, and besides, those three know how to take it," Ferran says of Oriol, Eduard, and Mateu. "It's like when you get mad at your family members.") seems to them like an assault on the hierarchy. They want their chefs to be treated with respect at all times, even—especially—by the chef above them.

Yet for all their embrace of tradition and rank, many of the stagiaires long for some kind of direct relationship with Ferran. It's not that they expect to be pals with him—only Diego, who, on the day he turns twenty-eight, dares to jokingly ask Ferran what the chef had gotten him for his birthday, describes his relationship with Adrià as friendship. ("He calls me Messi," Diego offers as proof, a reference to the star Argentine player on Barcelona's soccer team.) But they had hoped for something more. Although one stagiaire recounts how Ferran bought his table dinner when they both ended up at the same restaurant on a night off, others report running into him in Barcelona and getting the distinct impression that he didn't know who they were. Many are bothered that he doesn't greet them at the restaurant. Gabriel Vidolin, a sensitive, cuddly stagiaire from Brazil who arrives halfway through the 2009 season, gets a chilly response when he attempts to show Ferran a short video of some of the dishes he prepares at his restaurant back home. Ferran is his greatest hero, Gabriel says, and he is anxious to hear his advice. The response is crushingly brusque. "I don't interact with stagiaires," Ferran says. A few minutes later, Mateu rushes over to Gabriel. "What did you say to him?" he demands. "You want to talk to someone, you talk to me."

In many ways, the apprentices' disillusionment is a product of generational differences. Fifteen years ago, no stagiaire would have expected anything from his chef except distance, and perhaps disdain. "When I was *staging* in France," says Dan Barber, who spent half a year working at Michel Rostang, "it would never have occurred to me to approach the chef unasked." Other prominent chefs recount a similar attitude. "Are you kidding?" asks Claude Bosi, chef of the two-star Hibiscus in London. who apprenticed with Jean-Paul Lacombe in Lyon. "He would have smacked me if I talked to him like that."

In truth, Ferran knows more about the stagiaires than he lets on. His memory is prodigious, and he maintains a mental record of at least their bare biographical facts, if not their actual names. He is given to referring to some of them by nationality: The Argentine, The Japanese. It's a characteristic that Juan Pablo, who has come to elBulli after years teaching in a culinary school in San José, will discover when, fifty-eight days into his *stage*, Ferran calls him over to meet chef José Andrés. "He's Chilean," Ferran explains to Andrés before shuffling him off to the dining room to start his forty-course meal. "And a prof." That night, as excited as any adolescent girl with a crush, the thirty-five-year-old writes in his journal, "He remembered me!" And once a stagiaire has gone on to a job of his own, Ferran is unfailingly generous and kind. "He is incredibly supportive," says Redzepi. "But that's once you've left elBulli."

Still, many of elBulli's stagiaires find Ferran's self-imposed distance disappointing. That is a reflection in part of the expectations that elBulli itself creates, with its emphasis on first names and no insults. It is also a sign of changing times, as even the most haute of haute cuisine restaurants succumbs to a certain degree of democratization. The fame accorded the celebrity chef probably plays a role as well: through his own books and the innumerable articles about him, the conference talks and television appearances, Ferran—like an increasing number of famous, media-friendly chefs—foments the illusion among his admirers that they know him. But his remoteness is one of the stagiaires' most common complaints, the uneasy product of their perhaps unrealistic expectations. Mateu puts his finger on it. "They come here," he says with a rueful smile, "thinking that they're going to learn to cook from Ferran Adrià."

o o o

"Luke, do you have any brothers or sisters?" Sergi, the teenage stagiaire from one of the local culinary schools, asks with a grin. It is late at night, nearly the end of August, and everyone is standing around outside, waiting for word that they can go home. The others turn to Sergi, expecting a punch line that quickly comes. "Because I could run an entire restaurant with just two or three of you," Sergi says with a guffaw.

All the stagiaires laugh, including Luke. But the expression on his face exposes a faint trace of doubt: Are you laughing with me or at me? Until this point in the season, Luke has never questioned what he is doing at elBulli. He knows that he doesn't quite fit in with the rest of the stagiaires: his lack of funds prevents him from going out very often after work, and both his Spanish and his English are limited, making it hard to communicate as fully as he would like. And his efforts, so superhuman as to earn him the moniker "the Machine" also distinguish him, even in this hardworking place. As someone for whom efficiency and effort come almost naturally, he knows that he is sometimes critical of those who in his opinion fail to meet the restaurant's standards. It's not unusual for him to play enforcer at the center table, a self-appointed second in command to Eugeni, noticing when other stagiaires lose focus, chastising them with a silent shake of his head when they talk on the line, correcting them on any work that is less than perfect. But he has never doubted that this was the way it should be, that this was what it means to be a disciple.

Yet, two months into the season, Luke admits what is to him a shameful secret: he is tired of spherifying. Each day, he and two other stagiaires create thousands of globules. He has been doing it since the start of the season, eight weeks ago now. The year before, when he was at elBulli for two months on that impromptu *stage*, he spherified too. "I know it's an important job," he says with a guilty smile. "It's just—" He pauses over the treasonous thought before blurting it out. "It's just that I'd like to learn something new."

It's a benign complaint, but it signals a larger discontent. When he started the season, Luke was convinced that elBulli—and Ferran—were the highest pinnacle to which a young cook could aspire. "It's the perfect restaurant," he said then. "Just perfect." When he was put in charge of spherification, he took the assignment as a sign that his devotion had been recognized. The same held true for his seating position at family meal: of all the people at elBulli, he was chosen to sit next to Ferran. All these gifts he accepted with modesty and grace, along with a driving ambition to prove himself worthy. He has worked harder than anyone else. He has monitored the others, trying to encourage them to meet his own efforts. And he has made it clear that, given his druthers, he would continue at elBulli indefinitely, dedicated to it forever like Marc or Oriol.

At the end of August, Eduard tells Luke that he will be given new tasks. He is excited by the news; not only does it represent a chance to learn something new, but perhaps it will also mean the dreamed-for increase in responsibility, the first step toward acquiring a permanent position in the restaurant. He has already proven that he is ready to oversee other people's work. That's why, for example, he chewed out Lorenzo for not hosing down the landing properly and why, when he saw Gaël drift off in the middle of lentil production, he opened his index and middle fingers in a "V," brought them to his eyes Robert De Niro–style, and pointed accusingly to the bowl. (Gaël straightened up, but not without a scowl; you could almost hear his inner voice asking who Luke was to tell him what to do.) But Luke doesn't care. "There are a lot of really strong-minded people here, and it can be hard to work with them—everyone has his own way of doing things. But we have to work together, and in the way that we're told," he says. "Otherwise, the quality suffers."

Maybe, he hopes, the new tasks mean he is being auditioned for a permanent position. At the beginning of the season, Luke told Marc that he was interested in returning the following year as a line cook.

Marc made a note of it, but since then Luke has heard nothing. Still, he was optimistic. ElBulli seemed to him an environment not very different from the army, and hadn't he been promoted there? Surely, he thought, Ferran would recognize his efforts, his submission to the good of elBulli.

But the two new jobs that Luke is assigned fall short. The first is to prepare the Parmesan "pasta" that forms the shell for the ravioli dish. To make it, he pours hot Parmesan serum—made by melting cheese and separating out the solids and fats—in a thin sheet across a plastic tray, lets it harden, and then cuts out a thin, translucent circle with a ring. Thanks to the addition of agar-agar, the disks have the consistency of gelatin and are extremely fragile, so transferring them from tray to the drying rack on which they will be lightly dehydrated requires a bit of finesse. Luke slides his offset spatula under each one and then, as he goes to retract it, adds the little flourish, the barely perceptible twist of the wrist, that makes his work look simultaneously more mechanical and more balletic. Three hundred times he does this, over and over, until all the Parmesan disks are removed. The second task is simpler. He sets up the equipment for the lentils: bowls filled with ice water and topped with a strainer, syringes at the ready. Luke attacks both assignments with characteristic gusto, but it takes him only a day or two to recognize that they are no more challenging than his old ones, and impart no greater responsibility. One day he catches Marc at family meal and asks about next year. "We haven't made any decisions yet," Marc responds. His tone is gentle, but Luke gets the definite sensation he is being blown off.

"I'm disappointed," he says. "So much time, working so hard." Luke is too disciplined to let his work be affected by his own setbacks, but it does make him wonder, for the first time, about his priorities. Ever since that cooking competition back in Seoul, he has been on a clear path of his own making, and he has been relentless in its pursuit. From the army to the slaughterhouse to the nights sleeping on the bare Turkish ground to the long hours in the elBulli kitchen, he has followed the plan he first devised in the general's kitchen years ago. And just as he never stopped asking, in restaurant after restaurant, what is the most important thing for a chef, so too has he never stopped repeating to himself to always work harder, to always be faster. But now, though he is a little afraid to admit it, he realizes he may have been wrong. All that discipline may not necessarily get him what he wants—a better job, recognition, acceptance, embrace as part of Ferran's team. He may never gain access to elBulli's inner circle. In Luke, the first seeds of rebellion stir. Every now and then, as he squeezes out lentils or scoops up Parmesan disks, he pauses and stares pensively into space.

four

September, or **Risk**

One afternoon, Oriol presents Ferran with a refined version of a dish they've been working on for a couple of days. It's simple: a swath of black sesame paste swirled through a pool of transparent white yogurt water and served in a shallowly indented bronze-colored plate so that the whole concoction looks like an abstract painting set in a frame. Ferran takes a spoonful and begins to rapidly nod his head up and down in the idiosyncratic gesture that signals approval. "It's magic!" he proclaims, then smiles slyly. "Thirty percent of our clients will hate it. But it's magic!" He and Oriol decide to call the dish Petroleum, in honor of its oil-slick appearance.

Throughout this conversation, Andrea Correa has been quietly weighing dollops of sesame paste and jotting down the quantities in her pastel-colored notebook. As with almost all exchanges between Oriol and Ferran, her physical proximity to Oriol—as his assistant, she is rarely more than a few inches from his right side—enables her to listen carefully, and now a flicker of disbelief crosses her face. She is far too respectful to ever ask Ferran himself, but she can't help but wonder at the statement. As soon as her fellow stagiaire Kim is within earshot, she recounts the interaction, then whispers an urgent question under her breath. "What kind of chef serves a dish he knows a third of his clientele won't like?"

What kind of chef indeed? ElBulli is not impervious to its clients' tastes; servers are required to take note of any dish that goes largely or entirely uneaten, and the instances are recorded on one of the restaurant's many forms. (In 2009, the most frequently returned dish—even one prominent food writer barely touched it—was the artichoke rose.) But as Ferran likes to say, elBulli is not a "normal" restaurant, and part of the abnormality stems from its ability to be more cavalier than usual about diners' response to individual dishes. "What they like comes second," he says. "Creativity comes first." Pointing to the exciting but undelicious Petroleum, he continues, "We don't ask if a dish is 'good' or 'bad.' Here there's no such question. Our question is: Does it make your hair stand up on end? Is it magic?"

In theory, Andrea agrees. She has worked in enough important restaurants to appreciate the thrill that comes from a dish that breaks new ground. She admires the inquisitiveness and daring that go into the high-wire act that elBulli sets for itself each year. And as someone who tends to describe dishes in terms of their aesthetics, she implicitly understands the value in creating something that is beautiful, whether it be a painting or a plate of pasta. But still, she can't help wondering why a chef would risk alienating his clientele. The fact that this issue troubles her makes her wonder about her own creative abilities; maybe, she thinks, she wasn't cut out for this kind of cooking. But she can't shake a more fundamental doubt about elBulli. Aren't restaurants about nurturing people, about making them feel cared for? Why, she wonders, would you want to risk that?

o o o

One afternoon in September, just before the start of service, the entire staff gathers for a group photo. Like almost everything at elBulli, the brigade is recorded and archived, and if you could go back and look at the annual photos from the past twenty years, you would find among

Andrea Correa
(Francesc Guillamet)

them the young(er) faces of some of the best chefs in the world: not just Redzepi and Aduriz but Grant Achatz, Joan Roca, Jason Atherton, Quique Dacosta, Will Goldfarb, José Andrés, Nuno Mendes, Josean Martínez, and many others. Maybe that sense—that the photograph constitutes a kind of confirmation that each stagiaire has been part of this history-making restaurant—explains the giddiness in the air that day. Or maybe it is simply that, like grade school children who get out of class for their annual portraits, mise en place was cut short by thirty minutes. In any case, there is a joyfulness to the event, as the chefs gather on the hill outside the kitchen and jostle one another as they get into position. Marc has come in for the day and is trading wisecracks with the chefs de cuisine. Juli is making his habitually strange, if humorous, comments, and even Ferran, taking his place at the front, is in a jovial mood. As the house photographer, Francesc Guillamet, snaps away, a sense of bonhomie emanates from the group, as if they are all the dearest of friends involved in something much larger than themselves.

The reality is a little more complicated. For one thing, they don't all know one another. Now that the season is halfway over, several of the original stagiaires have left. Some, such as Laia and Sergi, have returned to their culinary schools; others, such as Ralph and José Luis, were slated to stay only three months. Miguel Alexander was supposed to stay the entire season, but his pregnant girlfriend, at home in Venezuela, made him think better of that decision. In his and the others' places are new stagiaires, including Eduardo Carmona from Mexico and Alfonso Gómez, a cook in the Spanish navy, who occupies the position that the restaurant (in homage to Ferran's own history) reserves each year for someone from the military. Short-term stagiaires have also begun arriving. For the rest of the season, there will be a steady trickle of cooks who come for a few days or a couple of weeks to absorb what they can. Jung, from South Korea, is one of them.

The full-season stagiaires are sad to see their companions depart—Roger will miss seeing his now-serious girlfriend, Laia, and Miguel Alexander was one of Diego's best friends in the kitchen. But they are also relieved to have some fresh blood around. "Everyone was getting a little cranky, " Andrea confesses. "People were snipping at each other; you can tell they were just tired of being around each other." Antonio agrees. "We've all been getting a little bored and tired of being here," he says. "It's good to have these new people here, who are excited like we were a few months ago. They bring new energy."

The change also means, however, that people who had gotten used to working together now have to readjust. A two-tiered system emerges, as the new stagiaires struggle to learn skills the old ones have mastered and the old ones struggle to contain their frustration that it now takes the brigade longer to complete tasks it had only recently pared to a bare minimum of time. It also means that Eugeni's fierce attention to the center table, which had eased a bit in recent weeks as he became more confident that his charges knew what they were doing, is now back in full force. And it means that more mistakes are committed. Victor, from Mexico, has yet to get the right amount of pressure on the syringe for the lentils; during his first few days he often presses too hard, splattering those nearest him with olive green batter.

For the photo, Ferran adopts his habitually serious expression: a fierce gaze that makes him look as if he is challenging the camera to a duel. Everyone else smiles broadly. But if you look closely, you'll see something else, a certain slump to their shoulders that betrays exhaustion and torpor. Thanks to the long hours of physical labor, almost all the stagiaires are thinner than when they started, but their movements, compared with those at the beginning of the season, seem less athletic and determined. And although this is not evident in the photograph, a little time in the kitchen makes it clear that not everyone is clinging to the rules as meticulously as before. Over the course of a few September days, Eduard finds several *tapers* thrown accidentally in the trash. Iosu, though freed several weeks ago from the burden of the yubas, seems to be chafing under his new routine in *cuarto frio;* it's not unusual to see him roll his eyes after an instruction or mutter to himself under his breath. And when the month's four-day break comes around, the Italian stagiaire Luca—burdened by money and family problems at home and depressed by a job he finds crushingly tedious—confesses to some of the others that he is thinking of not coming back. "I'm bored," he admits sullenly. "In other kitchens you move around a lot more, they understand you're a student, you're there to learn, so you can go over to other stations, watch what they're doing. Not here. Here, you're not a student, you're a worker. A worker in a factory assembly line."

But if Luca's smile in the group photo is somewhat forced, Katie's is unquestionably authentic. A few weeks earlier, Felix returned to Roses for vacation and, while he was there, proposed to her, pulling out for the occasion one of the oversized candy rings made by the Barcelona sweet shop Escribà. They celebrated with dinner at Rafa's, where they settled on a Memorial Day wedding and decided to hold it in Roses so that Felix's family could attend. Already Katie has spent one day off scouting restaurants for the reception, and her mother will be visiting soon so that they can start tasting menus and choosing florists. Considering that she has a full-time job until the end of December and is going to move to a new city and begin the preparations to open a new restaurant immediately after, planning an international wedding might seem a lot to take on. But with the same buoyant faith she brought to the task of mastering the croquant, Katie is sure she can get it done.

° ° °

Andrea was not sure why she was chosen to be Oriol's assistant, as precision, she knew, was not her strong point. On other cooks, the chef's jacket had the crisp, tailored lines of a double-breasted suit, but on Andrea, who was tiny to begin with, it slouched off her narrow shoulders and bagged around her waist, making her look smaller still. At work she wore her strawberry blond hair pulled back in a high bun with one of a seemingly never-ending array of brightly colored headbands, but strings of it often escaped and flopped carelessly around her neck. Her shoulders hunched slightly, and her apron wasn't always spotless. She met her husband, Andrés, a pastry chef, when they were both in culinary school, and for a short while they worked together. The fledgling relationship barely survived the experience. "There would be crumbs," she admitted. "Or I wouldn't wipe everything down spotlessly. He would get really mad. Pastry chefs are *such* perfectionists." Even when cooking at home, the couple squabbled about what Andrés saw as her sloppiness.

Nor did Andrea see herself as wildly creative, at least not in the elBulli model. She had never invented a restaurant dish, had never really even tried to come up with a surprising combination of flavors or textures. "What I love about elBulli, what I see as the magic here, is how they play with your emotions: it's like a painting or a great movie. But it's not what I cook. The flavors are good, they're just not the kind of thing I want to eat very often." She pointed to the Parmesan ravioli—made from agar-agar and Parmesan serum—that Luke was meticulously scooping up with his spatula. "I love that dish," she said. "But I love a plate of shaved Parmesan cheese just as much."

What *did* Oriol see in her? Her former boss René Redzepi calls Andrea "extremely talented, a great cook," but Oriol, who tapped her when she had been at elBulli only a few days, had no way of knowing that at the time. He was guided by more pragmatic concerns; specifically, he needed someone who spoke Spanish well and was an especially hard worker, since he or she would be required to show up an hour or two earlier than the other stagiaires. But what Oriol really seemed to need was someone whom he could—in his quiet, joking way—boss around. Oriol Castro is the gentlest of souls, but doing his job means constantly telling someone else what to do—and not the impersonal mass of the brigade but a single individual. Whether conscious of it or not, he was looking for someone he could trust to receive his orders uncomplainingly.

Even-tempered in the kitchen, Andrea rarely let the pressure of the job get to her. A hundred times a day, Oriol called for her to do something— write down the proportions of a recipe he had just invented, peel a piece of squash in preparation for testing it, fetch the tray of mushrooms she had just, on his orders, returned to the walk-in—and she always responded with the same cheerful *"Oído!"* Sometimes he would call her name and she would stand there, waiting, until he remembered what he wanted. Yet even then she responded with equanimity, never letting frustration creep into her voice. Perhaps that was because she knew how lucky she was.

Andrea's parents, both psychologists, divorced when she was four. With no siblings, she lived alone with her mother, María Teresa, in a small house in a middle-class neighborhood. Her mother was not a great cook, and they weren't a great food family. "She knew how to make some things, but it was pretty basic—rice, beans, arepas, plantains," Andrea recalls. "It was the same thing every day. And she hated it. She thought cooking was a form of slavery." Her mother was repelled by the sight of blood in meat and, anytime they had steak or hamburger, would cook it until every trace of pinkness was gone. Even now, when Andrea goes home and tries to convince her mom of the gustatory pleasures of, say, a steak cooked medium well, María Teresa resists. "She always says, 'Put more sauce on it so I can't see it,'" Andrea says, rolling her eyes ever so slightly. In that environment, restaurants provided a happy escape: for her mother from the drudgery of cooking and for Andrea from the numbing monotony of rice, beans, and overcooked meat. Her mom would take her out a couple times a month—often to a crêpe place they both liked—and Andrea was always enchanted. "I loved restaurants," she remembers. "Not just the food, though I loved that. But everything—having people wait on you, the way everything was set out so perfectly, the way the food looked so artfully laid out on the plate." When she visited her father, a more adventuresome eater, she got to go out even more, though in those cases the pleasure was tempered by her father's tendency, as a confirmed Marxist, to see the occasion as a case study for the inequities of the capitalist system.

Andrea wouldn't realize that anything was unusual about her childhood until years later. It's true that there were always men with machine guns outside the crêpe restaurant, and she was never allowed to roll down the car windows. Nor could she leave a bag on the car seat, walk alone outside, or visit certain parts of the city. But it never occurred to her to ask why. It was just how things were when you grew up in Medellín, Colombia.

o o o

It's easy to forget how dangerous a kitchen can be. One night in September, the stagiaires get a reminder. Service this evening has been unremarkable; tables arrived properly spaced apart so that no one felt particularly rushed, plating is going smoothly, and Eduardo hasn't had to raise his voice more than a couple of times to quiet everyone down. Now, at 11:30, the first tables are beginning to ask for their checks. Savory dishes are still going out, though they have slowed enough by this time for the center table to seem almost calm. Finding himself without anything to plate, Jung, the visiting stagiaire from Korea, decides to get a head start on cleanup. He bends down at the flattop and empties the grease trap into a pot. The dirty oil is still extremely hot, but for some reason—maybe he forgets, or maybe it is shyness brought on by his inability to speak Spanish—Jung fails to say "Quemo" as he stands with it and turns. He bumps into Jorge, and the container of near-boiling oil spills down the latter's leg. Jorge lets out a scream that stops service cold. In an instant Oriol and Eugeni are on him, ripping off his pants. From the knee down, his skin is lobster red, and angry welts are already starting to bubble. There are a few seconds of chaos until it is determined who will take him to the hospital. Laia runs for her car, and together a few of the stagiaires lift their injured companion into it. With Jorge still screaming, Laia rushes him down the road to Roses.

The doctors who treat Jorge inform him he won't be able to work for several weeks. Marc Cuspinera tells the stagiaire he can go home to Venezuela and return the next year, but Jorge is determined to see the season through. He spends the next couple of weeks lying in bed in the cramped, dark room he shares with two other stagiaires. Every morning, one of his housemates takes him to the clinic so that he can have his bandages changed; another routinely cooks him something to eat. The rest of the time he is alone in the dingy apartment, trying to distract himself from the pain by watching bad Spanish soap operas and checking his Facebook page. Usually he dozes off sometime around 11 P.M., only to wake when his roommates get home around 2 A.M. The days stretch out in front of him excruciatingly.

For about thirty minutes after the accident, the kitchen is a shambles. Getting Jorge out of the kitchen and on his way to the hospital is relatively easy; harder is getting the large oil slick up off the floor while cooks are still swirling past the stove and plates are still going out. Eugeni goes at the spill with a mop and hot, soapy water, trying all the while to keep everyone clear of the slippery spots. Eduard takes Jung aside, purportedly to chew him out. The offense is serious enough that, in some restaurants, the stagiaire would be fired on the spot. But Jung is so obviously miserable about what he has done that Eduard doesn't have the heart. With a stern warning about the importance of saying *"Quemo,"* he pats him on the shoulder and sends him back to work.

By this point in the season, *quemo* has become something of a joke— so habitual and ubiquitous, so routinely used just to get people out of the way—that the stagiaires consider it practically meaningless. But it escapes no one's attention that the worst kitchen accident most of them have ever witnessed was caused precisely by someone failing to say the word—and say it, most notably, when it was true. As service finishes that night, the mood is noticeably somber. Every cook in that kitchen is thinking it could just as easily have been him.

o o o

When Andrea was growing up in the 1980s and '90s, Medellín was the home base of Pablo Escobar, leader of one of Colombia's two warring drug cartels, and one of the most violent cities in the world. Gangs and paramilitary groups fought openly in the streets for supremacy, and police didn't dare enter many of the poorer, crowded neighborhoods that crept up the sides of the surrounding Andes. In 1991, the year Andrea turned eight, there were 6,350 murders in her hometown, or 381 for every 100,000 people. Drug traffickers regularly hired gangs of assassins to detonate bombs in public places, killing scores at a time, though point-blank shootings were also common. In one particularly gruesome incident, hooded gunmen forced their way into a nightclub frequented by the adult children of wealthy businessmen, forced the male patrons to lie facedown on the pavement outside, and shot twenty-six of them. Kidnappings also skyrocketed; in 1990, the number reported nationwide rose to 1,274 from 789 just the year before. For much of Andrea's childhood, Colombia was the world leader in the crime.

Her family was hardly immune to the violence. Her father had left Medellín years earlier for the relative safety of Bogotá and would later move even farther away, to Mexico. One of her uncles, who had stayed in Medellín, began receiving extortion demands. He tried to ignore them until he noticed one morning that he was being followed on his way to work. He was on a plane for the United States the next day. None of this made much of an impression on young Andrea until one night when she was twelve years old and sleeping over at a friend's house. Early the next morning—she remembers it was still dark out—her friend's mother woke her to tell her she had a phone call. She stumbled to the phone in her pajamas. It was her mother, and her voice was panicked. "There was a bomb," she said. It had exploded outside the residence of a former governor, next door to the house of Andrea's grandparents. Her grandfather had been gravely injured in the attack. Her grandmother had been killed. As she waited for her mother to come get her, the twelve-year-old watched the news over and over on television.

Andrea was devastated to lose her grandmother, and she remembers weeping inconsolably at the funeral. But she wasn't scared. In Medellín, violence was so omnipresent and so random that you couldn't really fear it—it was just the backdrop against which your everyday life unspooled. The fear would come later.

Like many middle-class Colombians, Andrea grew up assuming she would spend some of her adolescence in the United States. Most of her cousins had gone off to study English for six months or a year, and so, when she graduated from high school at age sixteen (in Colombia, there are eleven years of preuniversity study, and Andrea finished them one year early), she moved to Atlanta, Georgia, to live with her uncle while she studied the language. She arrived there alone, speaking not a word of English and knowing no one beyond her uncle's immediate family. They gave her a room in their house and sent her to school at Georgia State University, which offered a program to prepare foreign students for college. It was only then, in suburban Atlanta, with its machine gun–less malls and unguarded classrooms, that Andrea realized how dangerous her childhood had really been. It was only then that she started to feel afraid.

o o o

There are no muses at elBulli. The commonly held image of the artist as a tortured soul waiting for fickle inspiration to strike has no place at a restaurant whose reputation depends on constant, steady reinvention. Maybe in the beginning, with some of those earliest ideas—to transform the most classic of Spanish dishes, a gazpacho, into a plate that made the diner question if he really knew what gazpacho was, for example, or to pass a purée of white beans through one of the siphons habitually used for making whipped cream and thus invent, in 1994, the first of those infamous foams—maybe those were born from the unpredictable lightning bolt of inspiration. But at least since 2002, when elBulli did away with à la carte menus, Ferran has not had the luxury of waiting for a bout of creativity to hit. After all, he has set a remarkable challenge for himself, which is to come up with a hundred or so new dishes a year. And the longer he successfully meets that challenge, the more his diners' expectations grow. People now come to elBulli at least in part because they know they are guaranteed a meal that will surprise them, even—especially—if they've eaten there before. The pressure on Adrià to innovate is therefore intense; there is no room for the equivalent of writer's block in his world, so he has developed an elaborate system that eradicates the terrifying possibility that he could ever simply run out of ideas.

At elBulli, people talk about creativity as if it were a tangible commodity, or at the very least a skill one can learn and practice. "We're starting creativity next week," Ferran said back in June, in the same tone that a department store buyer might use to communicate the arrival of that season's swimsuits. In other restaurants, words like *research* or *test kitchen* or *idea development* or *brainstorming session* are used to describe the process of invention. But those phrases are too inconclusive for elBulli. "Testing" and "research" imply the possibility of failure; they run the risk that nothing will come of them. And that is a risk that elBulli cannot take.

Each year, the restaurant starts its menu from scratch, consciously rejecting or diminishing the role of techniques and ingredients that played starring roles in the previous season and looking for something new. (For example, although Ferran is perhaps most closely identified with foams, he has not actually served them in several years. "Airs," however, are a different story.) For that kind of reinvention to happen, creativity can't wait for something so fleeting as inspiration; it has to be codified. And indeed, one of elBulli's ironies is that the more widely Ferran is defined as an artist, the more businesslike his approach to creativity has become.

That approach usually begins with a single departure. Because of his reputation for high-tech wizardry, many people believe that Ferran starts his inventions with a new piece of technology or, at the very least, some arcanely philosophical concept. The truth is that, like most chefs, he usually begins with a product. One Friday early in September, Eduard asks Oriol for his shopping list. Oriol tears a hastily scribbled page out of a notebook and hands it to him. It reads:

Mató cheese
White dragonfruit
Finely ground flour
Angel hair squash
Duck eggs
Cranberries
Monkfish liver
Tofu
Mini kiwis from Figueres

The combination of ingredients is unlikely, but Eduard doesn't bat an eye (though he does pause to ask Oriol if he wants the tofu normal or extra-silky). It is part of his job to make sure that he keeps a steady supply of new ingredients flowing into the restaurant. Some of those new ingredients come from the travels that Adrià and his team make each year during the off-season: Japan, Thailand, Korea, Norway, and the Amazon have all proven rich sources. Some come from producers with whom the restaurant has worked in the past and who by now know that Eduard is always happy to receive a box of finely crafted smoked butter or surprisingly sweet lemons. And many come from Eduard's own searches, his regular visits to farms and fishermen, where he is always on the lookout for new possibilities.

Whether they arrive through serendipity or active search, all new products eventually end up on the pass, awaiting testing. On this particular Friday, the selection of products is especially promiscuous: a box of herbs; a pair of disgusting-looking fish livers, soaking in a liquid that has by now turned pink; a bottle of elderflower juice from Ikea; a couple of round, green squash the size of basketballs; and a big plastic bag filled with what appear to be Japanese candies—the junky, fluorescent-colored kind of candy that the Spanish call *chuches*. Ferran unwraps one and puts it in his mouth. He makes a face. "I have no idea what that is."

So maybe it won't happen with a Japanese *chuche*. But many of elBulli's ideas start with nothing more than this: a new vegetable, a spice no one has tried before, a condiment from some far corner of the globe that, when tasted, sparks an unfolding chain of ideas. The rose is a perfect example, but there are numerous others this season, too. Pàmies, Spain's main supplier of exotic vegetables and herbs, has sent in a supply of ficoïde glaciale, a lemon-flavored lettuce whose dense, juicy leaves appear covered in dew. The "glaciale" in the plant's name prompts Ferran to think of ice, which leads him to the idea of an ice salad. After a few trials, Oriol hits on a version he's happy with: he places small rocks of crushed ice in one of the restaurant's handmade gold bowls and dots the interior with ficoïde, watermelon cubes, purple garlic flowers, and drops of balsamic vinegar. Visually, it's stunning. Ferran looks at it appraisingly. "We're the most poetic cooks in the world," he says, "But we don't advertise it. Because to be creative you have to be very pragmatic."

Pragmatic enough to throw out a dish because something—some ephemeral, impossible-to-explain thing about it isn't right. The ficoïde goes out for maybe three nights, then disappears from the menu, never to be seen again. Still, Ferran can't get the idea of an ice dish out of his head. At one point when he and several other Spanish chefs were in Brazil earlier in the year, trekking through the Amazon on a culinary tour, they stopped in a dusty town, and as the group stood sweltering in the sun, one of their hosts sprinted off to a street vendor and bought them all cups of shaved ice, doused with Coca-Cola. Maybe it was the blend of perfectly crushed ice and syrupy soft drink, or maybe it was just the heat, but Ferran was enchanted. "Ice," he says, recalling the moment. "You bite it, it breaks. A totally unique texture." That was all it took: he decided then and there to do something with ice on his next menu. He thought the ficoïde, with its evocative name, would be it, but he was wrong. "It can take a day or a month or a year to get things right." He gestures toward the now-discarded salad. "I can't even tell you what's wrong with it. But something is. It's just not magic."

Instead, he and Oriol revive an ice dish they tested earlier at the *taller*—the workshop near the Boqueria market, where they develop ideas during the six months each year that elBulli is closed. From the restaurant's local citrus grower, Eduard has recently received a supply of thin-skinned mandarin oranges no larger than Ping-Pong balls. At Ferran's behest, Oriol begins to work with them. At first he uses tweezers to place small pieces of the same crushed ice—as close in texture as the restaurant can come to the Slushee of Ferran's memory—on a flat plate, but Ferran wants something that looks a little more haphazard and tells him to use a spoon. Seven tiny mandarin segments are laid in the spaces in between. Again balsamic vinegar is dotted over the dish; this one also gets a drizzle of olive oil and a bit of salt. Ferran takes a bite and rapidly nods his head yes. "But ten segments, not seven," he corrects. The first ice vinaigrettes go out that night.

The dish's simplicity holds a clue to how recipe development at elBulli works. When a product is new to Ferran and Oriol, they tend to manipulate it very slightly. In its first incarnation in 2008, the obulato, the translucent paper made from potato starch, was used merely as a support for the asparagus canapé—unadorned, it functioned the way a slice of bread might. But now, in 2009, they have to do something more complicated with it. They play with its texture by baking it into crisp, sugar-coated sheets for the pineapple pastry. They experiment with its size and shape by molding a massive sheet into the *pañuelo*. Then they draw attention to the obulato's one great weakness—that it dissolves in liquid—by creating the Shabu Shabu, a dish that requires the diner to dip the filled obulato in liquid and eat it before it disintegrates. "Next year," Ferran asks not at all rhetorically, "who knows what complicated form the obulato will take?"

Some products resist manipulation—in fact, they resist creativity altogether. Meat has proven notoriously difficult for elBulli to reinvent. "What are you going to do with it?" Ferran asks. "You can cut it different ways, you can cook it different ways, but it's still a chunk on a plate." In fact, proteins as a whole present a challenge, and the innovation in those dishes tends to go toward the elements served with them rather than the protein itself. The "risotto" may be made from corn germ and foie gras fat, but the baby cuttlefish that sit atop it are still plain grilled cuttlefish. Every now and then, the chefs will find a way out of the protein trap—in 2007, one of the last courses before dessert was a hare with apple that consisted of a bowl of intensely flavored, thickened rabbit stock with a bright pink apple gelatin in the center, a concise reversal of the normal meat in the center surrounded by sauce. And one of the great innovations of 2009 was to create a sequence of game dishes, so that the diner moved from a snifter filled with squab consommé to a rabbit loin with cocoa-dusted foie gras ravioli to rabbit brains in hare "juice." But mostly Ferran gets around the protein problem by using cuts of meat that no one else would. This predilection goes far beyond the taste for offal that is so trendy today. Rather than calf's liver and pig's feet, elBulli serves cow tendons and goat kidneys and tiny little bunny tongues. There are woodcock heads, served with the beak intact (the better for clutching while you suck the brains out of the skull). There is cartilage, taken from the back of the chicken and deep-fried, so that it is both crunchy and gelatinous. And there are those rabbit brains— fried, poached, sautéed. Once, while a chef was visiting from the United States, Ferran opened a box of chickens that had just arrived from France and pointed to the carcasses—head and feet still attached, plump bodies wrapped in white muslin—and said, "That is the best chicken I've ever eaten." He proceeded to explain that the bird was a breed that dated back to the time of King Henri V and had been on the verge of extinction when a pair of farmers in southwest France decided to try to save it. The chickens were raised on pasture, their diet consisting solely of grass and grubs. The result, Ferran emphasized again, was "the best chicken" he'd ever eaten. "Better than Bresse," he said, referring to the famed, dark-footed birds of Normandy. Given this effusive praise, the visiting chef asked reasonably, "So this is the chicken you serve in the restaurant?" Ferran looked at him as if he were crazy. Brushing the suggestion away with a flick of his wrist, he scoffed. "What the hell am I going to do with a whole chicken?"

Sometimes, an idea, for all its incarnations, won't go anywhere at all. That was the case, a few years ago, of a risotto Oriol tried to make from sunflower seeds. "We spent two weeks on that thing, and in the end . . . nothing," he says, still visibly annoyed by the failure. In 2009, the snack they call *ninfa* looks to be going the same way. The idea for it had come from the flavored meringues that the restaurant was shaping into mini-baguettes, dehydrating until crisp, and then slicing and filling first with apples and almonds, then later with squash and truffles, so that they became the "bread" in a "sandwich." Now they're using the same technique to make the *ninfa*, but the shape and texture are giving them problems. Oriol first tries piping the meringue in concentric circles, but Ferran doesn't like the look. He tries wrapping a piped line around a tube to create a kind of meringue cannellone; Ferran thinks it's not artistic enough. He tries shaping it into a kind of boat, which he then fills with puffed quinoa. Ferran takes a bite and says, "Better. But it needs to be smaller. The first bite is good, but, because there's no liquid [liquid would make the meringue soggy], you get tired of eating it." Oriol presents it again, smaller this time. Now the quinoa bothers Ferran.

"Do it with nuts," he says.

Oriol objects. "But we already have nuts in the Shabu Shabu and the mimetic peanuts."

"Okay, then do it with pistachios." Ferran replies.

"Pistachios?" If Oriol knows that these too are a kind of nut, he keeps that information to himself. "What about sunflower seeds?"

"Sunflower seeds?" Ferran shakes his head, perhaps in memory of that ill-fated risotto. Then he reconsiders. "Okay, do it with pistachios first and then sunflower seeds. "

Ferran turns away, obviously still occupied with the meringue problem. "The level is there, but something's missing," he says distractedly. They'll try a few more versions, but the *ninfa* won't be making it onto the menu anytime soon.

This process of trial and error, in which one variable is changed at a time, is the most important thing that elBulli does, the basis of its creativity. Roberto González, a cooking instructor and food writer who did a *stage* at the restaurant in 1998, remembers the first time they got agar-agar, which by now is one of the standard gellifiers that elBulli uses. The substance had been used in Japan since the fifteenth century and made its way to the West in the late nineteenth century, when it became part of the repertoire of industrially produced foods. But at elBulli, González recalls, they had no idea what to do with it. "They had learned that it was used in Japan as a thickener, so they ordered some," he says. "The problem is that they ordered it fresh. They were basically starting with a big pot of seaweed, trying to use it to thicken sauces." There were a lot of briny-tasting false starts before Ferran and the other chefs figured out that they had to dry the agar-agar first, then grind it into powder.

Even then it wasn't perfect for every application. Agar-agar can turn most any liquid into something semisolid and, unlike gelatin, will maintain its texture even when heated. It opened a world of possibilities, including the restaurant's famous ham noodles, made from ham broth. That application is still on the menu; in 2009, the restaurant was making the pasta for ravioli from nothing more than Parmesan serum and agar-agar. The rhubarb and sea cucumber dish comes with a garnish that looks like a piece of crumpled cellophane but is even more minimalist: water and agar-agar. But the substance tends to make liquids fairly solid, and Ferran wondered if another additive existed that might be more subtle. He asked a scientist friend if there weren't something else besides agar-agar, and in response, learned about xanthan gum, a thickener made from cornstarch. Used in almost imperceptible amounts, Xantana, as it would become known once elBulli began to market it commercially, allowed the chefs to gently thicken any liquid, regardless of temperature, without affecting the flavor or smell. "I could add it to water, and you wouldn't know it's there," says Ferran. "It would just be ever so slightly thicker than normal."

There are few unintended discoveries at elBulli, few times when a cook accidentally drops, say, raspberries into wasabi, only to discover that they actually taste good together. Most new dishes start with an interrogation: What happens if we freeze-dry foie gras? Can we come up with a new way to thicken a sauce? What is the best way to highlight the tartness in a lulo or the variety of flavors in soy? As the famously creative

American pastry chef (and former stagiaire) Will Goldfarb explained to the *New Yorker* writer Bill Buford, the "operating principle was always 'What if?' A custard has always been made with milk. What if it's made with cream? (The result is drier and richer.) A chocolate mousse has always been served cold. What if we warm it? (You taste more) . . . What if? What if? What if?"

But every now and then, the chefs surprise even themselves. That same afternoon, with a little spare time on his hands, Eduard begins idly poking through the products on the pass—the elderflower syrup, the fish livers, the horrid Japanese *chuches*. He picks up an angel-hair squash, which in Spain is most commonly eaten candied and stuffed into pastry, and cuts it into chunks. He removes the black seeds from the white flesh, trims away the dark green peel, then stands back and contemplates the vegetable. He slices it thinly. Then, for a reason he doesn't really understand, he decides to boil it. He sticks a few fan-shaped slices into a pot of water, covers them with parchment, then promptly forgets about them. An hour and a half passes before he remembers to remove them from the water. By now the flesh is translucent and has partially separated into filaments. He dries the squash and puts a slice onto a plate. "What kind of fish is that?" Oriol asks. "It looks like shark fin."

They each grab a spoon and taste. The squash doesn't have much flavor, but the texture is pleasantly meaty. Excitedly, Oriol sends Andrea to the walk-in for some chicken stock, then yells after her, "And get some Asian stuff, too." She comes back with everything she can think of: soy sauce, sesame paste, ginger, tofu, dashi. He plays around with the seasonings before deciding on a simple broth made from stock, ginger, and lemongrass. He spoons a bit onto a plate, then sets a fan of angel hair into the pool. He brings it to Ferran. "Shark fin squash," he says. Ferran tastes it and beams. "No," he says. "Land fin." It will go onto the menu as that—*Aleta de tierra*—but when he talks about this spectacular, and spectacularly simple, dish, he will sometimes call it "ecological shark's fin"—a reference to the real shark's endangered status.

Naming, too, is a big part of the creative process at elBulli, and, as the case of the Shabu Shabu proves, the words that describe a dish routinely go through as many iterations as the ingredients that make it up. "Naming is where the psychological work happens," Ferran explains. "I'm not exaggerating—it's very intellectual. You want the name to reveal something that opens the door to the dish, that allows people to enter. But without forcing them. Because it's always up to them to decide: Do I enter the game or not?"

o o o

Although Andrea was safe in the United States, she quickly chafed at the constricts of living with her uncle and his family in the Atlanta suburbs. Six months after arriving, she moved to a new apartment downtown, which she shared with two male roommates ("My parents really loved that," she recalls). After she passed her language courses, she was ready to enroll in college and soon had to choose a major. With her eye on a career in business, she first picked math, but a few months into that program, realized she wanted to do something more artistic. As she pondered a future career, she kept coming back to all those times she had gone out to eat with each of her parents. It wasn't so much the food that had drawn her then—though she certainly enjoyed that—as the atmosphere. The lovely tables and chairs, the flattering lighting, the pristine table settings: between the physical beauty and the conviviality, restaurants engendered a sense of well-being she felt in few other places. She determined to become a restaurant designer and began taking classes at Georgia State's hospitality school.

To earn a little money and get some hands-on experience, she also took her first restaurant job, as a server at the American Café. The place was nothing special—a casual restaurant located in one of Atlanta's many malls that served a lot of burgers and fried mozzarella sticks. But it had a few house-made specialties that were tasty enough, including a potato soup heavy on bacon and cheddar. Andrea didn't love waiting tables, so in her spare time she asked one of the restaurant's Mexican cooks to teach her a few recipes. It was the first time she had ever really cooked, and she enjoyed the experience enough that she soon began looking for an externship in a restaurant kitchen. She landed at the Buckhead Diner, an upscale diner owned by the city's most important restaurant group; to this day, it is one of Atlanta's most popular restaurants. On paper, many of the dishes were the same as those served at her previous job, but the quality was much higher and the recipes more sophisticated. At the Buckhead Diner, the meat loaf was made with veal and wild mushrooms, the potato chips were house-made and topped with Maytag blue cheese, and even the burger came on a fresh-baked egg bun. Andrea was entranced, and not only because she had started dating the sous chef. "I thought I was making the best food in the world," she says.

When her externship was over, Andrea decided to combine her newfound passion for cooking with her lifelong desire to travel. She enrolled in a cooking class at the Sadler, a restaurant in Milan, and left, early in the summer, for Italy. It wasn't until she arrived—and paid the $2,000 tuition—that she learned she wasn't exactly in the right place; the other students were older than she and conspicuously better dressed. It soon became clear to Andrea that the place was a cooking school for rich tourist housewives who wanted to watch the chef make ravioli. Andrea was crestfallen—and mortified. Taking pity on her, the chef got her a *stage* (and a refund), and she spent the rest of her summer working for real in his kitchen. It was her first time on the continent and her first inkling of what would turn into an enduring love for Europe.

When she got back to Atlanta, Andrea fed her new infatuation by leaving the Diner for an Italian restaurant run by the same company. The pastry chef at Pricci was pregnant, so Andrea stepped in to cover for her and was put to work making tiramisù and biscotti. She wasn't crazy about the work—it was her first real taste of the precision that pastry requires—but it was a real, paying job in the kitchen, her bosses liked her, and she was actually in charge of something for the first time in her life. If there were any doubt left about her future, she settled it then. She would be a chef. Preferably in Europe.

Andrea graduated from the Georgia State program in 2004 and went to culinary school in Chicago (her first choice, the Culinary Institute of America in New York, was too expensive). She compensated for her disappointment about being in the Midwest, however, by focusing her energies on finding a way to return to Europe. One of her classmates told her that she should talk to another pastry student who had recently returned from a *stage* at this crazy restaurant in northern Spain whose name she couldn't pronounce. Andrea looked him up and was delighted to learn that not only was he from Colombia but his name was Andrés. Best of all, he knew exactly how she should go about getting to Europe. How could this not be fate?

Within a few weeks, Andrea and Andrés, the two Colombian pastry chefs, were dating. Together they took jobs at Charlie Trotter's in Chicago to earn some money—though Andrea started as a stagiaire (Andrés was hired outright, making him her boss of sorts), her work was impressive enough that within a week she was offered a paid position on the hot line. A year or so later, they both decided to request *stages* in one of their dream restaurants. Located in a renovated warehouse on the docks in Copenhagen, noma had, by 2008, rapidly gained a reputation as one of the most exciting restaurants in the world, thanks to the efforts of its talented, passionate young chef, René Redzepi. Initially both Andrea and Andrés were thrilled to work there, although Redzepi's managerial style would eventually dismay Andrés. But Andrea remained enamored. "The food he made was so beautiful," she says. "It was unlike anything I had ever seen, or even imagined. I didn't know food could be like that." One dish in particular stuck with her: a tartare made from locally raised musk ox, pressed into a perfect rectangle and topped with neat rows of sorrel leaves, so that the whole thing looked like a tiny field of clover. "We had to individually select and place each leaf," she recalls, "and make sure their stems were all turned to the same direction. René always said it had to look like a living thing." Andrea loved that you had to pick up the square of tartare with your hands and feel the tickle of leaves against your fingers. She loved the swath of juniper dust that added a bit of crunch and pungency to the cold, rich meat. But mostly she loved the sensuality of the dish. When she talks about it now, you would think she was before a Michelangelo fresco or an alpine sunset. "It was so *beautiful!*" she exclaims.

Andrea wasn't particularly drawn to avant-garde cuisine. Asked what she would cook if she had her own restaurant, she responds, "A really good pasta with tomato sauce." But beauty, the complicated, sometimes breathtaking, aesthetic pleasure a talented chef can achieve on the plate—that was something worth pursuing. It was why she had once wanted to be a restaurant designer, why she had fallen in love with restaurants in the first place. It was also why she decided she wanted to do a *stage* at elBulli, even though it would mean being apart from Andrés for six months. Maybe far apart—he was trying to get a job in Asia, and the two had been planning to move there together. But when Andrea got word she had been accepted at elBulli, she didn't hesitate. Andrés wasn't initially happy about the decision, but he supported her and postponed his travels to arrange a temporary job in Spain so that they'd be able to see each other on her days off. Going to elBulli was the most exciting thing, she thought, that had ever happened to her.

o o o

Naming is not is the final step in elBulli's creative process. Even after a dish is deemed magical enough to be served, Ferran and Oriol continue to tinker with it. Some of that tinkering is active—three months after it first goes out, the artichoke rose suddenly acquires a tiny square of silver leaf. But a lot of the development goes on in the minds—and notebooks—of Ferran and Oriol. "It doesn't stop," Ferran says. "We look for perfection in execution and in production, but in creation, there's no such thing. Take the sandwiches," he says, gesturing toward Jacobo, who is slashing through the meringue he just piped into breadlike shapes with strokes made to resemble the gashes in a baguette. "Now that we've got the idea down, there are five hundred ways to make it. Which is perfect?" It's a question upon which Ferran can cogitate endlessly. "There's no secret to it, it takes hours and hours. If you don't have time, you can't create. Right now," he says, "I have to feed everything into my head. Feed, feed, feed, so that later, the ideas will just spill out. Like downloading a chip."

When an idea spills out at elBulli, it is Oriol's job to catch it. In his nearly illegible hand, he archives everything: every product that comes in, every technique developed, every dish created. The information is typed up and illustrated with photographs he shoots with the camera he keeps in a drawer just off the pass. On each page he puts a description of the plate or product, information about the seasons in which it is available, its size, weight, and cost, and a full list of the preparations tried with it. Eventually, the recipes that go on the menu will be professionally photographed and the information about them entered into the catalogue that the restaurant publishes annually (or nearly annually; in the past few years, they've had a hard time finding the time to get the print edition out, though photos of most new creations are available online). Even the dishes and ingredients that don't make it—the magical Petroleum will be one—are carefully documented so that when it comes time to initiate creativity again at the start of a new season, there is a foundation from which to begin.

It is hard to imagine anyone better suited to this work than Oriol Castro. Thirty-six years old, with olive skin and thick black hair he wears in a brush cut, he is today the second in command at elBulli and the person whom Ferran calls "one of the five best chefs in the world." Not bad for a high school dropout. Having failed a year in school at age sixteen, Oriol was set to repeat the courses when a favorite teacher took him aside and asked him if he was sure that was what he wanted to do. Until then he had never considered an alternative, but in an instant he knew the teacher was right; more schooling wasn't for him. For a while he played with the idea of becoming a fisherman—he had always loved the sea—but his brother was a cook, and that seemed appealing, too. In fact, the work was so appealing to Oriol's brother that he had married the daughter of the local culinary school's director. Oriol opted for the family connection. He enrolled in the school and at the same time took a job cooking at a small restaurant nearby to earn some money. For the first time in his life, he felt enthusiasm for work, and even won first prize in a national pastry competition. After he earned his diploma, he decided to stay with it. He worked briefly in Martín Berasategui's eponymous San Sebastián restaurant outside San Sebastián, and in Jean Luc Figueras's restaurant in Barcelona (where Ferran himself had done a brief *stage* before entering the military). Then, in 1996, Oriol took a *stage* at elBulli. He has stayed on ever since, becoming chef de cuisine in 2001.

Oriol works with an intensity that belies his great warmth. He takes a personal interest in the rest of the staff, and is quick with a consoling pat on the back or a word of encouragement. He is the kitchen's great joker (although, per Ferran's rules, always discreetly) and its biggest gossip, playfully jabbing Eduard with a skewer, for example, as he interrogates him about how he and his girlfriend spent their days off. The stagiaires adore him, and more than one holds him up as a model. Oriol shrugs humbly at the praise. In one of his first jobs he had a chef de cuisine who kept order by berating and abusing his cooks—"he would purposely leave knives heating in a frying pan so they'd be burning hot when you picked them up," he recalls—and he determined to be different if he ever had the opportunity. "A big part of the job of chef de cuisine is psychology," he says. "But mostly I just act the way I want to be treated."

In his professional trajectory, Oriol is typical of the restaurant's permanent staff. Like Marc Cuspinera, Lalo Bosch, Mateu Casañas, Lluís García, and Ferran himself, Castro came young to elBulli and has spent almost all of his career there. But something about Oriol distinguishes him from the others. Ferran has had important collaborative relationships before, especially with Xavier Sagristà, who helped develop ideas during elBulli's first great period of invention, 1990 to 1994. But in Oriol he has found someone more like himself—someone with as fierce an insistence on asking "What if?" "I'm a complicated person, and so is he," Oriol says. "But Ferran and I understand each other. All we need is a look or a couple of words to communicate."

By now they share a palate—"I can usually tell when Ferran is going to like something or not," Oriol says—and a vast mental warehouse of recipes, successful and not. They also share the tendency to archive, to collect. Not only does Oriol keep close and detailed track of every product or technique they try, but he keeps tabs on possible uses for products that the restaurant has not yet explored. He takes advantage of the stagiaires from Mexico, for example, to draw up a list of all the uses of corn in their country, which he then organizes into a culinary flowchart of sorts, with ground corn leading to tortillas and tortillas leading to enchiladas and tamales. Later in the season he will develop more charts: one that tracks the uses of the potato-starch obulato, another that depicts all varieties of game and their characteristics. But he doesn't confine his collectionist impulses to food. He has also begun asking some of elBulli's more famous clients—the artists Miquel Barceló and Richard Hamilton, the designer Philippe Starck—to sign plates for him. They all agree, scrawling their signatures (and the occasional sketch) in black marker on one of the restaurant's white porcelain plates. He keeps them on a high shelf in the room he shares with Eduard. "They're for my daughter," he says, showing them off proudly. "One day, she'll be glad to have them."

More than any other trait, he and Ferran share an intellectual restlessness. While Oriol works, his head cupped in one hand while he jots notes or tilted inquisitively over a chunk of cooked squash, he is the picture of stillness. But his mind is always whirring. A chestnut purée being auditioned for a game dish reminds him of a candy he tried once in Japan, and within hours a crispy, sweet shell with the appearance of pulled sugar is wrapped around a warm hazelnut oil and sits on a plate, awaiting Ferran's opinion. Like all elBulli longtimers, Oriol is supremely modest and loath to identify the dishes that have originated with him. But spend even a few hours observing him at work, and it's hard to ignore the fact that many of them do. It is often he who comes up with the initial elaboration or takes a vague concept that Ferran throws out one day (*What if we put all the different incarnations of soy on a plate? What if we did something with those giant clams from Galicia called* urolas?) and turns it into a dish the next. Their process by now is routine: Oriol prepares an element and, when he's moderately satisfied with it, will take a bit on the end of his spatula to Ferran, who holds out his fist to receive a smudge (this allows him to taste without dirtying any spoons; he licks the item from his hand). Ferran then delivers a verdict—too salty, not interesting enough—and Oriol returns to tinker some more.

Back and forth they go, Oriol adjusting and Ferran tasting, until finally they have fine-tuned whatever it is they are working on. At that point, Oriol plates the dish as it's meant to be presented and formally serves it to Ferran, who on these occasions is always seated in his chair. Oriol rushes back with the camera to photograph the completed plate, then hovers over Ferran as he eats. Ferran finishes every bite, and they talk about his impressions before Oriol clears away the plate.

Imagine, test, evaluate, improve, document. This is what Oriol does with his days, both at the restaurant and, during the months when elBulli is closed, at the *taller*. The work is time-consuming, and he spends most of his time away from his wife and young daughter, who live about an hour south of Barcelona. Occasionally his wife will ask him why he and Eduard, who also works far from home, don't look for jobs closer to their families, even if those jobs aren't in a restaurant. Oriol's reply is always the same. "You know we can't do that," he says. "We live for cuisine."

o o o

Andrea and Oriol consult on a product they are testing. (Francesc Guillamet)

When Andrea first arrived at elBulli, she thought she would like nothing better than to spend the next few years of her career working there. The sleekness of the kitchen, the dazzling dishes that came over the pass, even the light that streamed through the glass—it was all so lovely she thought she would never want to leave. And she quickly fell in love with Spain itself, with the warmth of the people she met, the rugged landscape, the conviviality of the streets and bars, the fact that no one ever went to bed before 1 A.M. It was even better than Italy.

But there were things that bothered her. She was disappointed by Ferran's attitude toward his chefs; she was one of the cooks who was most appalled by his habit of chewing them out in front of the staff. She was also disappointed by the relative lack of camaraderie in the kitchen. Because of the long hours and stressful conditions—and the fact that they all lived together—the stagiaires were closer as a group than, say, the average bunch of office workers. But compared with other restaurants where she had worked, something of the esprit de corps was missing. She thought it might have something to do with the fact that there were so many of them: the stagiaires in Pastry and *cuarto frio* seemed to work together well as a team and actually enjoy each other's company (and surely the physical distance from Eugeni's watchful eye enabled them to interact a little more). But in the main kitchen, with so many people struggling to stand out, there was little sense of community. "It feels pretty competitive," she said. "Everyone's trying to prove themselves." As time went on, she found this wearying, and her enthusiasm for returning to elBulli waned.

Because of her position, Andrea didn't have to compete with anyone—she had, in most of the stagiaires' minds, already won. She had the kitchen virtually to herself when she arrived in the morning, and although her first task, spraying for flies, was admittedly unglamorous, she got to spend the rest of the day in close consultation with Oriol. Most of her work consisted of bringing out ingredients, measuring them, labeling them, and taking notes, though she also got to do some of the prep and cooking involved in Oriol's projects, peeling nuts or searing off a piece of meat. But the most important thing she did was to take notes, carefully jotting down the proportions and instructions in every new dish that Oriol and Ferran tried.

She had a front-row seat, in other words, to every new invention. At the end of August, when the chefs began revamping the menu again in preparation for fall's ingredients, she watched them develop several recipes, for example, with sweet potatoes. Ferran and Oriol had already shaped a purée of the stuff into a small quenelle that looked exactly like the edible part of a sea urchin, but they had a harder time with a dumpling-ish item they were trying to make. At first the texture was the problem: a large amount of butter made the purée too greasy and left an unpleasant feeling in the mouth. Then shape became an issue: at first it was just a mound of purée on the plate, but that was too messy and loose. They tried siphoning it first and then spherifying it, as if to make a yam version of the soft Japanese rice cakes called mochi. For a few services, the sweet potato went out like that: a large, single quenelle on the plate. Still, it wasn't right: not very attractive and hard to eat. So they quit using the siphon and began simply spherifying it. The end product resembled the polenta gnocchi they had been making the year before, and that resemblance, in turn, gave Oriol an idea for the rest of the dish. "As soon as he started treating it as an Italian dish, it fell into place," Andrea said. There were more experiments—they tried shaving tonka bean over the gnocchi before resorting to standard truffles—but two days later the gnocchi were going out with butter, Parmesan, and truffles, a barely reinterpreted rendition of the classic pumpkin ravioli. "And that was it. Ferran absolutely loved it."

Andrea loved observing the creative process, but she didn't feel a yearning desire to participate in it; she was fairly content with her routine of killing flies, prepping ingredients, and writing everything down in her pastel notebook. But one day Oriol fell terribly sick, leaving Andrea to work directly with Ferran. He had decided that day to revisit a raspberry cracker, which up until that point had always been made from the obulato—yet another incarnation of the season's star product—coated with a powder made from ground, freeze-dried fruit, spritzed

with water, then baked. That afternoon, however, he switched things
up a bit: he had Andrea mix the powdered lyo-raspberries directly with
water and paint the mixture over a stencil with round holes so that the
crackers came out perfectly circular. He told her to set the crackers in the
dehydrator, which was the normal technique for baking them, but for
some reason another possibility popped into Andrea's head. Until that
point, she had never actively tried to shape a dish or volunteer an idea;
her opinion was never requested, and it never occurred to her to offer it
uninvited. Despite her position as creativity assistant, she knew her job
was to prep and archive and clean up after the others, not to create, and
the times when she even got to play around with products—one day she
spent an hour or so piping meringue through different tips in the quest,
once again, to create the perfect *ninfa*—were few. But now, for some
reason, she spoke up. "Have you ever thought of freezing them?" she
asked Ferran. He raised his head and looked at her intently, as if seeing
her for the first time. "Do it," he said. Later Andrea would say that the
new cracker was "more of an accident than any idea that was clearly his
or mine." But they went on the menu that night, topped with a dollop of
creamy raspberry purée.

Later she would add this version of the cracker to the notebook, one
more item in a collection that gave her an authority the other stagiaires
longed for. Part of that authority was practical—a cook who hadn't quite
mastered a new dish would sidle up to her and whisper, "Now, how much
Xantana was I supposed to put in that?" and she would always have the
answer. But it was also symbolic: Andrea was the keeper of the keys.
Consequently she treated the notebook with the greatest care, as if it were
a living thing. There were no chocolate stains on it, no drops of water
smearing the text. It was, quite simply, the most valuable possession
she and the other stagiaires could imagine owning. Ironically, though,
she wasn't sure she would ever use it. Because the recipes it contained
were not her style of cooking, she saw it more as a memento of the work
she had done than as a guide to her future. When she thought about
the pressure that Ferran and Oriol put themselves through, when she

thought about the precariousness of a restaurant defined by constant reinvention, she shuddered a little. Andrea appreciated the importance and grace of elBulli, but risk was not what she wanted out of a life in the kitchen.

o o o

For all the systematization of the creative process, for all the diaries, notes, tests, photographs, and catalogues, ineffable it remains. That, at least, is the message the stagiaires get when they sit down for a creativity session with Ferran and the other chefs. The class meets at noon one morning—two hours before the stagiaires begin work. Attendance is optional, but everyone shows up, even some of the waiters—this, after all, is why they came to elBulli. They sit in the back dining room, blinking furiously at the sunlight pouring through the windows. There is an air of excitement, though it's hard to say whether it is from hearing Ferran reveal his secrets or sheer nervousness at being in such close proximity to him, without a knife or stove top between them. He begins by explaining his creative process, how he and the other chefs start testing recipes at the Barcelona *taller* and bring the results of those experiments to the restaurant for refinement once the season is under way. Beyond that there is no formal lesson. There is only brainstorming.

He starts with the soy dish that they have been working on that week. At the center of it is a yuba made, in the traditional Japanese preparation, from homemade soy milk rather than the cow's milk the restaurant had earlier used. Ferran is extremely proud that they have just started making their own soy milk; he says it's the best he's ever tasted. He adds that no other restaurant in the West makes their own—they all just buy it. Then, as if to prove his point, he asks the stagiaires if any of them have ever made soy milk. No one says a word. He points to Yoji, a Japanese stagiaire who has just joined the crew for a few weeks, on loan from Massimo Bottura's restaurant in Modena, and asks, "Even you haven't made it?" Yoji quickly shakes his head no. Satisfied, Ferran moves on, explaining the logic behind the recipe. "Okay, so this product is so unique we decided to make it the protagonist of the dish—that's where the concept was born. The next step was to add the fresh soybeans. Why did we do that? It adds a certain amount of poetry. We think about soy as something that gets transformed into something else. Soy milk. Soy sauce. But we rarely think about it as a legume, as a bean. And there are so many other elaborations of it—more than with almost any other food. That's why we put miso on the plate, and soy paste." He pauses to catch his breath. "What are some others?" he asks, peering around the room. "Can you come up with some others that aren't on there yet?"

During this animated discourse on the properties of soy, Daniel has mustered enough courage to raise his hand. "I've made soy milk," he confesses. "At Alinea."

Ferran looks simultaneously annoyed and crestfallen. "You've made it? With Grant?" he demands, referring to the Chicago restaurant's innovative young chef.

Daniel nods nervously, rapidly growing aware that his admission is perhaps unappreciated. "Yes, with Grant," he says weakly.

Ferran glares at him for a moment, as the stagiaires shoot wide-eyed glances at one another. When he speaks again, he has clearly made a decision to ignore this information. "Can you think of other elaborations for soy?" he repeats. The room exhales.

César suggests leaving the soybeans in their pods and confiting them. Yoji mentions having once putting a soy extract into an atomizer and spraying it like dew. But Ferran is hardly listening. He turns back to Daniel. "Okay, so you made it at Alinea," he says. "But it wasn't as good as ours, was it?"

Daniel does not need to be told the correct answer.

Few of the other stagiaires have spoken so far; ideas have been thrown out largely by Oriol, Eduard, and Mateu. Frustrated by the others' silence, Ferran turns to the room with a warning. "If you don't start speaking up, I'm going to call on you." The threat works. When Ferran asks if there are any other garnishes they should consider adding to the Parmesan ravioli, he gets an answer. Andrea goes first, perhaps because she feels that, as Oriol's assistant, she should be able to come up with an idea or two. "What if we shaved pine nuts over them to look like grated cheese?" she asks. The other stagiaires murmur approvingly, and Luca, who is Italian, joins in excitedly. "Yes!" he says. "You could bring them tableside and have the servers grate them as if they were Parmigiano." The momentum in the room gives Kim courage. She leans over and asks Andrea the word for "lettuce" in Spanish. "Or," she says, "you could mix the ravioli with lettuce and make a kind of Caesar salad." Oriol is assiduously taking notes, but it's hard to know what Ferran makes of any of these ideas. And in any case, he is already onto a new subject: What new products should they think about trying?

Diego, who has been waiting for an opportunity to speak, volunteers what he considers a brilliant idea. "Horse milk," he says earnestly, to a roomful of laughter. "Seriously. They drink it in Mongolia." Ferran tries to keep a straight face. Jorge raises his hand to suggest spherified beer but is cut off. "I don't want to hear the word 'spherified' again." Ferran says. "Or 'foam.'"

José Luis brings up hibiscus flowers. "Doesn't work," Ferran says. "We tried it." José Luis tries to point out that you have to dehydrate them first, then rehydrate them, but Ferran has moved on. Luca suggests a *macaron*, but a savory one with the flavoring of a caprese salad. "Tomato meringue," he says, inspired by the pumpkin "bread" that *cuarto frío* is turning out. "With basil and mozzarella sandwiched in between." The chefs like that one.

"Write it down," Ferran says to Oriol. "What else?"

"Whale fat," Yoji, the Japanese stagiaire, blurts out.

Again Ferran laughs. "That might actually be a harder sell than the horse milk," he says. "Next thing I know you'll be telling me to look into woolly mammoth meat."

The meeting adjourns with an admonishment to keep thinking and to come up with more ideas before the next meeting.

Later, when the stagiaires talk about the creativity class, they focus on how nervous they were when Ferran questioned them and how inspired they were to go home and try to come up with ideas of their own. "He said he'd look at our ideas if we wrote them down, so that's what I'm going to do tonight," Nico says excitedly as he walks back to the kitchen.

Ferran, however, is more skeptical about the experience. "We do it for them, because it's important for them to understand how creativity works. And because they want it so badly. But is it worth it for us?" He shakes his head dismissively. "Nah, we never get any ideas from it." And in fact, there will be no more creativity classes that season.

o o o

All restaurants carry risks. As business propositions, they are notoriously difficult: profit margins are dangerously thin, and in the United States an estimated 60 percent of all new restaurants fail in their first five years. Prices that are too high or too low, unreliable purveyors, bartenders who steal, an ugly room or bad location, a health inspector on the make, food that, in the end, just isn't very good—a million things can sink a restaurant. Avant-garde cuisine increases the challenge, and Ferran takes it further still, seeking not to diminish his risks but to compound them. By setting the goal of constant reinvention, he must continuously put himself out there in a way that a "normal" chef, who merely has to please his customers, does not.

Most chefs find two rewards, beyond financial viability, for the risks they take. Anthony Bourdain describes them in his inimitable way:

> I'm asked a lot what the best thing about cooking for a living is. And it's this: to be part of a subculture. To be part of a historical continuum, a secret society with its own language and customs. To enjoy the instant gratification of making something good with one's hands—using all one's senses. It can be, at times, the purest and most unselfish way of giving pleasure (though oral sex has to be a close second).

In other words, what you get out of it is the twin rewards of belonging to a group and of pleasing others. Ferran has ostensibly relinquished the latter. He always says, "We've been lucky. We do what we want, and people just happen to like it," and although Andrea doesn't know if she fully believes him (after all, it's easy for him to say that now, with three

Michelin stars and a reservation waiting list roughly a million names long), she knows that outcome wouldn't feel lucky to her; she *wants* to please people. For her the second great opportunity that restaurants offer is community. Yet here too elBulli has frustrated her; although she has made friends—even good friends—in the kitchen, she doesn't feel the kind of deep camaraderie she craves.

Then one day, toward the end of the sweet potato gnocchi birthing experience, something changes. She starts the day as she always does, by retrieving the ingredients that might be called into service that day and setting them neatly on the pass. Then she roasts several sweet potatoes, scoops out the flesh, and purées it in the Thermomix with the now-proper amount of butter. Already, she feels a certain excitement about the dish. "Right when we started working on it, I knew it was going to make it onto the menu, just by the expression on Oriol's face," she says. "And by now I could feel us getting closer." That isn't the only bit of intuition she has. Late in the afternoon, she picks up a tray full of dirty bowls and utensils and begins to carry it to the dishwasher. She is nearly at the doorway when Oriol calls out to her, "Andrea, on your way back, bring—" She waits for the conclusion of the sentence, but Oriol has been interrupted by someone else. Then she realizes that it doesn't matter; she knows exactly what he meant to say. When she brings the Microplane grater and sets it beside him, he doesn't blink. It is exactly what he wanted.

Andrea has long observed the connection that exists between Oriol and Ferran. Oftentimes, they don't have to speak—Oriol will bring a pan over to Ferran, spoon a sauce onto the side of his hand, and be able to tell, just by the tilt of Ferran's head or a shrug of his shoulders, whether it is too sweet or simply isn't going to work. She has learned that Oriol is extremely aware of how Ferran likes to eat. "He doesn't like to cut his food," she remarks, "So Oriol never gives him anything that would require a knife and fork." Flavors, admittedly, could be harder to guess. "There are a few dishes that Oriol thought Ferran would really like, and Ferran was, like, no way." For the most part however, they seem like an old married couple, able to communicate with a glance or offhand gesture. At first, their level of unspoken communication struck Andrea as remarkable, proof of the extraordinary creative and intellectual bond between them, and she longed to experience something similar. But in the moment she realizes that what Oriol wants is the Microplane, she recognizes that she has achieved it too. "I realized he didn't have to tell me things, that I just knew," Andrea says with a bit of wonder in her voice. "It's like we were family."

five

October, or **Expression**

Oßne morning Eduard stops Gaël as he enters the kitchen. The stagiaire looks as though he's had a rough night: the flip he mousses into his blond hair is a little lopsided, and his thick-framed, rectangular glasses are a little smudged.

"There's a package for you." Eduard says.

"*Comment?*" Gaël's Spanish has not progressed much. If he concentrates, he remembers to say "*Quemo*" and "*Vale*" and "*Oído,*" but, caught unprepared, the twenty-two-year-old slips back into his native French. Even now, four months into the season, when Eugeni tells him to do something, the chef stops for a moment and scans Gaël's face to see if he's understood.

"A package," Eduard repeats, then grasps for the word in French. "*Un cadeau?*"

Gaël doesn't quite know what to make of this news, but he dutifully follows Eduard into the office, where, sure enough, a neatly wrapped brown package is waiting for him. He looks at the handwriting. "*C'est de maman,*" he says, blushing slightly.

Eduard tries to suppress a smile. "Well, open it."

Inside are two tightly wrapped pieces of cheese and a number of jars and bottles. His mother, it seems, has sent him a care package. There's a note as well. *"Recette"* it says on the envelope in elegant blue ink.

"It's a recipe for fondue," Gaël whispers, his cheeks flushing even more.

"Great," Eduard says. "You can make it for family meal."

Gaël takes the box downstairs and unloads its contents on the pass. A block of Gruyère; a slightly smaller one of Vacherin; a thin bottle of kirsch. Next to them he places several jars, each capped with red-checked fabric and tied with raffia. The labels on them are written in the same neat hand as the *Recette* envelope: cornichons, pickled mushrooms, pickled garlic. They are the condiments to eat with the finished fondue; Gaël's mother has canned them herself. They will sit on the pass that day next to the Szechuan buttons and the marinating fish livers and the prehistorically large cardoons, an incongruous jolt of home.

Gaël Vuilloud
(Pierre-Alain Gschwend)

o o o

In October, it begins to rain. The temperature drops, and with it the lower needles of the scruffy pines on the road up to elBulli start turning brown. The cutting wind that Catalans call the *tramuntana* picks up, and the tree-bending force of its gusts, coupled with the shorter days, make the journey to and from the restaurant a wholly different experience. Suddenly the lovely, if dramatic, drive along the coast becomes a more perilous adventure: it is dark, the sharp curves in the road around the cliffs are slick, and the winds are strong enough to make you wonder if cars are ever blown over the edge. With the tourist season over, you can make the entire drive without ever passing another car. The sun is setting much earlier too, so that the clients no longer just leave the restaurant in darkness but arrive in it. To them the restaurant, with its warm yellow lights shining at the end of an otherwise unlit road, must seem inordinately welcoming.

Listening to the wind howl, Ferran is gleeful. "This is much, much better," he exults, congratulating himself on the decision to change the time period during which the restaurant is open. "Much better for creativity. So much more tranquil." Much better too, he thinks, for increasing the sense of risk that accompanies a meal at elBulli. He loves the idea that the dark, rain-soaked drive might unnerve some diners. He loves the coziness of their being seated indoors on their banquettes while the wind whips outside. And he loves the fact that with the vacationers gone, his clients are much less likely to be the type who have come to elBulli simply to check another restaurant off their list. There are now, he says, a lot more serious diners, and indeed, the reservation list seems to bear him out. In a one-week period, critics from Spanish, Italian, and British newspapers all come to eat (there is no such thing as anonymity at elBulli), as do Diane Kennedy, an authority on Mexican cuisine, and the chefs Johnny Iuzzini and Heston Blumenthal. So too does Barbra Streisand; Oriol, still building his collection, gets her to sign a plate. But not all of the restaurant's diners are famous or wealthy. When one reservation cancels at the last minute, the table is given to a taxi driver in

Roses, who each year saves up his money for a meal at elBulli and waits hopefully for the call.

Perhaps the guest most valued that month—if not all season—is Ferran's brother Albert. Early in October, he comes to dinner, along with Silvia, his partner, and eight friends, to celebrate his fortieth birthday. Until that year, he would never have chosen to hold the festivities at elBulli—after all, it was where he worked, and besides, before 2009, it was never open when his birthday came around in the fall. But now that he has left the restaurant, it is the perfect location. The staff sets up the table in the back room, and Ferran ensures that a steady line of courses—everything in the current lineup, plus a few dishes still in development—flows out to it. All in all, the party eats forty or so different courses before it is time for cake. Hardly a service goes by at elBulli without a birthday, and normally they are celebrated with a plate of artfully arranged fruit and a massive card that unfolds to display a cake with candles (after so many courses, no one wants to eat a slice of yellow cake with chocolate frosting). But this time, Ferran has Albert and his friends led into the kitchen where, in the dark, all the cooks stand in a row, each with a lit candle, and burst into "Happy Birthday." "It's a living birthday cake," Ferran says excitedly as he embraces his brother. Albert looks thoroughly touched, but Ferran is even more emotional. "I've never seen him so happy," says Andrea.

The fall menu is now in place. Gone are the mimetic almonds, made from an almond praliné and encased in a thin, hard shell of mannitol; they have been replaced with mimetic pistachios. Corn is out of season, which means, mercifully, that the stagiaires no longer have to squeeze out its germ for risotto. Instead, they have to separate out the pulp of mandarin orange flesh in order to make a risotto from that. "They're always coming up with something like that for us to do," comments Lucho dryly. The pond and the artichoke rose are still there, but much of the rest of the menu has been given over to decidedly autumnal dishes. It's exactly what Ferran said he wanted to do back when he made the unprecedented decision to change the season from spring and summer to summer and fall. But the possibilities opened up by the season's products, and the success of the dishes created with them, surprises even him. Fresh cèpes are wrapped like gifts in a cellophane papillote and cooked in tiny iron skillets. Orange daubs of puréed squash are spooned into the shape of sea urchin flesh. Woodcock is on the menu, and that sweet potato gnocchi. A translucent, chestnut-colored liquid is brought to the table in a snifter, where the server mists it with Armagnac—the diner thinks she is getting liqueur, but she is, in fact, drinking a perfectly clear squab consommé, redolent with the scent of the autumn hunt.

The corps of stagiaires has undergone more changes. Saurabh Arora, a cook from Bangalore, joined the group at the beginning of the month—elBulli's first Indian stagiaire. One of the Mexican apprentices, Victor, has gone home—his *stage* lasted only a month. But Luca is still there. Contrary to everyone's predictions, including his own, he returned to work after his crisis of faith and economics, a decision motivated both by his own sense of responsibility and his extensive knowledge of just how small and gossipy the restaurant industry is. "If I start something, I want to finish it," he says. "Plus, I don't want to get a reputation for being unreliable. Chefs talk to each other."

In some ways, the kitchen has become more rigid, more set in its ways. The stagiaires on the center table can no longer get their own water, for example; they have to ask Lucho, who is now Eugeni's assistant, to bring it to them. And whereas before the cooks could simply tell Eugeni when they were going to the bathroom, now they have to ask him for permission. For some of the apprentices, there have been subtle improvements. Emma, for example, has finally risen in Eugeni's esteem. Although during the first three months he targeted her frequently for criticism, by October he is holding her up as an example to the others, praising her work ethic when he spies others slacking off. Her assignments have improved as a result. A semihidden hierarchy of tasks exists at the center table, and by now, all of the full-season stagiaires are fluent in its calibrations. For not always obvious reasons, some tasks within the self-enclosed world that is the center table have acquired greater prestige. "If you're good, you get upgraded," Emma explains. "When Eugeni moved me from mandarins to bone marrow, I knew I was doing well."

Other stagiaires are beginning to show signs of the strain. Katie's mother comes to visit from the United States, and they spend her four-day break visiting potential sites for her wedding reception and checking out florists and photographers as well. It's fun, but it also feels rushed. "I feel like I have four days to plan my whole wedding," says Katie. "It's a little stressful." Stress wears on Iosu as well, although in his case it seems more closely tied to work. He doesn't socialize much with the rest of the group and seems to live only for his girlfriend's monthly visits from Bilbao. He's been losing weight and muttering to himself in the kitchen; he flinches visibly when one of the chefs corrects him. Meanwhile, half the kitchen is sick (and, yes, still working; it is only when a stagiaire begins vomiting that he may decide to stay home), and things get so bad that a morning meeting is devoted to the restaurant's version of health care. Oriol takes it upon himself to do another hand-washing demonstration, while Eduard warns the stagiaires not to stand too close to one another when talking. (At that, Lorenzo and Antonio exchange glances. Don't stand too close? They spend fourteen hours a day pressed shoulder to shoulder.) Eduard himself falls ill one day but, in his typically stoic way, works through the pain. The only sign he is off his game is the way he occasionally clutches his temples during service.

Ferran's enthusiasm for the new season, then, is perhaps not echoed by the stagiaires. They are certainly pleased to be working with new dishes and thrilled with many of the new recipes, but they are also growing increasingly tired of the grinding routine. Still, all the weariness and influenza in the world can't hide the fact that the season is halfway over, and that fact alone gives a lift to many of the stagiaires. "It's all downhill from here, " says Mateu as he pipes one more sheet of mint leaves with chocolate. Mizuho, César, and Daniel, all within earshot, smile to themselves. "I'm counting the days," says Sunny.

The stagiaires are starting to think about what comes next. Emma knows she will eventually be working as sous chef when Corey Lee, her former chef at the French Laundry, opens his new place in San Francisco—she's just not sure when that will be. Katie has her own restaurant to plan. Txema will take over his parents' restaurant in the

Basque Country. And Alfonso knows he'll be going back to the navy. But other than that, few of the apprentices have plans.

o o o

At twenty-two, Gaël Vuilloud is one of the youngest stagiaires. Tall and skinny, he has imperfect posture that at times makes him look like a walking question mark. Outside the restaurant, he wears sleeveless sweatshirts and artfully ripped jeans, but inside he is one of the apprentices whose jacket is always perfectly pressed. His thick blond hair, swooped up in a flip at the front, and his glasses, with their thick rectangular frames, can make him seem like either the coolest of hipsters or the nerdiest of geeks. But Gaël is definitely not a geek. Within the admittedly insular world of Swiss cuisine, he is already a star.

Before he came to elBulli, Gaël had never lived more than a few miles from his home in Monthey, Switzerland. Located a bit inland from Lake Geneva and the elegant, well-manicured resort towns of the Swiss Riviera, Monthey is more working-class than its neighbors but still offers spectacular views of the Alps and enough proximity to the world headquarters of Nestlé in nearby Vevey that many of his friends' parents worked for the multinational food conglomerate. Indeed, in that part of the world, a preoccupation with food is almost unavoidable. In addition to the bountiful bakeries and *traiteurs* that seem to dot each of Vevey's streets, there is a giant fork, designed by the Swiss artists Jean-Pierre Zaugg and Georges Favre, its tines plunged into the water of Lake Geneva, and, thanks again to Nestlé, a popular museum dedicated to the history of food. Growing up in that environment, Gaël knew he wanted to be a chef. His earliest memories are of standing by his mother, who worked as a hairstylist but nevertheless cooked all the family's meals, and begging her to let him light the stove. The family couldn't afford to dine out very frequently, but they ate well at home: not only Swiss classics like fondue and rösti, a potato pancake often prepared with onions and bacon, but also roast chicken and veal navarin. His mom even made pizza—"the best pizza in the world," he says—from scratch, following a complicated recipe that took the better part of a day to complete.

His father, an electrician, was not initially pleased with the thought of his only son spending his life in a kitchen. When Gaël was thirteen, M. Vuilloud did the only thing he could think of to dissuade his son from his chosen profession: he got the boy an apprenticeship as a cook in a local pizzeria owned by a friend. Every day after school, Gaël would go to the restaurant and put in several hours chopping vegetables for sauce and preparing dough. It was a lot of work for a boy who was still in school, and he got to hang out with his friends a lot less than the average teenager. But he was ecstatic. "I just loved being in the kitchen," he says. "At the end of each night, I would walk home with this huge smile on my face."

If his father was disappointed that his plan to distract Gaël from his chosen career had failed, he didn't show it and, from that point on, played an active role in helping his son prepare for his professional future. The following year, he helped the boy get a full-time *stage* during the Christmas holidays at the Hôtel Restaurant Le Saint-Christophe, in Bex, a town located southeast of Lake Geneva, near several important ski resorts. The chef there, Mauro Capelli, was impressed enough with Gaël's work to offer him a full apprenticeship, though because Gaël was so young, he needed his parents' permission to accept it. The offer opened the door to becoming a real chef; in Switzerland as in France, the usual launch for a career in the kitchen is with a formal apprenticeship that begins usually when a boy is still in his early teens.

Gaël's parents took the decision seriously: they traveled to Bex to meet Chef Capelli and see the working conditions to which their son would be committing himself. In his eagerness to accept the apprenticeship, Gaël didn't notice any problems, but his mother was another story. Mme. Vuilloud didn't appreciate the chef's apparent disregard for women (he insisted on addressing only Gaël's father, not his mother) and promptly put an end to Gaël's fledgling career. "That," she said tartly as the family got back into their car, "is not what I want my fourteen-year-old exposed to." Her husband took up the search for a new apprenticeship.

He eventually found one at the Auberge de Vouvry, an inn not far from home, with a formal restaurant and one Michelin star. Gaël spent a month in the kitchen as a stagiaire before Martial Braendle, the auberge's owner and chef de cuisine, offered him another salaried apprenticeship. With only a blessed few months of obligatory schooling left, Gaël quickly accepted. He soon learned, however, that he wasn't done with studying; Switzerland, like many other European countries, strictly regulates apprenticeships, and budding chefs are required to spend one day a week at culinary school. There he received three hours' instruction in mathematics and language studies and six hours in culinary theory. "That part was boring—I already knew how to cook," Gaël says. "Most of the other students couldn't even chop an onion."

The practical lessons he received at the Auberge de Vouvry were much more to his liking. With its classical menu, the auberge has its apprentices spend a good deal of time peeling potatoes for dauphinoise and shucking oysters for bisque. But gradually Gaël worked his way up and began moving through the restaurant's different stations: garde-manger, sauces, fish, meat. Along the way, his salary jumped, from a risible 400 euros a month to an almost livable 800 euros. He was such an apt pupil that in 2002, Braendle entered his young protégé in a contest for the best apprentice chef in the French-speaking cantons. When he was interviewed for the local paper about Gaël's chances, the chef replied, "Gaël is a very fast learner. And more important, everything he makes tastes great. He knows immediately what's missing in a dish— that's a crucial quality in a chef, and either you have it or you don't." In the contest, at least, Gaël had it. Required to prepare two rabbits and some vegetables for eight people, as well as invent his own interpretation of an orange bavaroise (a cold egg custard), he impressed the judges with his well-balanced flavors and won first prize—an eating trip to Paris.

Culinary competitions are important in Europe, and several countries, such as Norway, France, and Sweden, expend huge amounts of money and energy to send their top young chefs to the Bocuse d'Or, a biennial event held in Lyon, France, that is the world's most prestigious cooking contest. With his initial success, Gaël found himself being pushed in that direction. He competed in three more contests before entering, at age nineteen, the Junior Culinary Olympics, for the chance to represent

Switzerland. By then he had finished his apprenticeship and entered the ranks of the profession, working full-time at the auberge as chef de partie. In his time off, he prepared for the contest. Most competitions require participants to prepare a dish around an assigned ingredient, and this one was no exception: Gaël was required to work with *fera*, a mild white fish indigenous to Lake Geneva. After several trial runs, Gaël hit on his dish: he would serve the fera raw, in a tartare, with a sauce made from Noilly Prat vermouth. It came out perfectly, the fish cold and sweet, its flavor balanced by the acidity of the sauce. As the competition wound down, rumors were flying that Gaël would win. But when the judges announced their decision, he learned he had come in second. The problem, he would later hear, lay with one of his garnishes: he had adorned the plate with cubes of gelée made from Campari. Some of the more traditional judges, it seemed, didn't like the texture of the cubes—they considered them too avant-garde. But others, more open to innovation, secretly came up to the young cook after the contest was over and told him he should have won. The Olympics would be his last competition. If he couldn't win by cooking in his own style, he decided, he didn't want to compete.

o o o

Having established himself so clearly as an artist, Ferran is often viewed as a genius detached from any context, national or culinary. Yet he is, of course, the product of his environment. Even after he took over the kitchen at elBulli, he was a "normal" chef for many years, working within the boundaries set by nouvelle cuisine. His culinary transformation began in 1989, when he experimented with that most iconic of Spanish dishes, gazpacho. By deconstructing the soup so that its components were discrete entities exposed on the plate, he initiated a process of inquiry—*What are our expectations of food?*—that continues to inform what he does in the kitchen. Yet, as he is the first to explain, any rupture he may have provoked was simultaneously an evolution, a gradual turning away from nouvelle cuisine's repertoire and toward something new.

Culinary history provides a context for what Ferran does, but so does European history. It is probably no coincidence that he shares many traits with that other internationally recognized Spanish artist, the filmmaker Pedro Almodóvar. Their media are, of course, different—spherified olives and Parmesan air for one; sex, drugs, and neurotic women in stilettos for the other. But the reckless joy of their careful creations, the provocative art disguised as humor and excess, are the same. So too is their shared drive, relentless but unstrained, to continually create anew. Only a few years before they burst onto the scene, Spain was ruled by Francisco Franco, one of only two World War II–era dictators to see his authoritarian regime survive into the 1970s. In the course of his nearly forty-year rule, Franco had managed to transform Spain into a staunchly Catholic, nationalistic country. Women were not allowed to work without their husbands' or fathers' permission, while homosexuals, regionalists, and political dissidents were routinely thrown into prison. Spain's food, to judge by the stuff that makes up the classic cookbook of the late Franco era, Simone Ortega's *1080 Recipes* was almost as staidly depressing as the culture: cauliflower in béchamel; tuna canapés; paella made with canned peas.

Almodóvar and Adrià changed all that. Although they worked in spheres distinct from the politicians who enabled the peaceful transition to democracy, they nonetheless participated crucially in Spain's liberalization in the years following the dictator's death in 1975. Whatever else it may be, the unique intensity of their creativity is undoubtedly a powerful response to the grim atrocities and quotidian frustrations of the Franco dictatorship. Together their work represents one face of repression's effects: radical invention as a rejection of conformity, unbridled exuberance in the face of numbness and fear, a quest for absolute liberty.

Movies are different from food, of course. However important motion pictures may be to how we think about ourselves and the world, we don't expect them to represent tradition, to nurture and comfort us, to carry the weight of identities both national and individual. Almodóvar may have initially shocked his viewers with his explicit but celebratory films about masochists and heroin-addled hookers, but he was still doing what directors have always done, which is to tell a story. With Adrià, it wasn't so clear. If he was a revolutionary, a genius, an artist, could he still do what chefs do, which is to feed people? If his dishes were art, could they still be dinner?

o o o

Not long after he came in second in the runoffs for the culinary Olympics, Gaël experienced another break in his professional trajectory. Switzerland requires its young men to serve in the military, and at age twenty, he was conscripted. He would spend the eight months working as an army cook, but he has little memory of the work. He does remember getting drunk on his days off—so drunk that, when he showed up at home wasted one weekend, his furious mother pushed him into the car and drove him straight back to the base. Only one good thing, he says, came out of his experience in the military: it gave him time to reassess the path he had been on since childhood. He had always known he wanted to be a chef and had taken steps as early as possible to make that happen, but he had never considered *what kind* of chef he wanted to be. "I had never really thought about it," he recalls, "never thought about how I wanted to cook or what was good." Now, as his time in the army drew to a close, he found himself pondering a question his chef, Braendle, had asked him before he enlisted: What do you want to do next? He knew he could go back to the auberge and continue to work his way up the brigade. Or he could try something new, push himself further. He wasn't sure which path to take until Braendle intervened. "Why don't you go work for my friend Denis?" the chef suggested. "He doesn't have the same conception of food as I do, but at least you'll get to see something different."

The Denis in question was Denis Martin, who, a few months before Gaël joined him, had earned two Michelin stars for his eponymous restaurant in Vevey. Swiss cuisine in its *haute* incarnation is practically indistinguishable from French, but Martin had broken with tradition by looking south for inspiration rather than north and west. Here was a chef who used siphons to create airy mousses without gelatin and a

Pacojet to turn escargot into frozen "dirt." Some of his menu items, such as the "Gin Tonic," read as if they could have come straight from elBulli. Yet there were marked differences. Martin says he began experimenting thirty years ago, which would mean his experience with avant-garde cuisine predates Ferran's. Although his dishes display the same cleverness found in some of elBulli's creations, the humor in them is broader and less cerebral, more Adam Sandler to Adrià's Woody Allen. His Gin Tonic, for example, comes in the form of a globe that fits into the palm of a man's hand, and that, remarkably, glows in the dark. There is a dish called Nothing, the culinary version of John Cage's "4' 33'"' composition (which consists of four minutes, thirty-three seconds of silence), in which an invisible substance is poured into the bottom of a shallow bowl. When the diner takes up the spoon and puts it in her mouth, she very clearly tastes dill and cucumber. To serve the final savory course in Martin's twenty-two-plate tasting menu, waiters hand each diner an airmail envelope. Its contents make it lumpy and disconcertingly warm. Inside is a second envelope, this one plastic, which is to be cut open with an artistically designed pair of scissors. In truth, the plastic is a sous-vide bag, which contains a perfectly cooked squab breast in a rosemary-scented reduction. The dish's cleverness derives from its plating and its name: it is called Homing Pigeon.

Martin's restaurant is more irreverent—and makes more of a show of its irreverence—than elBulli. Fond of music metaphors, when asked whether he considers himself to be cooking in the same style as Adrià, Martin responds, "Do U2 and AC/DC make the same kind of music? Of course not. But they're both rock and roll." Here, instead of flowers, a plastic cow noisemaker—turn it over and it moos—tops the tables, and a meal ends with diners popping big, brightly colored circus balloons to release the white chocolate and pepper candy inside. But his method of working (he has a test kitchen on-site) and his desire to use cuisine to provoke memories and emotions are similar. He has adapted a distiller created for the giant food conglomerate down the street, for example, so that it produces a clear, tasteless liquid that smells deeply and perfectly of the ingredient—lemon, strawberry, toasted bread—from which it is drawn.

Gaël was entranced. Before arriving at Denis Martin, he'd had only one exposure to the phrase "molecular gastronomy": a newspaper article that featured a dish composed of lines of wasabi and an almond foam, served on a black slate plate. He found it extraordinary; the idea that food could be about more than sustenance and simple gustatory pleasure had never before occurred to him. But at Denis Martin, it didn't take long before he had assimilated the concepts that gird avant-garde cuisine: food as provocation, food as art. Before long, Martin was encouraging him to experiment on his own and giving him greater responsibility. At the time, the restaurant was open for both lunch and dinner, and Gaël would work from 9 A.M. until 1 A.M. "I think he was just glad to have a new kid in there, because there was too much work," says Gaël. But soon, he discovered that he shared his chef's enthusiasm for innovation. In 2007, Gaël came up with a dish that is still on Martin's menu: a savory cornet, tinted black with squid ink, filled with an herbal mousse, and topped with strips of fried calamari—a play on the boardwalk newspaper cone filled with fried fish. Not long after that, he began making regular public appearances with his chef, first at culinary conferences in which he would demonstrate dishes for other professionals and later on a Swiss television show called *Imitate the Chef*. There, as Martin watched approvingly, asking questions and complimenting his technique, Gaël prepared a barely poached ravioli in which the filling was made from regular button mushrooms but the "pasta" was thinly sliced pieces of kohlrabi. As he cooked, he calmly explained what he was doing and why, unnerved by neither the camera nor the watchful gaze of his chef. He moved with the graceful confidence of a veteran.

They had conflicts, nonetheless. "Gaël is very stubborn, very strong," says Martin, no slouch himself in the backbone department. Once when his chef corrected him, Gaël snapped back, an unthinkable breach of kitchen protocol and hierarchy. Martin immediately froze and gestured menacingly to his cook to follow him. He took Gaël, whose moment of pique had by now transformed itself into abject remorse, down to the wine cellar—the confessional, as Martin calls it. It was cold and dark in there, and Martin couldn't tell if Gaël was shaking from the temperature or from fear. "Look, you want to take me on, we can do that," the chef said to his protégé. "We can fight, and I'll throw you out. Or you can decide to respect me and do what I say, in which case, I'll continue to help you." Gaël chose the latter. He survived the Oedipal conflict intact.

Martin held up his end of the bargain. He knew that Gaël was still somewhat drawn to the traditional cuisine he had prepared at the auberge, and this concerned him—not because he had anything against classical cooking, but because he was worried that Gaël's unwillingness to invest himself wholly in one style of cuisine would prevent him from fully developing as a chef. One day he took the twenty-one-year-old aside and told him he needed to try other places so that he could make a decision. "I said that if he was leaning toward traditional cuisine, I would get him a *stage* at Guy Savoy or some other classic three-star," Martin recalls. "But if he wanted to commit to avant-garde cooking, to my style of cooking, he should go to elBulli." Gaël chose the latter.

o o o

When the backlash against Adrià came, it was deeply shocking—even traumatic—to many members of Spain's normally convivial fraternity of chefs. Receiving a prize in May 2008 for his new book, *The Kitchen Laid Bare*, the three-star chef Santi Santamaria, who himself had greatly shaped Spain's culinary history from his restaurant Can Fabes, about ninety minutes down the road from elBulli, criticized his colleagues for "legitimating forms of cooking that distance them from the traditional" and railed against "cooking with chemicals like methylcellulose whose consumption could be dangerous." In case anyone missed the reference, he got specific: "I have an enormous conceptual and ethical divorce from Ferran; he and his team are going in a direction contrary to my principles." It wasn't the first time Santamaria had played the Rabelaisian populist, speaking earthy truth to gastronomic power (the previous year, he had told a chefs' conference that "All good meals end with a good shit"). But this time his words—so clearly intended to provoke—were met with outrage. Within days, Euro-Toques International, a European chefs' organization, issued a statement expressing its indignation at

Santamaria's "act of aggression." Fermi Puig, Ferran's old navy buddy and today the chef of Barcelona's Drolma, wrote in *La Vanguardia* that the debate had pushed the public's respect for chefs back a decade. Sergi Arola, a former elBulli protégé who holds two stars for his restaurant Sergi Arola Gastro in Madrid, accused Santamaria of mounting a personal vendetta "out of envy." Was it petty rivalry that was driving him? The quest for publicity for his book? Or did he really believe this stuff? In some ways it didn't matter, because the end result was the same.

Ferran tried to avoid a public response but eventually went on the record as saying that he regretted the damage Santamaria's comments would do to Spanish cuisine's reputation abroad. And indeed, although at home the press was confined largely to delighted chortles over the so-called War of the Stove Tops, in other countries, such as France and Italy, things soon took a more pernicious turn. Although Joël Robuchon, possibly France's most important living chef and an early and steadfast elBulli supporter, went out of his way to defend Adrià (in an interview, Robuchon declared, "I eat at elBulli all the time, and my health is impeccable"), others used the occasion to resurrect the pettiness and ire first provoked in 2003, when *The New York Times Magazine* had crowned Spanish cuisine—and especially Ferran's—the most exciting in the world, thereby displacing the French, who had held that title since pretty much forever. Now some French chefs took the opportunity opened by Santamaria to denigrate the use of additives as "not really cooking." In Italy, a documentary-style television program went undercover in the kitchen of Massimo Bottura at the avant-garde Osteria Francescana in Modena and filmed the chef adding methylcellulose to a sauce. The show's air of shocked outrage—what insidious foreign corruptions were contaminating Italian food?—was persuasive. In 2009, the Italian government banned the use of hydrocolloids and other additives from restaurants (despite the fact that they were still permitted, and widely used, in industrial food), and it wasn't long before the *carabinieri* were busting into restaurants and confiscating cans of Texturas—the collection of additives sold under the Adrià name.

The virulence of this reaction pushed Ferran into a stance he never wanted. He had begun his career cooking what was essentially French food, and he continues to see the kind of avant-garde food he now makes not as emerging from an abrupt break with the past but as a natural evolution from nouvelle cuisine. It isn't he who is saying classic French cuisine is dead (that would be *The New York Times*); in his mind all he has done is open up the category of haute cuisine to include new, liberated forms. He is also accustomed to the suspicion that molecular gastronomy excites among some critics, and he long ago grew used to their mockery of the foams and liquid nitrogen that are now ubiquitous in restaurants throughout the world. But this latest incarnation of antagonism has forced him to defend himself.

Now when journalists show up, eager to see the wizard at work, he quickly dashes their expectations. One day an unsuspecting reporter for a French newspaper is in the kitchen, doing a story on the latest dishes. Ferran marches over to him as he stands at the pass, notebook at the ready. "Do you see any test tubes?" he demands. "Any Bunsen burners?"

"No," the reporter replies a little nervously.

"What about machines? Do you see any big, scary machines you don't recognize?"

The reporter admits that he does not.

"This is another of the great myths about elBulli," Ferran says, his words rushing together as he warms to his subject. "That I'm a mad scientist and this is my laboratory. Does this look like a lab? Do I look like a mad scientist?"

At this particular moment, Ferran's untrimmed, disheveled curls are bouncing and he is animatedly making a characteristic gesture—his erect index finger *thwop*s along the bridge of his nose—that makes his eyes look as though they might pop from his head. He also has a bit of sauce on his face from a recent tasting. The reporter makes no comment.

The additives at elBulli, he points out, are flavorless and used in minute quantities—a gram here, a smidgen there. "And they're natural. What is Xantana made from? Corn. How is that more processed than sugar? Do you know what they do to get sugar? Or wine?" Here he retrieves a bottle and turns it to expose the label.

"What does that say? Sulfites." He nods insistently. "Eh? I'd much rather eat a little Xantana than a sulfite."

The reporter scribbles furiously, afraid, perhaps, that he will be made to do just that. But Ferran is on to another topic of outrage.

"Everybody says that I don't cook, that I just use technology. Do you want to see my technology?" he demands. "There's my technology." With that he pulls the reporter behind the pass and takes him to the center table, where the stagiaires, their fingers red and sore, are meticulously shelling fresh pistachios.

o o o

Gaël was only twenty-two years old when he left for Spain, but he had already spent seven years in the restaurant business and was chef de cuisine at a Michelin-starred restaurant, where he earned roughly 3,000 euros a month. So it came as something of a shock to be reduced once again to shucking oysters as an unpaid stagiaire at elBulli. Still, the indignation would come later; his first sensation was fear. He was one of the youngest cooks there, for one thing, and his language skills were severely lacking; Eugeni would get after him during training, telling him to listen, listen, but all the listening in the world didn't matter if Gaël couldn't understand the words being spoken. "When I got to Spain, the only words I knew were *gracias* and *cerveza*," he says with a smile. "I couldn't understand a fucking thing they were saying to me."

It wasn't until the first service that his fear began to give way to anger. As Ferran called an early dish, Gaël joined the scrum at the center table to begin plating it. But Eugeni, convinced that the stagiaire's lack of Spanish comprehension meant he didn't know what he was doing, took the cup out of his hand and told him to get behind the group and watch. "I understood what to do," recalls Gaël indignantly. "And I wasn't there to just watch. I wanted to do things."

It took a while before the permanent team realized that Gaël's lack of proficiency with Spanish was not equivalent to a lack of proficiency in the kitchen. Convinced that the Swiss stagiaire was a bit slow, Eugeni kept urging him to go faster at tasks, whether peeling nuts or shucking oysters. Watching this exchange one day, Oriol proposed a little test. "Eugeni," the chef de cuisine called out, "let's see who can do them faster—you or Gaël." A pile of shellfish was placed in front of each man, and on Oriol's signal they began to shuck as quickly as they could, taking care not to nick the flesh inside. Gaël, who had spent years of his apprenticeship perfecting this particular skill, won easily. "Eugeni wouldn't speak to me for the rest of the day," he says with a small smile.

Gradually, through actions more than words, Gaël convinced the chefs at elBulli that he knew what he was doing. Eugeni made him his assistant for a while, and Oriol and Eduard began to give him more responsibility. The artichoke rose, for example, became "his" dish. After Emma moved on to the center table, Gaël took over the blanching and pressure cooking of the petals and found that he liked the precision of the dish. "You have to have an intuition for it," he says. "A bit too short, and they're raw. A bit too long, and they're overcooked. It's a matter of seconds." Over time the chefs would look to him to say how many roses he would need for service each night. Even Ferran noticed. "He seems like he's spaced out," he said one day in reference to Gaël. "But he's actually paying attention to everything."

Well, not everything. Gaël was frequently so focused on what he was doing that he failed to notice things going on around him. The night Jorge was burned, for example, Gaël was assisting at the Starters II station and was so deep into the task of cooking the ham canapé that he had no idea the accident had taken place—even though it occurred about three feet away. "I didn't even hear anything," he recalled. Nor did the tensions and outbursts of a normal service bother him. "For one thing, whenever someone starts yelling, I can't understand what they are saying," he said. "But I also like stress. I like it when someone gives me shit if I fuck up. Don't say, 'Oh you poor thing, are you having a bad day?' Get in my face."

In August, he began to consider putting his name in for a job the following year. It would mean leaving Vevey, his job and his girlfriend for another six months. But a position as chef de partie at elBulli would also offer a challenge that was hard to resist. "I want to see if I can do it," he said, explaining his decision. "I want to see if I can run a station in the best restaurant in the world."

Run a station and further his artistry. At Denis Martin, where he was already chef de cuisine, Gaël played roughly the same role that Oriol did at elBulli, coming up with new dishes, testing new ideas. This to him was the whole point of cooking, the thing he hoped to get better at by returning to Roses. He already knew how to treat food as an evolving canvas, so that it might surprise, delight, unnerve. But another stint at elBulli, one in which he was in charge of something, might teach him, he thought, the responsibility of an artist. "Some people, they just want their food to be about love," he said. "But that's not enough for me. I want it to express me, my ideas, my vision." Like Oriol, Gaël had no desire to own his own restaurant one day. "I don't want to run a business," he said. "All that worrying about costs and staff and keeping the building maintained—I'm not good at that. I just want to cook." I just want, he might as well have said, to create. Like Oriol, he imagined he would be happier alone in his lab, testing new ideas, than in the messy, mediated job of running a restaurant.

Like almost everyone producing avant-garde cuisine, Gaël dislikes the phrase "molecular gastronomy." ("What does that even mean?" he asks. "All food is made up of molecules.") But he loves the opportunities it affords to experiment, to confound expectations. And he wholly embraces the idea that a chef can be an artist. Cooking, in his mind, is like painting—there are house painters, and then there are painting painters. He sees himself fitting into the latter category. "I don't want to be cooking to feed people. I want to cook to shock them." Asked if he ever questions his talents—about whether he is good enough to be a painting painter, he says he has no doubt. "I've never met anyone with more passion for cuisine than I have."

o o o

Along with the issue of additives, a new—or at least newly chic—direction in haute cuisine has increased the scrutiny to which elBulli's food is subjected. Although European chefs have practiced locavore, or farm-to-table, cuisine for centuries, an emphasis on exotic ingredients and year-round availability in recent decades had displaced what was once a necessary tradition. Now, as that old kind of eating becomes fashionable once again and an ever-growing number of chefs seek out heirloom vegetables and pastured meat, the product itself has assumed greater importance. Santamaria, who has always featured local, Catalan ingredients and techniques in his cooking but certainly isn't averse to serving a tomato in February or importing oysters from Normandy, appropriated the rhetoric of this new movement in his attack on avant-garde cuisine.

Here too, Ferran feels compelled to defend himself against misconceptions about what goes on in his kitchen. Yes, he serves Japanese tofu and Ecuadoran roses and Dutch succulents and French smoked butter. "But did you taste this?" he will ask, holding out a raw leaf, or smearing an uncooked dab onto your hand. "It's the best in the world." Like any other decent chef, Ferran can get very excited by a product that does nothing more exotic than taste good. And he can be just as disappointed when it doesn't live up to his expectations, no matter how rare or unusual it is. When a shipment of Lola tomatoes that he tasted a few weeks earlier finally comes in—the fruit elongated like a jalapeño and packed preciously in straw—he opens the box with the joy of a child at Christmas. Immediately, he grabs a knife and starts slicing into a tomato. One piece, then two, then another; the tomato has disappeared, and still he can't stop eating. He starts in on another.

He pauses to issue the usual verdict. "These are the best tomatoes in the world," he says before taking another slice.

This time, however, something stops him, and he pauses in midchew. "There are seeds in this. Last time there weren't seeds." He chews a little more, then picks up a whole tomato and looks at it skeptically. "They're good, or even very good, but . . ." His thoughts trail off, but he closes the box; for the moment, Lola tomatoes don't look to have a future at elBulli. "This is the most stressful part," he shrugs. "You never know what the product will be like."

Lola tomatoes come from a producer a few hundred kilometers down the Mediterranean coast, in Alicante. Does that make them local or not? The question doesn't trouble Ferran. His policy has always been to start close to home and work his way out, letting quality, more than any other factor, including price, be the chief determinant. If he can get better-tasting tomatoes from Alicante than he can from a farmer in the nearby town of Figueres, he will choose Alicante. And in fact the shopping list for the restaurant forms a series of concentric circles expanding ever outward in space and time—daily shopping at the market in Roses, every other day in Figueras, twice weekly at the Boqueria in Barcelona, once-a-week shipments from everywhere else. If the restaurant imports its organic milk from Germany but gathers pine nuts from the trees just outside the kitchen door, it is because those products, he says, are the best.

Amid the snark and the side taking of the Santamaria *escándalo*, one important point about elBulli's cuisine has been obscured. It is not uncommon for critics to characterize some of Ferran's most iconic techniques—the foam, the spherification, the liquid nitrogen—as mere novelty for the sake of novelty or showmanship for the sake of showmanship. But ask him why he invented these techniques, and his answer will always come down to the chef's holy grail: flavor. Foam, that early revolution, was designed in the quest to make a mousse without gelatin or cream. Liquid nitrogen creates a sorbet without the sugar that would normally be necessary to keep it from forming hard, icy crystals. Xantana allows a cook to thicken a sauce without flour or butter. Spherification permits the diner to eat liquids, not drink them. The things that chefs traditionally add to a preparation to transform its texture—butter, sugar, cream, vegetable purée, flour—may be delicious, but they also dilute the flavor of the primary ingredients. Yet if you add Xantana to chicken stock, you'll have a sauce that tastes of nothing but chicken. Turn the juice from shucked oysters into foam using nothing more than a siphon, and you'll have a mousse that tastes solely of the sea. Freeze a mango purée with liquid nitrogen, and you will get a sorbet that tastes shockingly of only ripe fruit.

Ferran uses hydrocolloids and high-tech machines because they allow him to make a product taste more like what it is. But he is just as likely to set those additives and technologies aside if they don't bring anything to the plate. Although it took a few years, he has by now learned that he doesn't necessarily need them to create the provocative, magical dishes he adores. One of the most beloved dishes of the 2009 season, for example, perfectly captures the essence of autumn and enchants diners by forcing them to reexamine their preconceptions, but is also startlingly simple: a large, empty wineglass filled with a scandalously abundant amount of fresh white truffle, shaved tableside. It is a ridiculously luxurious dish, made all the more so by the fact that the diner isn't meant to eat the unadorned truffle, only smell it. Truffles don't have any real taste, Ferran explains, only aroma; smell them deeply, and you'll have a fuller experience. Chef Denis Martin, who tried the dish on his annual visit to elBulli, agreed. "It's a cretinous idea—truffles alone in a glass!" he ranted. "Idiotic! Stupid! But it's pure genius." Especially because, after the table has had its fill of the scent, the servers bring out plates of sweet potato gnocchi, sauced with butter and sprinkled with more truffle shavings. The diners sniff the glass, then take a bite, intensifying the flavor of what is in their mouths into a near frenzy of truffle-ness. On this, as with the liquid nitrogen sorbet or Xantana-thickened stock, the point is always the same. "It's about purity," Ferran says. "Purity of flavor."

With those words, he exposes the lie behind the now-common tendency to position what we might call a cuisine of the product against a cuisine of elaboration. In its most virulent form, the tendency pits "organic," "farm-fresh" cooking that "respects" the ingredients against cooking that is "technical," "molecular," "manipulated." (The virulence runs both ways—not long ago David Chang provoked a minor firestorm in culinary circles when he accused San Francisco chefs of doing nothing more than setting some "figs on a plate.") But as Ferran points out, all cooking—even splitting open those figs and drizzling them with a little honey—is manipulation, and to attempt to assign a value to the degree of elaboration that occurs in the kitchen is an impossible task. Product versus Manipulation is a false dichotomy.

Yet Ferran is not content simply to emphasize flavor. If he were, he would be serving that liquid-nitrogenized mango sorbet alone in a bowl. He combines pure flavors in new, provocative ways and brings new techniques to the same task not just because they are amusing or taste good but because, in doing so, he allows his diners to reexamine their expectations of what food is and what it can be. Manipulation, in other words, is where the art happens. It is this ambition, this sense that his dishes are reaching for something more than simply tasting good, that irks his critics. His crime is less that he breaks or refuses to acquiesce to long-established rules (savory comes before sweet; sauce is liquid, not solid) than that he dares to ask, *demands* to ask, really, can food be art? Behind the rivalries both personal and nationalistic, the purportedly antagonistic ideologies of manipulation versus product, lurks this question.

Can food be art? Adoring diners have declared chefs since Marie-Antoine Carême worthy of the title *artist*, but it sometimes seems that until Ferran, no one really took the question seriously. Indeed, when Ferran was invited in 2007 to participate in Documenta, an important contemporary art fair held every five years in Kassel, Germany (his contribution was to serve dinner to a couple chosen daily from among the fairgoers in Kassel and sent to elBulli for the night), his inclusion prompted outrage among some critics precisely *because* he was being treated like any other artist. Skeptics complained that including a cook signaled the banalization of Documenta. "Both Adrià's participation and contribution seem ridiculous to me," sniffed the art critic Robert Hughes, adding definitively, if reductively, that "food is food." Even the show's organizers seemed unwilling to make a conclusive statement on the question. "We aren't saying that cooking is a new art form. We're saying that Ferran Adrià shows artistic intelligence," said the curator, Ruth Noack. "And besides, compared to [Jeff] Koons, who's banal? Banality in art isn't a question of medium but of complexity." Although Ferran is frequently and commonly compared to Pablo Picasso, Salvador Dalí, and Antoni Gaudí—all three radical innovators with ties to Catalonia—the question "Is he an artist?" still circles back on itself, never conclusively resolved, yet impossible to avoid, and occasionally polarizing in its implication that one chef, at least, is more of an artist than any other.

Ferran's own evolution on this question has been striking. During the early years of his renown, he was most closely identified with scientists. Much of this reputation was surely enflamed by the media, who loved to depict the chef holding bubbling test tubes aloft or working fixatedly with centrifuges. But Ferran himself encouraged the connection by actively seeking relationships with scientists, especially the chemist Pere Castells, who first introduced him to xanthan gum. In 2004, he became a founding member and director of the Alicia Foundation, a Catalan institution dedicated to studying the intersections of science and food. He still remains involved with the scientific world; in 2010, he helped teach a course in Harvard University's science department. Yet over time, he has moved slightly away from this identification or at least complicated it; he has in fact admitted that his original hope for Alicia— that the foundation would advance the technique of haute cuisine—has not borne fruit. His formerly close relationship with science has been, if not replaced, at least pushed aside to make room for a connection with the art world.

At the time of Documenta, when he was asked whether he saw himself as an artist, he refused to answer the question clearly. He took care to emphasize that other media, like photography, had encountered artistic resistance when they were first introduced, but overall said he preferred to stay out of the debate about whether what he does is art or not. "That's for other people to decide," he said at the time. "Cooking is cooking. And if it exists alongside art, that's wonderful." But that was in 2007. These days his primary connections outside the culinary world proper—at least the ones that most excite him—are with the arts. In 2009, he was invited to participate in more than a dozen arts conferences, was the subject of a well-received Parisian opera, and has been involved in a couple of films that have little to do with cooking per se. "I could fill my entire schedule just with the art shows I'm invited to participate in," he said one morning, clearly pleased with the development.

The stagiaires who come to elBulli are drawn by Adrià's creativity.

Like everyone else, they refer to him as a genius, an artist, and they spend their six months of indentured servitude hoping that some of the talent that has made him unique will rub off on them. But most of them say they do not want to cook like him. It is a curious truth that although they are thrilled to acquire the techniques and fight to have the opportunity to learn to use the Pacojet or the alginate bath, the great majority of stagiaires have no plans to produce avant-garde cuisine themselves. Sunny is typical. "Nah, I want to go back to basics," he says one day when he has arrived at the restaurant early so that he can go down to the beach to meditate before the start of mise en place. "Delicious food, beautiful ingredients, made with love." Begoña, from Bilbao, echoes his words, albeit in a different cultural context. "A good stew, a creamy rice" is how she describes what she wants to cook. "Food you eat with a spoon." There are exceptions—Luke adores the most conceptual of Spanish cuisine, and Nico is always jotting down ideas in his notebook for cocktails that separate into layers before the diner's eyes—but asked about their own style, most of the stagiaires work in the words "good," "product," and "love."

What is interesting is that they see it as a choice, an either/or, between the avant-garde and something more nurturing and delicious. In other words, they unwittingly subscribe to the dichotomy laid out by Santamaria. Yet, as many elBulli alumni have discovered, a chef need not choose. Having come through elBulli, Andoni Luis Aduriz, René Redzepi, Paco Morales, and Nuno Mendes have all chosen to weight the balance a little more toward the product, but they also judiciously use modern, "molecular" techniques to heighten flavors. Their food is less self-consciously artistic than Adrià's, and because all of these chefs maintain gardens and forage for wild ingredients, it tracks closely with the locavore movement. But a foam here, a frozen sand there, "dirt" made from ground burned hazelnuts—all owe a profound debt to elBulli. Theirs is, in other words, a third way.

Some of the stagiaires don't seem to realize that they don't have to choose between one and the other. "I'm interested in learning about molecular gastronomy," says Emma. "But it's not me. I want to really cook." "Really" cook. What does that mean? Is it not "really" cooking if it involves a distillatory or a centrifuge? If it includes hydrocolloids or sulfites? If it requires you "only" to put some well-grown vegetables on a plate? Yet however much they may reject Ferran's approach to cuisine, the stagiaires have nonetheless internalized the ethos that drives it. Like the young women who accept without question the gains in employment and opportunities that feminism has brokered but reject the moniker "feminist," they expect their food not only to make others happy but to say something about themselves. They see cooking, in other words, as a form of self-expression equal to writing poetry or painting sunsets. Even if they are loath to call it by that name, they have come to see cooking as art.

o o o

As Gaël struggled to decide whether he wanted to apply to return to elBulli, the question of art weighed on his mind. He had come to Roses already experienced in the ways that food could shock and amuse. But his time in Adrià's kitchen had given him a larger context for that knowledge. Like a provincial painter who finds himself in the workshop of a great master, he saw now that, for a chef, cooking could be about even more than expressing your own vision. It could also articulate a more global vision, a profound challenge to the status quo. But for food to do that, and do it consistently, required the unswerving determination and dedication of a revolutionary. Did he want to be part of a revolution?

All day, that row of homely ingredients for fondue sat on the pass: the cheese, the garlic, the raffia-tied jars, each of them somehow out of place next to the dark-tinted bottles scrawled in obscure alphabets, the unlikely vegetables, the mysterious pastes oozing from their cellophane. Finally Eduard pulled Gaël from the line and told him to start cooking. Although he had made fondue countless times before, the Swiss stagiaire was nervous as he prepared it and worried that he would make a mistake. Always so intently focused on his own work, he didn't realize that he was not the first stagiaire to suffer this anxiety. At other points in the season, other apprentices had found themselves in the simultaneously exhilarating and terrifying position of having to cook a typical dish from home for Adrià and his staff. For Luke it was kimchi, for Katie it was her grandmother's barbecue sauce. Luca had had to prepare tiramisù, only to have Ferran and Oriol set about deconstructing it in an effort to come up with a savory version.

Now it was Gaël's turn. Oriol sent Andrea over to watch, instructing her to take careful notes of everything the young Swiss cook did. So, as he worked, Gaël explained each step, just as he had on the television shows he had shot with Chef Martin. He lined up all his ingredients— the cheese, the kirsch, a bottle of white wine, cornstarch, pepper, a clove of garlic, a little baking soda. He grated the cheese and put it into a stainless-steel pot but noted that a clay one would have been better. Fondue, he said, should never be stirred with a metal spoon, only a wooden one. And it had to be stirred thoroughly, to ensure that no

The Easter egg is frozen in liquid nitrogen (Francesc Guillamet)

cheese remained undisturbed on the bottom of the pan, where it would burn. As Gaël talked and cooked, Eugeni, Eduard, Oriol, and even Ferran wandered over to observe. From the intensity of their interest, you would have thought that Gaël was at work on an elaborate preparation of some rare and unprecedented dish, like spherified ortolans. But no, it was just melted cheese. Still, for these Spanish chefs, fondue was unexplored territory. They stood at the stove top with Gaël, dipping their cubes of bread into the finished sauce and laughing as they licked gooey cheese off their fingers.

Did Gaël recognize something valuable in the moment? Or did making fondue remind him of the kind of cooking he didn't want to do? The next day, he asked Marc to consider him for chef de partie the following year. A few days later, his fondue inspired a new version of the Easter Egg, this one made with Gruyère cheese.

six

November, or **Sacrifice**

At 4:05 in the afternoon, Kim Floresca is preparing the sauce for the abalone dish. She peels several pieces of ginger and puts the peel into a *taper*. She slices the ginger, then turns and checks a stock she put on the stove top earlier. She walks around the corner to *cuarto frio*, grabs the Thermomix, brings it back to her station, and plugs it in. She walks to the other side of the kitchen, gets a jug of mineral water, measures out the proper amount, and adds it and the ginger to the blender cup of the Thermomix, which she covers in plastic wrap. She caps the plastic with a lid and turns the machine on. As it works, she takes another *taper*, filled with enoki mushroom stems, to the small refrigerator and comes back with saucepan and whisk. Now she sprints in the other direction to the *plonge* and returns with a small colander, laying out all three items in a neat line at her station. She checks on the Thermomix, turns back to the stove, pours water into the saucepan, opens a bottle of sake, and pours some into a cup. Nico interrupts to ask her a question about the sauce he is working on, and she pauses to inspect his labor. Satisfied, she grabs a spoon, turns back to the Thermomix, turns it off, and strains the contents through the colander. The remaining juice goes into the pot.

She drops the used colander into the dishwashing tub stationed beneath the salamander, notes that the tray is full, and carries it to the *plonge*, returning with an empty one. She then takes the pot of ginger purée, mixes it with the sake she has measured out, and puts the whole mixture on the flattop to cook. Eduard asks if she's doing okay. She barely hears him, because by then she is on her way back to *cuarto frio* to grab another Thermomix. When she returns, she is also carrying a slab of frozen lardo wrapped in parchment. She places them at her station, turns, lifts the lid on the saucepan, and checks the contents. She whisks the ginger purée a bit, then tastes the stock, which is quietly simmering beneath its paper lid in another pot. She turns back to the slab on the counter, picks up her knife, and carefully begins to slice. The lardo is hard enough to make slicing difficult, so she turns to heat her knife on the flattop. First, however, she stirs the ginger purée again. With the knife hot, she turns back to the lardo, cutting the slab into paper-thin slices, which she sets aside. She dips her spoon into the ginger purée and tastes, then returns

Kim Floresca

(Francesc Guillamet)

to slicing the lardo. Once she has enough, she wraps up the remainder in its parchment, then covers that with plastic wrap. Using the blade of the same knife, she bruises a handful of lemongrass bulbs, then adds them to the saucepan. After stirring it a few times, she takes the ginger purée off the heat, covers it, and takes it to the refrigerator, along with the unused lardo. She takes the slices she has just carved and dices them into cubes. She has done all this in the span of five minutes; the time is now 4:10. Oriol looks over at her and shakes his head in wonder. "You're a machine, Kim."

o o o

By November, everyone is coasting. The long months really have turned the stagiaires into a kind of machine, each person knowing exactly where he or she should be at a given time and exactly what to do. They have learned not to look at the clock when making the lentils and have developed a rich vocabulary of glances and smirks that silently communicate their frustrations and jokes. By now they have learned exactly how much work they must do to keep Eugeni's ire in check and, conversely, how much they can get away with not doing. Everyone still makes sure to put cloths under the cutting boards, smell shellfish after opening it, and wipe down the counters obsessively. But wiping out the *tapers* before using them? Not so much. Other minor rules have also fallen by the wayside. Diego has shaved his head into a kind of flat Mohawk and, in contraindication of the rule against facial hair, has grown a soul patch; he looks like a Hare Krishna hipster. Iosu, who has moved from *cuarto frio* to the center table, where his habit of talking to himself drives Emma crazy, is openly scornful of his chefs; criticized or even just given instructions, he will smirk at Eduard and talk back, though always out of earshot. And Lucho, who has been working for more than a month now as Eugeni's assistant on the center table—his job, he says, "is to make sure everyone has what he needs so that no one ever has to stop"—has earned himself a bit of a reputation as a delegator: there are some tasks now that, when assigned to him, he quietly refuses to do, passing them along instead to more recently arrived stagiaires. The chefs try to stem the decline but have only sporadic success. One morning Oriol chastises the brigade for failing to clean a cart during the past five days; Eugeni stops Frederico as he carries a plastic tray from the *plonge* in one hand, warning him that he is going to drip water on the floor. Frederico looks at the tray, then looks at the floor; both are perfectly dry. Eugeni doesn't care. "Trays are carried in two hands," he says, though without, perhaps, the same conviction as before. The chefs too are exhausted.

For some, this mild relaxation of the rules is liberating, a freedom from the rigidity and the uncomfortable sense of being always on edge that marked the early months of the *stage*. For others, it's a disappointment. Having learned that no one appreciates his corrections and least of all his outrage when he finds foods improperly wrapped in the walk-in, Sunny has resigned himself to just getting by. "I find myself not caring or not making the extra effort because no one cares if I do," he says. "I hope it doesn't change me."

Now that the season is winding down, there are also a lot more short-term stagiaires and even casual visitors in the kitchen. Two Austrian cooks who have won an award—their prize is to spend a week working at elBulli—show up for two days but then, apparently put off by the tedious nature of the work, disappear. Cooks from other restaurants come for a few days to pick up new techniques. If they're young and fairly inexperienced, like Ainhoa from Sant Pau and Pilar from El Celler de Can Roca, they are put on the center table to work along with the other stagiaires. But one set of visitors, the entire crew of the Japanese restaurant Shunka in Barcelona ("The best nigiri in Europe!" Ferran says of them), is treated like esteemed guests. For two days in November, they are given the full run of the kitchen and allowed to observe what they like. They stand as erect as military recruits, their hands clasped politely before them, as Oriol demonstrates the sunset-colored sheet that is pressed trout eggs and Mateu shows them how to spin sugar on a drill bit for the *muelle*. Occasionally Ferran will pop over to interrogate them, asking their opinion, for example, about the soy milk the restaurant is making. "Here, taste this," he says, handing the head chef a slice of tofu from a package that was bought earlier that day in Barcelona. "It's the best in the world." The chef takes a bite, then nods his head politely. "Actually, there's one other that's better," he says hesitantly. Even Ferran must concede to the occasional greater authority; he calls Eduard over and has him write down the name.

The restaurant is also populated these days by cooks who did *stages* at elBulli in earlier years and have since gone on to hold jobs in other kitchens. With a lifetime invitation to return, they come to brush up on their skills and to see the latest innovations. Rubén García, the chef de cuisine at José Andrés's minibar, comes for a week; Rafael Zafra, who runs the kitchen at the Hacienda Benazuza, the elBulli-affiliated hotel outside Seville, for two. Terry Giacomello, who now works at Quique Dacosta's restaurant, has been returning for a couple of months each year since finishing his *stage* in 2005. With their uneasy status between stagiaire and chef, these visitors tend to alienate the real stagiaires, who resent their presumption (*This is how we did it in my time*) and the fact that many of them simply step out of tasks they don't want to do. But just as the kitchen absorbs the Japanese chefs, it somehow absorbs them, too.

The kitchen also continues to absorb new dishes, though the pace has slowed considerably. Late in October, for example, it occurred to Eduard that if he cut a cherimoya (a custard apple with green indented skin and a creamy white interior) into thin slices, the flesh looked like crabmeat; now a dish with cherimoya and spider crab is on the menu. A new autumn cocktail, made from pomegranate seeds soaked overnight in sweet wine, is also going out. And because Ferran likes for one corner of the chocolate box always to hold something new, Mateu is working on a fantastic new candy that looks exactly like a Parisian chocolate *macaron* but yields wobblingly in the mouth—it's actually a lime-flavored marshmallow, coated with cocoa and filled with a breath-chilling mint chocolate ganache. Although the word has no Spanish translation and does not lend itself easily to a Catalan accent, Ferran is delighted with the marshmallow. *"Este,"* he says, *"es el mejor* marshmallow *del mundo."*

Officially, though, the 2009 menu is closed and any dishes developed from this point on are for 2010. Oriol is now at work compiling the year's catalogue. "It's been a good year," he says, "very poetic." Flipping through the pages of the blue binder, he comments on its importance. "This is where ideas come from. When you sit down and go through this, you remember things that didn't quite work out or think about other alternatives. Writing everything down is monotonous, it's incredibly boring. But like Ferran says, you have to have monotony to have anarchy."

For the moment, Oriol's own ideas are running toward the anarchic. "Remember the chips we made this year with vanilla? They were clear, with black specks," he says, jabbing a finger at the page. "Looking at this here makes me think, could we do them in black, with white specks? What kind of batter would we need? Or thinking about the game dishes, what if we made a game *macaron*? We could use the meat to flavor the meringue, just like we do now with the *bocadillo*. And then make an apple ganache as the filling, because fruit goes well with game. But it would be savory, not sweet." And so he goes, turning pages that represent the better part of a year's work, and thinking. Two days later, he has produced the *macaron*. It won't be on the menu for at least another year, but it doesn't matter. "At least now I've got the idea."

The stagiaires have more practical concerns than game-flavored cookies. With the end of the season just weeks away, they are now uniformly concerned about their immediate futures. About a dozen— including Gaël, Luke, Jacobo, Nico, Diego, Gabriel, and Roger—have asked to be considered for chef de partie positions at elBulli the following year, though so far nobody has a clear idea of how many slots will be open, nor what they'll do in the intervening six months. Javier, one of the stagiaires who replaced the three who left abruptly in the first month, has made it clear to the others that he doesn't want to work at elBulli because he doesn't like the food. Others too have decided that they'd like to master a new form of cooking. Andrea is one of them; although she wants to stay in Spain, she'd rather be working someplace else. She has met a chef, Paco Pérez, whose restaurant Miramar is a few miles up the coast and has one star; he's expressed interest in hiring both her and her husband, Andrés. Andrea is thrilled by the possibility; she's dying to stay in Spain, and Pérez, she says, "is really special. I can tell by the way he treats us." But Andrés, who used to work in Hong Kong, is eager to return to Asia and is applying for jobs in Singapore. Andrea isn't keen on the idea, but she wants to be with her husband. So she keeps hoping that Pérez will come through with the jobs before Singapore becomes an issue. He has to sponsor them for visas, but thus far he hasn't completed the paperwork.

o o o

With her ramrod posture, her unflagging discipline, and the long black hair that she always wears in a tightly coiled bun—even on days off—it's easy to see that Kim is a woman with the military in her past. Indeed, her father worked for most of his career building reconnaissance computer systems for the U.S. Air Force, moving his family around several times as he was transferred from base to base. He insisted on strict discipline for his entire family. "If he said we were leaving at nine o'clock, then you were there, ready to go at 8:59," recalls Kim. Her parents met while her mother was working at a base hospital, her relatives all have at least one member of the family in the military, and her sister enlisted right out of college. "Everybody assumed I would do the same thing," she says. "*I* assumed I would do the same thing."

In fact, while she was in high school Kim visited several recruiting offices in preparation for her presumed career. But something always something held her back. Her family never cared much about food; her mother, she says diplomatically, "makes some things well," and her father doesn't cook at all. They did enjoy the local cuisine during the time they were stationed in Germany, but while Kim was growing up, none of the family spent much time cooking or eating out. Still, from an early age she was fascinated with a couple of shows on the Food Network, and she clearly remembers standing in the kitchen one day with a box of cake mix, a can of whipped cream, and some chocolate sauce and narrating her actions to an imaginary television audience as she pretended to whip up a "gourmet" cake for the cameras. Much to her embarrassment—and her family's continued delight—her father and sister were listening outside the door. That year, her dad gave her a chef's coat for Christmas.

By the time Kim decided to go to culinary school, her father had retired from the military and was working for Hewlett-Packard and the family was living in a California town about half an hour from Lake Tahoe. She visited a school that was opening in Roseville, not too far away, and, while she was there, met the pastry chef. He was busy working on a confectionary statue of Eve (as in Adam and) that amazed Kim. "I didn't know you could do that—express emotion in a face made of white chocolate," she recalls. "I said right then, 'I want to do this.'" She started classes and, when summer came around, took an externship as part of her degree at the Ritz-Carlton hotel on Amelia Island, in Florida. But she hadn't been there more than a couple of weeks when she received word that her school, still in its first year, had closed for lack of financing. Scrambling to find another place so she wouldn't lose her credits, she found a culinary program at American River College in Sacramento. One of her chefs from the previous school was working there at the time and convinced the administration to admit her, even though it was the middle of the year. Her new school required a daily three-hour drive in each direction, but her father's office wasn't far away and the two decided to carpool together. With the ingrained aversion to even potential lateness inculcated by years of military life, they would leave home at 3:30 A.M. and arrive in Sacramento just as the sun was coming up. More often than not, they had time to stop by a market or café one or the other of them wanted to explore. In the evening, before undertaking the return trip, they tried new restaurants. Her father had always taken his children apple picking and fishing, and those daily drives turned into another opportunity to bond over food.

Food wasn't just a means of connection; it also became an arena in which she could express some of her values: the ingrained sense of discipline, the desire for competency above all else. It became, in other words, a place no less efficient than the military for proving herself. In her new classes, Kim excelled, bringing a steely exactitude to every task from turning vegetables to taking out the trash. Within a few months her chefs encouraged her to join the school's culinary team competing in the Junior Culinary Olympics that year in Las Vegas. She took their advice, was quickly promoted to team captain, and led her team to fourth place—not bad for someone with only a few months of culinary training behind her.

When she finished school, Kim took another externship, this one at the Broadmoor, a stately old hotel in Denver, Colorado. Within a few months she had done so well that she was offered a job as a line cook. One of her colleagues at the time describes her as "the most committed and driven cook I've known. She really is an archetype with her laserlike focus and singularity of vision." She was excited by the work of her chef, Rick Aco. "It was the first time that I saw dishes that weren't made according to some old, hidebound set of rules," she recalls. "It was where I saw what cooking can be—how it can be an expression of free will." Noting her enthusiasm, Chef Aco introduced her to Daniel Ryan, a like-minded cook working in another Broadmoor restaurant. Within six months they were living together. "We just knew," she says. For her part, Kim was drawn to Dan's certainty, his drive. "He knew what he wanted and how to go about getting it," she says. "Plus I had never met anyone who loved food as much as I did." The two spent their time off poring over cookbooks; Thomas Keller's *French Laundry Cookbook* was a favorite. They began planning their careers together.

○ ○ ○

In comparison with other restaurants, the hours at elBulli are not particularly onerous. In general, the restaurant is open only five days a week, and after one of the monthly ten-day stretches, a luxurious four days off follow. Furthermore, since 2001, the restaurant has served only one meal a day. "I remember when we were doing lunch and dinner," says former stagiaire Roberto Gónzalez. "You would finish service at one or two in the morning, and it would take you half an hour to get home. You'd have to leave at eight thirty to be back in time for mise. Half the staff wouldn't take off their clothes at night because it saved time—you'd roll out of bed and go. It was insane." These days, with roughly twelve hours off between the end of one workday and the start of another, the stagiaires have time between shifts to do laundry and go out for breakfast. They no longer sleep in their clothes.

But if the stagiaires have something approximating a normal work life, the same cannot be said of the restaurant's chefs. During the six months that elBulli is open, Ferran is there practically every day and night. "This is definitely not normal," he says with that raised finger. "How many chefs do you know who are always in their kitchen?" He has a point. Most chefs who enjoy even a modicum of Adrià's renown spend far more time these days doing media appearances and traveling among their various restaurants than cooking. So common is their absence that the Tom Colicchios and Alain Ducasses of this world make news precisely when they go back *into* the kitchen. But Ferran realizes that a diner who spends years trying to get a reservation isn't going to be pleased if, when she finally arrives, the chef is not in the kitchen. On the few days during the season when he has to absent himself, Ferran makes sure his staff knew why he is gone. "It's the tenth anniversary of Sant Pau," he says one day as he prepares to leave, referring to Carme Ruscalleda's three-star restaurant an hour down the coast. "I wouldn't go if it were for the prime minister. But for Carme . . ."

Ferran also maintains that the level of exactitude of elBulli's cuisine requires his presence. "If not," he says, "you lose the rhythm." Here too he may have a point. On the day Ferran leaves for the Sant Pau celebration, Tato, who was a stagiaire the year before and has returned to refresh his skills after months working for Martín Berasategui, interrupts his lentil making at the center table to peel and eat a tangerine. Eduard catches him and calls him on it, but a few minutes later, Tato insolently puts more slices of fruit in his mouth between squeezes of the syringe. The chefs too are visibly more relaxed. Oriol, who usually delivers his wisecracks in whispered asides, is almost giddy. Even Eduard smiles more, and when a cook comments on how he seems more relaxed when Ferran is gone, he actually winks. "You think?"

Oriol and Eduard sacrifice the most during the season. Mateu works just as hard, and his hours are just as long, but he at least is from Roses, and at the end of each day he goes home to his family. Oriol and Eduard, however, live about an hour south of Barcelona, a three-hour drive from the restaurant. While elBulli is open, they live at the restaurant in a room tucked between the staff dressing room and the staff bathrooms. (Ferran says he lives at the restaurant as well, but he means it a bit more metaphorically: he and his wife, Isabel, have a comfortable home across the street that they bought from elBulli's original owner, Marketta.) The room that Oriol and Eduard share is small and cluttered, littered with cigarette butts and furnished with little more than a couple of mattresses and a desk. The two chefs shower in the staff bathroom and get their morning coffee in the restaurant. If they eat any meals besides staff dinner, no one ever sees them do it. In summer, the breezes off the coast keep their room reasonably comfortable, but because this year the restaurant is open for the first time in the fall and early winter, the two chefs find themselves struggling to keep warm. They bring in a space heater, but it hardly suffices against temperatures that occasionally drop into the low forties. Some nights, it's bad enough that Oriol goes into town and sleeps on Eugeni's sofa. Eduard stays at the restaurant and shivers through the night.

It's no wonder, then, that as soon as soon as the last service before a break ends, Oriol and Eduard are in the car, heading south—even if it's two in the morning and they won't arrive home until 5 A.M. When Eduard goes home, he stays with his parents, though lately he's been going to Barcelona instead to visit his girlfriend. Oriol's case is more difficult, as he has a four-year-old daughter and his wife, a nurse, is pregnant with their son. They have never really considered uprooting themselves to Roses, because his wife's job is in Tarragona, as are her parents, who provide much-needed child care. Instead, Oriol spends six months away from his little girl, Julia, who doesn't take his absence lightly. He calls home every night, but lately she's been in a punitive mood and refuses to speak to him. One night his wife tells him that Julia woke the previous evening because she heard a noise and thought it was her daddy coming home. He runs a hand through his hair as he recounts this. Oriol wasn't home the first time the new baby, a boy they will name after his father, kicked in the womb or when his daughter began telling everyone she met, "My brother's name is Oriol."

Living at the restaurant is not their only sacrifice. In the ten or fifteen years that Oriol and Eduard have worked at elBulli, Ferran has mellowed considerably, but they still bear the brunt of his anger when anything goes wrong and get little of the credit when it goes right. In exchange, they get a reasonable but not extravagant salary, the chance to work at the top of their field, and Adrià's gratitude—Ferran frequently says that without Oriol, Eduard, and Mateu, he could not run elBulli and that he doesn't have it in him to train a new set of chefs. Their situation is not wholly different from that of any chef de cuisine who runs the kitchen for a famous executive chef: they do the grunt work, he gets the glory. Like unsung chefs everywhere, the names of Oriol Castro and Eduard Xatruch are known to few outside the innermost culinary circles. But their loyalty—to Ferran, to elBulli—is remarkable in a profession where a young chef is expected to move on. Ferran knows it: "The idea that someone would stay for ten years, like Eduard or Oriol—that's not going to happen anymore. Nowadays, if someone stays for a year, it's a long time." Asked why they do it, each shrugs with a gesture that is part embarrassment, part conviction that the interrogator wouldn't understand. They both swear that it doesn't bother them that their names aren't known and, like Mateu, emphasize that they wouldn't rather have their own restaurant or be their own boss. "This way, I'm a part of history," Eduard says.

In the course of their careers, few of the stagiaires will be asked to make the kind of sacrifices that the chefs at elBulli have made. But there will still be sacrifices, many of them significant. Christmas Eves and Valentine's Days will be permanently surrendered. Nights and weekends will go, too, making it nearly impossible to have a normal relationship, simply because their work schedules will prevent them from ever seeing their partners. Twelve hours of physical labor a day takes a toll on chefs' bodies: herniated disks, bad knees, varicose veins—to say nothing of the psychic pressure that working under stressful conditions produces. Even after they have worked hard enough and been lucky enough to own or run their own restaurants, with their own chefs de cuisine and partie below them to take care of the daily operations, they will still bear the ultimate responsibility. They will go in on their days off when a sous chef calls in sick or turns up in jail and be blamed for bad reviews. Their marriages will be likelier to fail, their businesses will be likelier to go bankrupt, their chances of becoming an alcoholic will be higher by far than those of the average population.

Easing the sacrifice just a bit is the second family that forms in almost any restaurant kitchen. A sense of shared purpose can deepen the connection among cooks, but in its essence forms simply from proximity: fourteen hours a day spent together working, cut off from the rest of the world (no cell phones in the kitchen!) and in situations of immense stress. Both the bonds and the rivalries can be intense.

o o o

Dan's background was very different from Kim's. Instead of frequent moves and exposure to new cultures, he lived until age eighteen in one house in Baltimore, Maryland. Instead of a strong father figure, his mother played the pivotal role in his life; his father died when he was four. And instead of the military rigor and discipline that marked Kim's family, Dan's was a much looser entity. As a full-time school nurse, his mother would still be at work when he got home from school, so Dan took care of himself much of the time. Something of a loner, he didn't get along with his brother, a few years older, who was much more sociable and into guns and other macho pursuits (he would eventually become a security cop) that didn't interest Dan. No one had much time for or interest in meals—the family ate at McDonald's four days a week (and, except for Dan, was overweight as a result). Still, they had lunch every Sunday at Dan's grandmother's house, along with a dozen or so other relatives. "It was the typical dysfunctional Italian family dinner," he says wryly. Nevertheless, the attention his grandmother lavished on the meal was enough to provoke his first spark of culinary interest. "Sometimes I would make macaroni and cheese for when my mom got home. Or I'd marinate chicken breasts in Italian dressing and bake them." His cooking skills weren't highly developed or even encouraged, but that faint flicker of interest would save him.

Dan is a smart guy, but by his teens he was doing poorly in school and regularly getting into trouble outside of it—including a few run-ins with the law. But when he heard about a culinary school at the local college, he saw a way out of his downward spiral. He was accepted into the program and moved away from home to live in a dormitory. And much to everyone's surprise, including his own, he did well, becoming a serious student. "After all the partying I had done, dorm life was tame," he says. "And for the first time, I was really into what I was learning."

When Dan finished school, he began working immediately, and eventually got a job at the Broadmoor. By then he was interested in avant-garde cuisine, and his ambitions had grown. Soon after he and Kim began dating, he told her about a restaurant he had heard of in Chicago, which was being run by an elBulli alumnus who was doing really exciting things. It wasn't long before Dan had a job at Alinea and Kim was working at Rick Tramonto's progressive French restaurant, Tru. Cooking at two of the best restaurants in Chicago, both were happy— especially Dan, who liked how at Alinea, the savory and pastry kitchens weren't treated as wholly separate entities. But within eighteen months, ambition and a desire to expose themselves to other chefs and other styles of cooking spurred them to move again, this time to New York. Once there, Kim worked as a line cook at what was considered perhaps the best restaurant in the city, Per Se, while Dan moved through a series of jobs, helping open Eleven Madison Park (whose chef, Daniel Humm, would go on to win the 2010 James Beard award for best in New York), then working briefly for Daniel Boulud, before finally landing at Alain Ducasse's ill-fated restaurant at the Essex House hotel. They had, in the end, opposite responses to the experience. Kim loved her work at Per Se, especially the restaurant's devotion to precision and dedication to the pursuit of perfection—they even had video screens mounted so that the chefs at the French Laundry could monitor what was happening in New York. She did not, however, like living in Manhattan. Dan, on the other hand, adored the city but was unhappy with all of the jobs he took there. When they discovered they'd won yearlong scholarships from ICEX, the Spanish bureau of international commerce, that included *stages* at elBulli, it seemed the perfect opportunity to make another change.

In fact, they had tried before to work at elBulli. The first year, Kim was offered the position, the second year Dan was, but they never managed to coincide, and because they were committed to staying together, they declined the offers. It wasn't until the ICEX award, which pays its fellows' expenses as they *stage* in some of the country's top restaurants, that they were able to coordinate joint positions: Dan in pastry, Kim in the savory kitchen. And because they wanted the full elBulli experience, they asked if they could stay on until the season ended, the last three months at their own expense. ElBulli accepted the proposal, and Kim and Dan flew to Spain in September 2008. Along with the rest of the fellows, they spent the first two weeks on an organized eating tour of the country's best restaurants. They got to visit the gardens at Mugaritz near San Sebastián and received a lesson in transforming oysters into shimmering titanium-clad sculptures at El Poblet just north of Valencia. In Segovia's Mesón de Cándido, they watched servers carve an entire roast suckling pig with a plate to prove its tenderness. At Marbella's Restaurante Calima, they learned how wunderkind Dani García turns simple gazpacho into a shimmering, ruby-colored "tomato." In short, they crisscrossed the country, dining daily in some of Spain's most avant-garde places and some of its most traditional. At each stop, they met the chefs and, in some cases, the producers who supplied them. It was a remarkable amount of fun after all their years of hard work.

With the trip behind them, Kim and Dan went to work first at Mugaritz, Andoni Luis Aduriz's two-star restaurant located in a village just outside San Sebastián. Kim in particular was enchanted with the ethos there; the chefs would regularly go out into the woods around the restaurant to forage for herbs. She also liked the fact that Andoni was so warm and approachable. Together she and Dan made a lot of friends, some of whom—Luke, Mizuho, and Begoña—would move with them to elBulli in June.

o o o

One of the main ways that the kitchen fosters a sense of family is with the daily ritual of a shared meal: every day at 6:30 P.M., the staff sits down to eat. For the stagiaires, this meal is pretty much the only food they put in their mouths during the twelve or fourteen hours they are at work. Not for them are the pyrotechnics of crisp-baked oblates and frozen foie gras. They eat carbs, and lots of them. Spaghetti with pesto, rice with rabbit, noodles with pork ribs, potato soup. It's hearty fare, and there's plenty of it. During the time that Diego is in the small kitchen, he takes it upon himself to step into the main kitchen after everyone is served and seated and cry, "*Buen provecho, señores.* There are leftovers for whoever wants seconds." Inevitably, this little flourish makes the longtime staff roll their eyes, like siblings who kick one another under the table every Thanksgiving when Uncle Leo gets up to tell his famous jokes. But there's a reason why staff dinner in restaurants is referred to as "family meal." It is the most obvious enactment of the bond that draws a collection of cooks together, a daily ritual that, like all daily rituals, unites them while it simultaneously reinforces the social order.

Family meal

(Francesc Guillamet)

In most restaurants, family meal is haphazard. The food itself is usually prepared from whatever items the kitchen has left over from service, a method that can lead—as any cook will tell you—to some decidedly strange dishes. And although servers usually have time to sit down and eat properly, the same is not always true of the kitchen crew. If your mise isn't done, if your fish has arrived late and still needs to be broken down, you may find yourself gulping down a few mouthfuls as you continue to work at your station. Not all restaurants operate this way; the family meals in Thomas Keller's Napa places were so well received that they became the foundation of his popular family-style restaurant Ad Hoc. And in the United States, where Latin Americans tend to make up much of the kitchen staff, family meal can often be excellent Mexican or Ecuadoran food. But by and large, family meal is an exercise in improvisation.

Not at elBulli. Here not only has the process of setting up and breaking down for family meal been systematized, with its assigned seats and dedicated tasks; so has the meal itself. Every platter that feeds the staff is deliberated over, tested, researched, and documented, just as if it were a new star dish on the restaurant's menu. The restaurant orders specifically for family meal, which means that instead of relying on the spontaneous inspiration of a cook as he throws a bunch of leftovers together in a pot, it must plan in advance what staff meals will be. And elBulli usually plans a year ahead of time. In August 2008, for example, it was already established that on August 19, 2009, the staff would be sitting down to a meal of pasta salad and pork tenderloin with teriyaki sauce—and so it did. Between the blue plastic covers of the family meal notebook are recipes for hundreds of dishes, most of them Spanish or Catalan in origin but some of them reflective of the diverse nationalities of the restaurant's cooks, as well as the travels of its permanent staff. Thus, although there is a lot of *escudella* and artichokes with romesco, there are also chicken with mole sauce, polenta with Gorgonzola, and pork with kaffir lime leaves. In 2009, the very first family meal of the year was gazpacho (strangely made with mayonnaise) and grilled fish; the last was teriyaki ribs.

For the past few years, Eugeni has been in charge of both preparing and documenting the family meals, and he keeps intimate track of every detail associated with them. Each dish gets its own sheet, complete with a recipe that details not only quantities and technique but problems to look out for and a photograph of how the finished dish should look. Nothing is left to chance—witness the recipe for a simple dish like grilled sardines:

Sardines on the Plancha with Refried Garlic

Ingredients

Sardines	13.1 kilos (236 units)
Sherry vinegar	42.9 grams
Garlic	429 grams (.43 kilo)
Olive oil	750 g (.75 liter)
Sea salt	10.7 grams
.4 olive oil	214 grams

Observations

Serve on violins [shallow oval platters with indented sides].

It's very important to take the fish out of the refrigerator and let it come up to room temperature ONE HOUR before cooking.

It's very important to have the planchas hot when it comes time to sear the sardines; otherwise dinner won't be ready in time.

Instructions

To clean the sardines: 4 hours before dinner, scrape off the scales, gut the fish, and remove the heads. Place on sheets of wax paper, cover tightly with plastic wrap, and return to refrigerator.

To make the fried garlic: 3 hours before dinner, slice the garlic thinly and fry in olive oil as if they were chips. Drain them on paper towels and set aside. Mix vinegar and the .4 oil and set aside.

Finishing and presentation: 1 hour before dinner light the plancha and turn to maximum heat. Bring the sardines up to room temperature. 30 minutes before: At exactly six o'clock, start searing the sardines, and, when finished, place them on the platters. Keep them warm, but be careful not to overcook them or let them dry out. At the last moment, mix the garlic chips with oil and vinegar, and drizzle sauce over each platter.

In addition to emphasizing exact timing and delineating every step in the cooking process, Eugeni also keeps track of the cost of every family meal, noting it on separate sheets organized by day. ElBulli generally spends between 150 and 180 euros per meal—not bad when you consider it's feeding seventy-five people. In 2009, the least expensive meal was cauliflower with béchamel and leftover chicken with store-bought mole sauce (113.25 euros total); the most expensive was spaghetti with tomato sauce and a second course of something called "Japanese Fish" (230.70 euros). Both of those numbers include a daily supply of not-very-good bread (10.80 euros), bottled water (36.00 euros), and excellent coffee (8.67 euros), which Debbie Sánchez or another member of the waitstaff makes to order.

An exceptional degree of quality control rules, and not all staff dishes meet with approval. Eugeni keeps track of meals that just don't work out, in addition to maintaining a list of family meals the restaurant would like to develop (*cap i pota,* a Catalan stew made from the head and feet of pigs; moussaka; and one of Ferran's sudden inspirations: lentils with cuttlefish). The Spanish potato salad called *ensaladilla rusa* was one of the rejects—it took too long to dice the potatoes. Oxtail stew was too expensive. Anything deep-fried was too messy. Ferran wasn't thrilled with a polenta that went out early in the season: too hard. At the end of the season, they were still debating whether to keep it in the recipe book.

But the occasional failed polenta aside, Ferran is inordinately proud of elBulli's family meal. And rightly so—it is mostly delicious food, for which the stagiaires are openly grateful. "How can you teach people about good food if you don't feed them well?" he asks. "How can you expect them to take care of others if you don't take care of them?" Should a visiting journalist show up around mealtime, he will be regaled with details of the meal's extraordinariness. *"No es normal,"* Ferran says: it's not normal that a restaurant actually orders food for its family meal; it's not normal that several staff people dedicate their first hours of work each day to preparing the meal. Nor is it normal that the chef sits down daily with his staff to eat the same food as they. The only difference between what he eats and what the rest get—a difference that Ferran does not comment upon but that is obvious to anyone who watches the bar where supplemental items sometimes appear (some leftover ice cream, a few panettoni sent by an Italian admirer) is that the chef *always* gets dessert. As the cooks line up in back to be served, he quickly passes the bar, swooping up a slice or two of cake before it runs out.

o o o

At elBulli, they had never seen anyone quite like Kim before. The restaurant has long employed a reasonable number of female stagiaires (though 2009, with its six full-season women and several part-time ones, would be something of a record), and most had proven themselves to be good workers. But Kim was different. She wasn't just better than the other women, she was better than anyone. Not only did she work cleaner and faster than any other stagiaire—she was able to break down a mackerel in seconds, and her station was as spotless as when she began—but she was methodical in her plating and absolutely precise in her knife skills. Yet for all her obvious talent, she wasn't arrogant: she was utterly comfortable with her lowly position in the kitchen's hierarchy. She never bristled at being told what to do, issuing her *oídos* with an unflagging enthusiasm that would have made you think she was volunteering for a second ice cream cone rather than agreeing to lug a crate of vegetables back from the walk-in. All the chefs had respect for her, and each one independently used the highest praise they could bestow on a cook. "She's a machine," Ferran, Eduard, and Eugeni all marveled.

In fact, in her work ethic she bore a certain resemblance to Eduard, who could most often be seen—chin tucked in, back erect—stoically moving from station to station as he monitored every aspect of the kitchen. Arriving as a stagiaire at elBulli when he was just seventeen after a year in culinary school, Eduard is, in Ferran's words, the most "Bulliesque" of the chefs, for he truly grew up in its kitchen. Now twenty-nine, he plays bad cop to Oriol's good one. Strict and often critical with the stagiaires, an attitude that derives from his role as the person ultimately responsible for ensuring that the kitchen runs properly, Eduard is highly disciplined in his own work. He expects those around him to show the same degree of dedication and frequently gets annoyed when they do not. But because he himself never hesitates to take on a job if it needs doing—even jumping onto the center table at times if a particular task isn't going quickly enough—the stagiaires have respect for him. "Eduard has a shitty job, the hardest one in the restaurant," says Nico. "But he does it really well."

Eduard Xatruch checks
the evening's menus
(Francesc Guillamet)

Despite her similarities to Eduard, Kim gets along especially well with Oriol. More than anyone else in the kitchen, he shares her adolescent sense of humor. In the moments when Ferran is out of the kitchen, he sidles up to her and punches her amicably in the arm, before delivering a scatological joke. Inevitably, she gives him a fish-eyed look of appalled disgust before bursting into giggles. Kim likes to think of herself as one of the boys (she once confessed to being initially suspicious of Emma because the latter dresses "like such a girly girl" outside work), and her jokes, which are often filthy and sarcastic, add to that impression.

Coupled with her tight bun and her tighter discipline, the tendency can make her seem sharp, even a little mean. For many weeks, in fact, Katie was convinced that she and Kim would never be friends. Yet beneath the tough exterior, Kim is quite warm, as given to mocking herself as others, and concerned with the welfare of those around her (she and Katie did indeed become closer). In fact, the only kitchen rule she breaks regularly is to slip other cooks a bite of food.

Kim's talents were tested early in the season. Luis Arrufat, who had worked at elBulli for four years and was now chef de partie for Starters I, learned in early July that his mother was gravely ill. The restaurant offered to let him go home right away, but he wanted to stay as long as he could. At the very least, he said, he wanted to help train someone to take over his station. Although Nico had been his assistant on Starters since the first week, it was Kim who was now put in charge of it. Just weeks into her *stage*, she was moved from the center table and began learning the dishes that came out of Luis's station. Nico was not pleased. "At the beginning," he recalls, "I hated her. *I* was Luis' first assistant, *I* knew all the dishes. I was, like, Who do you think you are? I was really annoyed."

But Kim won him over with her attitude. She didn't delegate, for one thing, leaving him the tedious tasks while saving the more appealing ones for herself. And she didn't order him around; she asked. "We shared everything," Nico says. "We were really a team." It didn't hurt that Nico shared Kim's sardonic wit and her skeptical view of the world. It wasn't uncommon to see them playfully shoving each other and joking under their breath. Within a few days, Nico started thinking that maybe she had been the right choice after all. She certainly had the organizational skills; suddenly it was her job to look over the tickets in the morning, count the number of dishes "sold," and make sure she did sufficient mise en place to cover them. It was her job too to memorize the recipes of anywhere from eight to twelve dishes at a time, from the relatively simple shrimp in two cookings (the head and torso of the crustacean deep-fried, the tail barely poached) to the complex abalone, which was scored and grilled so it looked like a three-dimensional checkerboard and served on a bed of enoki mushrooms and carefully trimmed codium seaweed made to look like a small heap of *fideuá*—the Catalan paella made from noodles. "The amazing thing about her is that she's not only watching over her own work, she's looking after the rest of the restaurant too," Nico says. "I have to learn to do that."

It's good she was so competent, because Luis's mother soon died and he left for the funeral, leaving Kim alone at the helm of Starters I. From the first, she performed brilliantly. Her dishes were, if anything, even more precise than Luis's had been, and they issued from her station with regimented timing. Even when Ferran and Oriol decided, a few days into her new position, to add a new dish, tempura potatoes, to her responsibilities, she performed admirably. Actually, "decided" is too deliberate a word for a process that began with their trying to come up with something to do with the tiny speckled potatoes that had sat on the pass for a week and ended, just as service was beginning, with the exclamation "Hey, that's good! Let's send it out tonight!"

It fell to Kim to get Oriol to explain the recipe to her step by step one night around 7:30 while she frantically took notes. Before she knew it, it was time to start frying the potatoes, which were served with a spicy kimchi in an elBulli take on the classic dish of *patatas bravas*, fried potatoes with hot sauce. As she prepared the first few batches, following only the sketchy instructions hurriedly issued by Oriol, she had to check in several times with Andrea and pump her for more details about how the potatoes should be made. In the end, all of the potatoes came out fine—perfectly fried and right on time—and to look at Kim's calm face as she prepared them, you would have thought that she was the picture of control. But to her, it felt as if she had descended into utter chaos. "That was bad," she said with a disappointed frown. "I like to know ahead of time what I'm supposed to be doing."

About ten days after she had taken over the station, Luis Arrufat returned to the restaurant. With his mother's funeral behind him, he had thought that work would be the best cure for his grief. His return came as a complete surprise to Kim, and for a day or so there was a bit of uncomfortable jostling as the two figured out their respective roles. But Luis was tired of being a line cook and was more than happy to surrender his post to Kim; instead, he would be a floating chef de partie, ready to jump into any station as needed. The job at Starters I was Kim's for the season.

It was gratifying news but also a little worrisome, because it meant that she was now permanently in charge. For all her competency, Kim had doubts about her abilities. For one, she didn't always trust her own palate. Frequently she would taste a sauce she had just made, then call over a chef to tell her if it was done correctly. But she was also worried about her new role as a manager of other people. Everything in her life had taught her how to take orders. What she didn't know was how to give them. During service, the other chefs de partie would grab stagiaires as they needed them, shoving garnishes at them and telling them what to plate when. But Kim found she had a hard time ordering people around and tended to do things herself rather than have to tell someone else to do it. At elBulli, however, there was just too much to do; for her to plate everything herself meant she wasn't there to finish one dish or start another. "I told her she just had to be a bitch, grab people, order them around," Nico says. "But she said, no, she prefers to work as a team." Accustomed to solving problems by herself (a surfeit of tasks meant she just had to work harder), she was hesitant to depend on anyone else, even though she was quick to lend a hand should anyone else need help. "I'm not good at leadership," she says simply. Yet she knew that she would one day be called upon to exercise it. Although they were working well together, she recognized that she might have to bear down on Nico one day; with his attitude and his pants bagging halfway down his backside, he didn't always share her impeccable work ethic. What would happen then? she wondered. Would she be up to the task? And if she wasn't, did she really have any business being chef de partie?

o o o

The kitchen's second family balances, to some degree, the pressure that the restaurant puts on everyone's first, or real, family, although the tension never completely disappears. Luca feels it acutely during his time at elBulli—his girlfriend, to whom he thinks of proposing, grows ever more unhappy as the months pass. It's why Miguel Alexander, with his pregnant girlfriend waiting for him in Venezuela, decides to leave. Even Katie, so upbeat and competent, feels the tension. About two months after she and Felix become engaged and one after her mother comes to Spain to help scout reception locations, Katie decides to postpone the wedding. "It was too much," she explains. "Working here every day, thinking about our own restaurant, and then planning a wedding on top of it all? I was going a little crazy." The news is greeted with disappointment and a little skepticism by Felix's family, who were looking forward to a May celebration in their hometown, but Katie is sure they made the right decision. "I feel so relieved now," she confesses.

Katie is lucky that Felix is in the same industry as she; someone outside it might not have been as understanding. Yet it is probably not an accident that all of the women at elBulli either arrive with or find there partners in the same field. "Where else do you have time to meet anyone?" Katie asks. She met Felix through José Andrés's restaurant. Begoña is dating a fellow cook at Mugaritz. Emma and Laia both find boyfriends among the cooks at elBulli. Andrea met Andrés in culinary school; they married in 2008. "It makes sense," says Andrea. "All we do is talk about food, and who besides another cook would want to do that?" Even for those who aren't involved with other cooks, the restaurant has played a matchmaking role. Eduard's girlfriend is a journalist, but they met when she interviewed Ferran on a trip to Japan. Oriol's wife, Julia, works in a hospital, but even she is connected to elBulli—they met when he got sick from some bad shellfish served at family meal and had to go to the hospital. She was the nurse who treated him.

For heterosexual men, the likelihood of finding a partner in the kitchen has increased with the growing number of women entering the profession. Nevertheless, the ratio of men to women in the kitchen remains highly unbalanced. Especially at the upper levels of the hierarchy, the percentage of women who are executive chefs or chefs de cuisine in the United States and Europe remains remarkably low (the U.S. Department of Labor puts it at 20.7 percent), and the percentage of world-class or, to be blunt, famous female chefs is lower still. Out of eighty-five three-star restaurants in the world, only five are helmed by women, and on *Restaurant Magazine*'s ranking of the 50 Best Restaurants in the world, only two women make the list. Even at the lower levels of the industry, the numbers remain troubling; although the percentage of women enrolled in all culinary schools in the United States is now almost equal to that of men, the ratio of men to women at the most prestigious school, the Culinary Institute of America, is still seven to three. People within the industry give all kinds of reasons for the disparity, from the physical difficulty of lifting heavy pots to the long hours that make a stable family life, especially with children, nearly impossible. But in these excuses, cooking is little different from surgery or airplane pilotry; they mask what is, quite simply, sexism and another source of pressure for those cooks who happen to be female. Despite, or most likely precisely because of, home cooking's reputation as a "feminine" craft, the world of the professional cook has long excluded women; in fact, the first chefs' guilds in Europe specifically banned women from practicing. Certainly the macho, take-no-prisoners culture of the professional kitchen doesn't lend itself to respectful sexual equality. Nor does it consist solely of practical jokes and talking smack; it also includes serious issues of pay and promotion. When Kim was working at the Broadmoor, for example, she discovered that a male cook, with the same skill level and less experience, was earning $30 a day more than she was. She approached her chef to complain, but he stalled her. "I said, 'This is bullshit—either you give me a raise, or I'll walk,'" Kim recalls. "He said, 'Well . . . ' and I said, 'There's no well. I'll walk.'" She got her raise.

Given the rigor with which it is run, it is hard to imagine a kitchen more open to women than elBulli. Most of the things that make up the salacious bits of the average chef memoir—the off-color humor, the hazing, the fornicating in the walk-in—simply have no place in Ferran's restaurant (it's hard to fit in fornication when you have to ask permission to go to the bathroom). The hours are, by industry standards, reasonable. Men and women alike strip down to their underwear in the single cramped dressing room, like professional dancers who are so accustomed to the proximity of each other's bodies that they barely notice when they're undressed. And, as Kim's situation illustrates, the restaurant has no problem promoting talented women.

Still, the female stagiaires struggle with what they take to be softer prejudices. Emma has followed instructions and makes sure she comes back from a trip to the *plonge* by carrying a crate of water bottles, but when Eugeni sees her lugging that much weight, he is immediately on her, reminding the stagiaires that if something is heavy, they should get another person to help. Andrea notices that the chefs are nicer when they yell at women than at men. Katie feels that Mateu is more solicitous of her and Mizuho than he is of the male chefs. Kim notices it too. She was the object of a lot of teasing when she was promoted, thanks to the politeness with which the chefs treated her in her new role. "The other guys would imitate Oriol and Eduard whenever Kim was around," recalls Andrea. "They were always saying in these cooing voices, '*Muy bien, Kim, muy bien.*'" Kim is hardly oblivious to the treatment. "Eduard was obviously brought up by a good mom," she says. "One day Sergio started putting in his order and Eduard stopped him and said, 'Where's Kim? She goes first.' It's good manners, I guess, but please don't single me out. I feel like all my coworkers are thinking I'm getting special treatment."

All of the women at elBulli live in mortal fear of doing the one thing for which women are notoriously blamed: crying in the kitchen. Katie, Begoña, Emma, and Andrea have all done it, either at elBulli or another restaurant, but they all hate themselves for it. "Look, it's what women do," says Andrea. "Men yell, women cry. But it's terrible when it happens, because it makes you look weak." Kim alone will not allow herself to break. "There's good and bad side to the sexism," she says. "The bad is when women live up to their stereotypes, when you have girls on the line that are really girly. You look at them and think, 'C'mon, did you really just cry on the line?' But the good is that people often have lower expectations for you, so you can really show them what you can do. And in the process, you knock down their stereotypes."

o o o

Earlier in the season, Kim, Dan, and the other cooks whose *stages* were subsidized by ICEX had spent one Sunday showing off their skills in a cooking competition and demonstrating a bit of what they had learned in the preceding months, both to each other and to the group of critics and culinary experts who made up the jury. They had been sent a list of products—all of them, from Andalusian olive oil to La Mancha purple garlic, indigenous to Spain—and were told to choose three to feature in their dish. From the moment he heard about it, Ferran had Oriol and Eduard help Kim develop her dish. She would come in early and they would do test runs, trying out ingredients, experimenting with platings. From the beginning she had wanted to do a modern take on a traditional Spanish dish, and she found herself drawn to the classic cod in green sauce. Originally she imagined a simple dish made from the loin, but under the chefs' guidance, she found herself working with the more unusual cod tripe. The salsa verde was straightforward—parsley, olive oil, and a fragrant dose of garlic—if you didn't count the tiny bit of Xantana. And Oriol convinced her to add, instead of the simple boiled potatoes that sometimes accompany the dish, three bacon-scented mochi, the slippery spheres made of spherified foam. On the side, as an added flourish, would go a crisp chicharrón, in this case made of cod skin rather than the pig skin that is normally used. At the morning practice sessions, they would time her (in the contest, she would have an hour to cook) and critique her presentation, and when it came time for her to depart for the competition, they loaded her with some of the restaurant's very expensive handmade glass plates so that her dish would look as good as possible. The chefs helped Dan, Mizuho, and Ralph as well, offering them tips and supplying them with serving pieces, but it was clearly Kim, the machine, in whom they had invested. "I like all of this, and I'm flattered," she said. "But it's not my dish."

The contest was held in the kitchen of a culinary school on the outskirts of Madrid. Most of the cooks had become friends during the first weeks of gluttonous travel, so now, even if they hadn't worked together in the intervening eleven months, there was still an air of happy reunion, which helped calm nerves and reduced the rivalry among competitors. The next year's batch of fellows had just arrived in the country, and they also were in the kitchen, helping out where they could and watching their counterparts with various degrees of awe as they wondered if they too would be able to do *that* a year from now. In gravity and tension, the competition had nothing on the Bocuse d'Or—it was far too congenial and festive for that—but still, the participants took it seriously.

At staggered intervals beginning at 11 A.M., each of the contestants started to cook. Kim had drawn a slot in the middle of the list, so she didn't begin until noon. She started with her mise, rapidly chopping the parsley and garlic she would need for the sauce and expertly removing the skin from her fish filets. Dan stopped by once to ask if she needed help, but she was so focused, so into herself, that she barely noticed him. She began to spherify her mochi, dropping the foam balls artfully into the alginate bath, a process that drew several impressed bystanders who had never seen the technique before. They asked her questions about it, and although she was right at the critical part of cooking her chicharrones, she managed to answer succinctly and civilly. As she fried off the skin, she moved with the same graceful efficiency that she displayed at elBulli, her eyes focused and expressionless, her movements reduced to a bare minimum. One of the new fellows, Paras Shah, who had worked with Kim briefly at Per Se, was reminded of how impressive a worker she was. "She's so fucking awesome," Paras said. "Honestly, there's nobody else like her."

Kim didn't win. In fact, she didn't even place in the top three (that honor, to the surprise of everyone at elBulli who had underestimated her, went to Mizuho, who came in third for her green tea sponge cake and green tea ice cream). But for those watching Kim, there was a moment during the competition that was far more revealing than any victory. Minutes after she had presented her dish to the jury and stood for the obligatory photo, she sprinted back to the kitchen to help Daniel with his. It was a complicated dessert with several different components. First was a cocktail made from cava and elderflower syrup, shot through the siphon so that the top layer turned to thick foam. Then came the main dish, in which Dan carefully interspersed torn pieces of the microwave sponge cake famously invented by Albert (chocolate, in this case), chunks of mango and passion fruit, and various creams and sauces. All told, there were about a dozen different elements, and put together on the plate they looked more like an abstract painting than dessert. One of the elements was supposed to be a small quenelle of ice cream, but the school's freezer hadn't been cold enough and the ice cream was too soft to serve. Dan made a fast decision to leave it out, then laid out all his plates on the counter and went down the line, delicately setting each ingredient in the right place. Maybe it was the ice cream snafu that got him off track, but it soon became clear that he was running out of time. Kim jumped in to help him plate, following him down the line, one ingredient at a time. It was just the two of them, and they were speaking English, but as he told her what to do, she responded invariably with the same enthusiastic *"Oído"* that she used at elBulli. To see them work together, you would never have guessed that they were boyfriend and girlfriend. She was just a *commis*, silently and efficiently helping her chef.

They are a curious couple. Against her starched appearance, he is more rumpled, his wispy hair falling unevenly over his collar and across his forehead. Whereas she is quick with a joke and often sarcastic, he is quieter, more introspective, and given to abstract thought. "He's got all the ideas," Kim says about Dan. "And I do all the hard work." Yet when he talks about his feelings for her, he is more effusive. One night, when they're out bullshitting at a bar, Luca asks Dan what he would do if Kim had to leave elBulli for some reason. Dan's response is immediate. "I'd go with her, of course. If I cut off my arm, elBulli wouldn't give a shit about me. But Kim will always love me." He accepts that she is much more outgoing than he, and more popular as well. "I'm used to people loving her," he says. "And wondering about me. They meet me and say, 'Oh, you're Kim's boyfriend,' like it's a question." Yet just as she did in the cold kitchen at the ICEX cooking contest, Kim defers to him on their careers. "He's the smart one," she says. "I'm the worker."

It's why she is considering Finland. For his next job Dan is looking for a conceptually sophisticated challenge. He has heard a lot about Scandinavian cuisine and has fixed his interest on a restaurant in Helsinki run by chef Hans Välimäki. Kim isn't sure she wants to move to Finland—it seems awfully far away—but she wants to support Dan, and she wants to stay with him. "We want to consolidate our relationship," she says. "So, yes, we're thinking about Finland." In her voice, there is the barest tinge of doubt.

o o o

In November, the American stagiaires, broadly defined (it was determined that Canada was close enough, and thus Emma was included in the planning, as was Luca, who had worked in the United States for several years) decide to celebrate Thanksgiving. On the actual holiday they will have to work, but they have the Sunday immediately following it off and can dedicate the day to cooking. A friend has offered her apartment for the occasion, and Katie starts drawing up a list of tasks, asking each person what he or she wanted to prepare. Sunny immediately starts plotting how to brine the turkey. Kim calls the stuffing. Dan chooses mashed and sweet potatoes; he will also make gravy. Luca wants to prepare an Italian-style apple tart. Katie, still overachieving, assigns herself a more traditional apple pie, brussels sprouts, biscuits, and creamed onions. Emma takes on some salads and vegetable sides; she will also make corn bread if she can find cornmeal. Pecan and pumpkin pies are out—no one can recall ever having seen the necessary ingredients in their Spanish supermarkets. Cranberry sauce remains a question mark; someone suggests they might be able to get Eduard to order the fruit from the Boqueria. The group invites the chefs, though all but Mateu (who promises to bring his wife and two kids) decline, out of either a desire to maintain the separation of rank or a simple preference for avoiding work-related social engagements during their meager time off.

The day before the dinner, some of the cooks get up early to go to the market before work. Kim had volunteered to get the turkey and bring it to the restaurant for overnight brining in the walk-in, as no one else had a refrigerator or a pot big enough. She had already established a rela-

Kim and Daniel cooking at
Thanksgiving (Sungho Jin)

tionship with Pedro, a poultry vendor in the Roses market, who supplies elBulli with chicken for family meal—and called him earlier in the week to request a *pato*, the biggest one they had, at least six kilos if possible. Pedro told her it wouldn't be a problem, so she is somewhat disappointed to arrive at his stall on Saturday morning and learn that the biggest he could find was just three kilos. Still, she adapts quickly and decides they will just have to cook two. The butcher cleans the birds and wraps them for her, and Kim happily carries them back to the car. But on the whole ride up to the restaurant, something—she isn't sure what—eats at her. *Pato, pato.* She drops the bag of fowl in the kitchen, then goes to change her clothes. The problem continues to gnaw at her. Three kilos—that's less than seven pounds, now that she does the math. Is it possible for a full-grown turkey to weigh only seven pounds? At home the turkeys always weigh at least fifteen. Maybe Spanish turkeys are scrawnier. *Pato, pato, pato.* As she mulls it over, Oriol is in the kitchen, opening the bag she left there. Seeing its contents, he bounds up the stairs and nearly collides with her as she, having just realized her mistake, sprints out, her stomach sinking. "I thought you Americans ate turkey on Thanksgiving," Oriol says. "What are you doing with a couple of ducks?"

Kim literally slaps her own forehead. *"Pavo!"* she cries. "Not *pato.*" She had thought her Spanish was okay, but now she has ruined Thanksgiving by getting one letter wrong. As she silently berates herself, Eduard arrives on the scene and Oriol gleefully relays the story. Kim fails to see the humor; she hates making mistakes, and this was a big one. The two chefs take pity on her. "Calm down," Eduard says, trying not to laugh. "I'll call Pedro." An hour later, Pedro is at the restaurant, a turkey—*pavo*—in his arms. He picks up the ducks and, with a chuckle, drives back to the market.

The meal comes off without a hitch. The stagiaires arrive around 10 A.M., taking over every inch of the apartment's narrow galley kitchen and using every bowl and spoon in the place (each has brought his or her own knives). The turkey goes into the oven right on time, and the stagiaires work out a schedule for the stove's few burners. Aitor has come with Emma but is suffering from kidney stones, so he spends the better part of the day on the sofa, where he organizes playlists on his computer. Katie rolls out a perfect pie crust, and Luca, who has brought an apron emblazoned with Hebrew words he cannot read, watches with mild fascination. Around noon, someone breaks out a bottle of cava. Emma Skypes her parents at home in Montreal and then walks around with her laptop, introducing everyone to them. Sunny insists on saying *"Quemo"* every time he passes behind someone in the narrow kitchen. Around 1 P.M., Mateu calls to say he won't be making it after all. Katie is disappointed, but his absence means that now César, the only person in Pastry who hasn't come, can attend. (Unbeknown to Mateu, César had decided that it would be unethical of him to attend a social event with someone for whom he no longer had respect. "I don't want to have to act normal with someone who doesn't treat me well," he said.) He shows up with a few bottles of good wine and another stagiaire, Gabriel, an hour later. With most of the meal in the oven, the group sits down to watch an episode of *Top Chef* in which Thomas Keller—a former boss of both Emma and Kim—is a judge. At the last moment, Mizuho, who has patiently waiting her turn at the oven, whips up a clafouti, though because of her accent, no one understands what she is making until it comes out of the oven. Throughout the six or so hours that they work, the stagiaires are noticeably happy, and a joyful, buzzy kind of energy fills the room. Emma puts it into words. "I'm just so glad to be *cooking*," she said.

When dinner is at last ready, ten cooks sit around a table covered in platters and bowls (with extra time on their hands, a few of the stagiaires have managed to come up with some extra dishes). Sunny carves his beautifully roasted bird, and the stagiaires compliment one another on their efforts. César says he is glad to learn that American food can be good. Katie passes a platter of golden biscuits around. "This is the best Thanksgiving I've ever had," she says. By then Kim has forgotten her mortification at her mistake. For just a moment, she lets herself relax and rests her head on Dan's shoulder.

seven

December, or **Reputation**

"**S**hit," Roger Alcaraz whispers to himself. "I am so fucked." As he tries to portion pieces of chicken cartilage for the canapé, a journalist from *La Vanguardia* follows Roger's every move. He has stacked pieces of wax paper, labeling each with a number and then a second "2" or a "5" that indicates the number of covers—and hence how many chunks of cartilage—for each table. Because of elBulli's reputation and the fascination its chef holds in the public imagination, there are often television crews, reporters, film directors, photographers, and bloggers in the kitchen; it is without a doubt the most media-documented restaurant in history. The cooks are used to having to work around the cameras and extra bodies, just as they are used to feeling like the figures in a diorama every time a high school class comes in during mise to see the great man at work and gawk at his minions. But this is something different. The journalist is from a Catalan newspaper and is focusing his story on the Catalan stagiaires. Which means that he is focusing on Roger. A month earlier, chef de partie Toni Moraga was offered a job at Carles Abellán's new Barcelona restaurant, Velódromo, starting immediately, and departed abruptly. Roger took over Starters II in his place. Just like Kim, he is now running his own station. But unlike Kim, who welcomed the chance to prove herself, Roger bears the pressure uncomfortably. Now he tries to continue prepping the canapés as he answers the reporter's questions but finds it hard to focus on both things at the same time. It would be easy to blow off the reporter—*Can't you see I'm working?*—but Ferran and the other chefs have told the stagiaires to respond willingly to journalists' requests. So Roger tries again. Asked, "Where are you from?" he puts down the piece of cartilage to answer. "Where did you work before?" He stops stirring the ham reduction. "What is it like to work here?" He pauses in midpivot, his body tense, and looks around guiltily to see if anyone has noticed. Finding no one, he answers at length. The reporter thanks him and shakes his hand. Finally the interview is over. Roger glances nervously at the clock, then turns around to glare at the pile of unfinished canapés waiting just as he left them. He feels his blood pressure rise further. "Shit," he whispers again. Is this what he signed up for?

Roger Alcaraz

(Francesc Guillamet)

o o o

Within the span of a single December morning, the season's great question is resolved: the stagiaires learn who will be returning to elBulli. In an unusually high turnover, all the chefs de partie except Luis, who will be Mateu's assistant in Pastry, have decided to move on. That leaves six slots to fill. They have been given to Roger, Gaël, Javi, and Jacobo, plus two other guys who were stagiaires in previous years. For Gaël, it will mean leaving his girlfriend behind and giving up his 3,000-euro-a-month salary in exchange for less than half that amount, but Denis Martin has promised to hold his job until he returns. Jacobo too feels as though he's worked out a good arrangement; he'll spend January through June working at Albert Adrià's tapas bar Inopia and then return to haute cuisine at elBulli in the summer. Javi is a bit less enthusiastic— he, after all, is the one who doesn't like elBulli's food and told everyone he wasn't interested in working there. But there's a recession in Spain, and he needs a job. Of the four, it's only Roger who has real doubts about what he's getting himself into. Having done the job for the past two months, he knows firsthand just how nerve-wracking a position as chef de partie can be. For him, it's the most stressful work he's ever done.

The other stagiaires who submitted their names for consideration are disappointed. For Luke, who feels that he has done everything in his power to show elBulli just how hardworking and dedicated he is, the rejection comes as a blow. Marc tells him it's because of his nationality: for years now, the restaurant has decided it isn't worth the trouble or expense to help foreign cooks get their visas and therefore hires only from within the European Union. But Luke, who made such sacrifices to work at elBulli, had hoped that in his case the restaurant would make an exception. He had chosen Ferran as his guru, someone to whom he could dedicate himself wholly. But it turns out that the guru doesn't want him as a disciple. "I give everything to them and work so, so hard, and it's not enough," Luke sighs. Instead, he will go back to Korea while he waits for a visa to return; Mugaritz, where he worked during the last off-season, has now promised him a contract. "Maybe it's better," Luke consoles himself. "Ferran was in the army, you know. I think that's why elBulli is so military. But Mugaritz is more like a family." Still, he can't hide his disillusionment.

Gabriel feels a similar sense of disappointment. He not only wanted to return for the following year but had hoped to spend the off-season as a stagiaire in the Barcelona *taller*. "I would have done it for free," he says plaintively. "All I asked for was a hundred euros a month to buy food." The Brazilian is discouraged by this outcome, but Sunny, his sense of outrage now easily pricked after months of being held in check, fumes openly on Gabriel's behalf. "Are they so cheap that they won't pay a hundred euros a month to someone who has just spent six months working for them for free?" he demands, deaf to explanations of labor laws and personality fit.

Of all the hopefuls, Nico expresses the most anger. After all, he was tapped from the beginning as the assistant to Starters I, a sign, everyone said, of his superior skills. He watched as Kim was promoted ahead of him, and later spent a crushingly dull six weeks doing spherification. He was ambitious and volunteered ideas—complete with diagrams—for new dishes. He worked hard. And Marc and the others made it seem that he had a chance. What happened?

Nico doesn't realize it, but up to the end he was being tested. The chefs realize he has strong skills and that he can work hard. But they have seen some of his flare-ups and know that he can lose his temper. They watched as Kim sometimes had to prod him to stop tinkering and get out his orders. For that reason, they postponed making a decision about him—they wanted to see which side of the balance he would come down on. "It comes down to attitude," Marc explains. Apparently Nico's isn't good enough. A former stagiaire named Ivan is given the job; he returns two weeks before the end of the season to train for next year. No one told Nico he was coming. To add to the insult, once Ivan is in the kitchen, Nico is asked to train him.

Is Ivan a better cook than Nico? It doesn't really matter. If best means the most talented, the restaurant doesn't necessarily hire the best cooks. If it did, it would be willing to endure the extra hassle and paperwork necessary to take on non-EU workers such as Kim and Luke, who have so clearly proven themselves. But the restaurant does not really consider a cook's palate, or whether she knows how to combine flavors well, or how strong his skills are, or even how hard she works because it does not need to. There is so much talent concentrated at the very top, and the system those talented chefs have created for production is so tightly controlled, that as long as the lower levels simply do what they're told, the kitchen more or less runs itself. ElBulli is a little like the old theological construct of the clockmaker God: create all the conditions for life on Earth, wind it up, then stand back and let it run. Still, it comes as a revelation to the stagiaires that the reputation of the best restaurant in the world does not rest on the talent of all of its cooks, only its top ones.

o o o

It is during one of the last days of December that the *Vanguardia* reporter and his photographer show up. The same day, about half a dozen people working for ONCE, Spain's national organization for the blind, are also in the restaurant, shooting an ad campaign in which Ferran will star. The ads will run both on television and in print, so there are cameras and lights all over the place, a director trying to track down his assistant, and a woman on at least two cell phones at once who has transformed the table just outside the dining room into a kind of command center. A mild-mannered professor of organizational management from Argentina is also on site, conducting research on how elBulli structures its staff so as to foster creativity. In other words, it is a normal day at elBulli.

When Ferran first began cooking professionally, the age of the celebrity chef had not yet dawned. Certainly there were chefs who were known and revered—Paul Bocuse had launched a brand of sorts from his home base in Lyon, and Ferran himself worshiped Michel Guérard—but the modern incarnation of the chef as superstar still lay in the future. In fact, it would take another decade before anyone began to refer to "celebrity chefs," and even then the phrase had a slightly oxymoronic ring to it. As late as 1992, when Wolfgang Puck opened an outpost of his buzzy Los Angeles restaurant Spago in the culinary desert that was Las Vegas, everyone thought he was crazy. Crazy too the cable channel (today's Food Network) that launched a few months later in the remarkable belief that audiences would watch twenty-four hours a day of food programming. The same word would also apply across the ocean, to a brash chef named Marco Pierre White, who by 1993 had not only become the youngest to earn three Michelin stars but had also earned another kind of reputation. "Those stories you heard about him, about how he would be shagging someone's wife upstairs while her husband was eating in the dining room downstairs," says Jay Rayner, a restaurant critic for the British newspaper *The Observer*. "That was the start of the rock star chef."

Twenty years later, the realm of the chef has expanded exponentially. Television shows, food festivals, outposts in Vegas and Tokyo and Dubai, cookbooks, spaghetti sauce labels, cutlery—even shoes and toothpaste—bear the names of some of the best chefs in the world; all this is part of the profession today. Chefs have become both brands and celebrities, to be sought equally by manufacturers eager to hawk their latest products and by fans (call them groupies) eager to track everything from a cook's latest dish to his latest failed love affair. In the process, the profession has changed tremendously, until it is almost unrecognizable to those who started in it just ten or fifteen years ago.

Of all the chefs in the world, perhaps none is as famous as Ferran. When he speaks about his latest dishes at chefs' conferences, people in the always-packed auditorium rise to their feet and cheer as if he were Mick Jagger. In his office, a wall twenty feet long is plastered with the magazine covers he has graced, and folding library stacks hold all the other stories written about him. He—or, better put, his effigy—makes a regular appearance on a satirical show on Spanish television in which public figures are played by puppets and gently mocked. When he makes an announcement about the future of his restaurant, every major media outlet in the world covers the news. He has achieved all of this without ever starring in a television show or opening any restaurants besides elBulli. But in order to keep his restaurant afloat—like most three-stars it loses money—he takes on lectures, sponsorships, and other paid gigs that, in turn, only spread his fame. He has served as a consultant for a

Spanish fast-food chain called Fast Good and one of the largest hotel chains in the country, NH. He has his own line of dishware, called Faces, and markets the Xantana and agar-agar used in the restaurant under the brand Texturas. He has hawked Lavazza coffee, Lays potato chips, and Pikolin mattresses.

And seemingly each year a new film or book about the restaurant comes out. In 2008, it was the coffee-table book *A Day at elBulli* (list price: 40 euros); in 2009, it was an eight-hour documentary for Spanish television on the history of the restaurant. Nor has he contented himself with the by now conventional ways of augmenting his reputation; as in everything else he does, Ferran is pushing even further the boundaries of the chef as public figure. In 2009, he was named the new face of a major Spanish tourism campaign and engaged in negotiations with a minor Middle Eastern country to launch a gastronomic campus there.

But perhaps the clearest sign of his fame is the stack of requests that each day, David López and Pol Perelló lay on his table in the kitchen. A woman sends a handwritten letter, begging Ferran to find a place in the kitchen for her son, who adores him (he invites the boy to visit for a day). Another fan writes to request a discarded chef's jacket. Every day also brings a flood of offers: to speak at a conference in Shanghai, to open a restaurant in Dubai. A law firm in Alicante, having heard about his "ecological shark fin," wonders if he has considered patenting the invention and requests a meeting. A publisher who sent Ferran an unsolicited book writes back to complain that that the chef hasn't acknowledged receipt. "In all my years of publishing the only person who never thanked me was Mother Teresa," the publisher writes in a tone of barely contained outrage. "And that's because she was dead by the time the volume reached her."

o o o

To the great amusement of Oriol and Eduard, Roger Alcaraz's parents are goat farmers. Early in the season, he brought in samples of the cheese and yogurt his family makes on their farm in the Pyrenees, and although the two chefs appreciated the product, they appreciated the humor even more, since "goat" in Spanish has all kinds of connotations, from asshole (*cabrón,* or "big goat") to cuckold (*poner cuernos,* or "to hang horns on") to hick (*cabrero,* or "goat farmer"). "Did you know that Roger's parents are *cabreros*?" Oriol would ask innocently. "No really," he would say, and then hold up a log of goat cheese as proof.

Twenty-three years old, with thick, curly brown hair and sideburns that reach nearly to his jaw, Roger looks as though he has heard it before. He was a teenager when his parents decided they had grown tired of the pressures of Barcelona life. In a reversal of the decades of demographic movement that had brought Spaniards from the countryside into the city, leaving abandoned villages all over rural Spain, Roger Alcaraz (senior) and Teresa Lagrava left their jobs—she was a secretary, he a water inspector for the city—and bought a goat farm high in the Pyrenees mountains, near the border with Andorra. The couple knew nothing about raising animals or making cheese, but a course organized through the local extension office helped resolve that. They started with sixty head and, within two years, were making a cheese that won a prize for the best in Cataluña. When the family left Barcelona to go live at the farm, young Roger took some ribbing from his friends. But much to his surprise, he found he liked living in the mountains and even liked tending the goats. He helped with the milking and in the winter fed the animals and cleaned out their barn. More than anything, he liked the quiet, the way he could walk out into the valley and feel utterly at peace.

When he was growing up, Roger's family was never into food. They might have lived in one of the culinary capitals of the world, but they never ate out—"pizza, if we were lucky," he says. His parents were terrible cooks. "Everything was bland, the spaghetti was always overcooked," he recalls. "Nobody cared about it. At home, eating was about getting full, not about taste." But one generation back, things had been different. Both his grandmothers were excellent cooks, specializing in the earthy casseroles—chicken with salsify and pigs' feet with snails— that characterize traditional Catalan cuisine. One of his grandmothers sold vegetables in the Boqueria market. At week's end, she would bring home the remnants, plus a nice rabbit or piece of beef for which she had swapped some tomatoes and lettuce. Standing in her kitchen as a boy, he would watch her go through the excruciating steps to a good casserole: slowly cooking down the tomatoes and onions into *sofregit*, slowly simmering a few bones and root vegetables into broth, frying the vegetables separately in oil, preparing the *picada*—a mix of nuts, garlic, and parsley that serves as both thickener and flavor booster—by hand in her mortar, and then mixing them all together and letting them come to the lazy simmer called *xup-xup* in Catalan. As tantalizing aromas rose from the dish, he remembers marveling at her patience.

o o o

"Only ten services left," Jorge says to Andrea one December morning as they share a ride up to work. They've just returned from their last four-day break, and they're not the only ones counting. "Do you know where I'll be exactly seventeen days from now?" Sunny taunts Gabriel. "Sitting in a café in Amsterdam." "Sixty-five thousand," Katie declares, having spent the morning doing calculations in her head. "That's how many pieces of chocolate we've made so far."

During this final sweep, the character of the restaurant changes once again. It's as if somehow, with only ten services left to go, the kitchen has reverted to those first days, when everyone was moving with exaggerated speed but without a very clear sense of where they were going. Or maybe they're just moving to keep warm. When the decision was made to stay open until December, no one apparently took into consideration that it's cold in December. Really cold. And the restaurant, which is expertly constructed in order to keep the kitchen cool in summer, has absolutely no insulation to keep in warmth in winter. When they're near the stove, the cooks are fine, but otherwise they're freezing. Everyone has sweaters on under their chefs' jackets, and the waiters are all running around in scarves and gloves as they set up the dining room. Oriol keeps going up to the stagiaires and telling them to feel his nipples—they're hard from the cold.

With the exception of Terry, the returned stagiaire who is still working with the pedantic vigor that has earned him the ire of many of the current ones, all of the short-term cooks who cycled through in November are now gone. In their place are friends of the house, come for a few days' visit to see what their buddy Ferran is up to. Each of them—and these are among the best chefs in Spain—will have a meal at the restaurant, but their real reason for coming is to go behind the scenes. Paco Roncero, of the two-star Terraza del Casino in Madrid, is there for a couple of days, lifting pot lids and watching with fascination the process for making the rose, which, upon eating, he too had thought was artichoke. Poking through the ingredients on the pass awaiting creativity, he opens one particularly unappealing *taper* and makes a face. "Every time I come here there's a fish in water on the pass," he says. Nandu Jubany, whose restaurant Can Jubany is famous for its game dishes, comes for dinner one night, then shows up the next with two recently shot wild hares as a thank-you. The start of service is less than five minutes away, but when Jubany offers to demonstrate how to skin them, Ferran, Oriol, Eduard, and a few others clear a space in the small kitchen and watch with as much fascination as if he'd just brought in a unicorn for butchering. Albert Adrià, who hasn't been seen since his birthday dinner, is back in the kitchen too wearing his chef's coat and experimenting with a new, show-stopping dessert that he plans to serve at a chefs' gathering in January. Marc has also returned, keeping track of everyone's coming and goings and overseeing the photo shoot for the year's catalogue, which means not only that a corner of the kitchen has been given over to camera, photographer, photographer's assistant, light kit, and backdrop but that a sample of every plate and bowl is now strewn across the kitchen table as Marc tests which setting best shows off each dish.

It's chaos, in other words. Yet those disturbances are nothing compared with the two days when Juan Mari Arzak and Pedro Subijana come to visit. Both are three-star chefs from San Sebastián; together, they were responsible for first initiating the new Basque cuisine that would eventually give birth to Spain's food revolution. Although older—Juan Mari is eighty; Pedro is sixty-two—they are two of Ferran's dearest friends, the people he spends his days off with. Subijana is the more subdued of the pair. He confines himself largely to observing the kitchen from in front of the pass and uses the time to reflect on what elBulli has achieved. On the subject of the restaurant's menu, for example, which he and Arzak will eat their way through that night, Subijana notes that he is envious. "A set menu allows you to be more organized and to control quality better because you always know exactly how much product you need. An à la carte menu can be more fun, because it's always unpredictable, but the products won't be as fresh. The problem is that ninety-nine percent of restaurants can't have a set menu because the client rebels; a set menu is the chef saying 'I know better than you what you should eat.' ElBulli gets away with it because it's elBulli."

Cigarette break after family meal
(Francesc Guillamet)

If Subijana takes an intellectual approach to the kitchen, Arzak is all about the sensory experience. He strolls past the flattops with a camera strapped across his chef's jacket like a jolly tourist, lifting pot lids, snapping photos, sticking in a spoon and tasting a sauce, constantly interrupting the cooks to ask what they're doing. He jokes with the male stagiaires and tries to get the female ones to kiss him, complimenting them extravagantly on their beauty. He then ambles over to the table where Ferran and Pedro are working and reports on what he has discovered. Noticing that Ferran is going through a stack of photographs of his dishes posted online, Juan Mari begins to opine on what he calls "those damn bloggers." "But what the fuck do they think they're doing?" he asks indignantly. "Doesn't anyone come to a restaurant just to eat anymore?" (Although Ferran shares Arzak's disdain for bloggers, he also makes use of their work. Every so often, one of his staff will present him with a stack of photos downloaded from Flickr. The images are of dishes snapped at leading restaurants around the world. "This way I keep up with what everybody else is doing," Ferran says. "Though I almost never find anything new.") Then Juan Mari is up again because, out of the corner of his eye, he has noticed someone doing something interesting with a squash. "What is that thing?" he asks no one in particular. Eduard is ready with its name, an obscure variety of squash. "Comes from Austria, thirty euros a half kilo, the pata negra of squash," he says, referring to the label given the best *jamón ibérico*. Overhearing the exchange, Subijana whistles in wonder—not at the squash but at Eduard. "You keep all that in the hard drive, huh?" he asks, tapping his temple. Eduard actually blushes.

The presence of the two great chefs makes everyone a little giddy. Most of the stagiaires have heard of Arzak and Subijana but have never met them or eaten in their restaurants; to be working in their presence is like having the Beatles drop by your high school band class. Even Oriol is excited. "They're maestros," he says. "To have them here, asking me questions, trying to learn from me, is incredible. I should be learning from them." For his part, Ferran is amused by the uproar Arzak and Subijana cause. Watching Juan Mari interrogate a stagiaire about how to open a cockle, then insist on posing for a photo with him, Ferran chuckles. "It's like the Marx Brothers in here." That afternoon, when Diego comes out of Small Kitchen to announce that yes, *señores*, there are leftovers, he is wearing a huge Basque beret in honor of the guests.

o o o

Maybe Roger's memory of his grandmother helps explain what happened
to the Alcaraz family, because the family who never used enough salt
and boiled their pasta too long all ended up, in some form or another,
in the food industry. There are his parents and their goat cheese, but his
sister too has felt the call; she is in culinary school, studying to become
a pastry chef. Roger's own trajectory started when he was sixteen. Until
then he had planned to become an engineer and was taking the necessary
preparatory classes in high school. To earn a little extra cash, he took a
summer job waiting tables at a friend's restaurant and, for the first time,
saw what food could be—how it could be more than just sustenance or
homey comfort. The restaurant served typical Catalan restaurant food:
fresh seafood, omelettes, sausages. But for the teenage Roger, one dish
stood out. "It was just grilled sardines," he recalls. "But the cook topped
them with *requesón* [a kind of cottage cheese] and honey." That dish, with
its unlikely ingredients melding brine and sweetness, its combination
of oily flesh, crisp skin, and creamy cheese, excited Roger. He asked his
friend, the restaurant's owner, if next year he could come back and work
in the kitchen.

Before he knew it, he was enrolled in culinary school. He was an
average student, but he managed to get an externship first at a restaurant
on the island of Menorca and then at La Broche in Madrid. It was a tense
time to be there. The restaurant's founding chef, Sergi Arola, had just left
the restaurant, and although by Michelin rules it was La Broche that had
earned two Michelin stars and not Arola, few believed that the restaurant
could maintain its ranking without its star chef. Roger's boss was the
new chef, Angel Palacios. Between the pressure of living up to the bar
set by his predecessor and his appointment as the Spanish candidate for
the Bocuse d'Or, Palacios could have created a horrible environment for
his new young cook. But thrust into this pressure cooker, Roger thrived.
It was his first exposure to avant-garde cuisine, and it turned out that he
had a talent for the exacting work it required.

That year, La Broche lost both its stars. Roger didn't care; he wanted to stay and work, but with his restaurant flailing Palacios couldn't afford to keep him on. The chef suggested, however, that if Roger really wanted to get ahead in the profession, a *stage* at elBulli would do the trick. He called Marc to recommend Roger personally.

o o o

The arrival of famous chefs is not the only source of disruption at elBulli in December. Luca, who during November's long break suffered a second bout of uncertainty about returning, has indeed seen out the season. But Iosu has suddenly disappeared. He calls Marc one night to tell him he isn't feeling well and asks for a day off. A few minutes later, he calls back, asking this time to speak with Marc the following day. That morning, Marc comes in to find Iosu and his father waiting outside the restaurant's back door. As Marc recalls it, Mr. Sainz told him that Iosu was suffering, that he felt stressed out all the time. He has made few friends within the group and has lost a lot of weight. There isn't much time left in the season, but Iosu doesn't want to see it out; he abruptly resigns. His father asks for a letter of recommendation for his son, but Marc declines. "What am I going to say, that we're pleased with his work?"

Gaël, too, has suddenly departed. One afternoon, about halfway through mise, he was called to the phone at the restaurant. His mother was on the line, telling him that his eighty-five-year-old grandfather was near death and not expected to live more than a few more days. Oriol told him he could leave right away, but Gaël decided to work through service and waited until the following morning to return to Switzerland. His departure was so abrupt that he didn't have time to say good-bye to many of his peers. It was also sudden enough to lead some of the stagiaires to speculate that Gaël was freaked out by being offered the chef de partie position and couldn't figure out a way to decline it. Even Marc has his doubts; for a few days he wonders if they've made the right choice in selecting the young Swiss cook.

In these last few days, several of the stagiaires fall sick: Sunny, who says he's never missed a day in any of his other jobs, is suddenly out with the flu. "I wouldn't have stayed home if it weren't the end of the season," he says, "but I figured I deserved it." César, too, after another run-in with Mateu, has been abruptly felled by illness. "At least that's what we think," says Katie, who notes that he's been out for a couple of days. "But someone said they saw him walking around town." With no creativity tests left to do, Andrea is biding her time during the day by typing up data for Oriol before preparing to work in the front of the house for the last five days of the season, a request she made months earlier because she wanted the chance to at least vicariously experience a meal at elBulli. Andrés Conde, Mateu's assistant in Pastry, has finally returned to work after a motorcycle accident a few weeks earlier, but in his absence the pastry crew has learned to work without him, and there's not much for him to do. Especially since Luis Arrufat, who has been floating in the main kitchen since returning to work in August, is now in Pastry, preparing for next year, when he will take over Andrés's job. In order to let Jacobo practice running Cold Station, which is what he'll be doing when he returns as chef de partie in June, Aitor has been moved to Starters I, where he is still working despite the agony caused by his kidney stones.

With him there, Kim has been moved back to the center table. She's been away from it for five months now, and many of the tasks are new to her. But it doesn't take more than a day before she is as bored as everyone else. The lentils in particular drive her crazy. "That has to be the worst project ever invented by Ferran Adrià," she says. The roses also vex her; she can't believe how much faster Sunny is at laying out the petals than she is. "I'm watching him, thinking, how is it possible he can be getting three done for every one I do? And I keep going faster and faster but I never catch up, and it's making me more and more frustrated." The other stagiaires watch this unspoken competition with amusement. Finally someone lets her in on the secret: Sunny is making small roses, and the petals, which are also smaller, are easier to mold. The larger petals, which is what she's working with, are floppier and therefore take longer. To pass the excruciatingly slow time, she, Sunny, and Emma start a game to see who can get the others to laugh. "But it has to be real laughter—enough to get us into trouble with Eugeni," she says. "Whoever wins, the other two have to name their next pet after."

o o o

At elBulli, Roger was in heaven. Placed initially at the center table, he was one of the few stagiaires who was never bored with the work. He loved the emphasis on perfection, the unsurpassed organization, even the commitment to cleanliness; he had never seen a restaurant so dedicated to its own betterment. "They never stop trying to improve," he said. It's true that he could find the labor tedious—he disliked having to open the cockles in particular because you had to pay such close attention to ensure that each piece was good—but there were plenty of tasks that allowed him to let his thoughts wander. The chestnuts, for example, required only minimum attention, which meant he could spend the time peeling them daydreaming about the bars he had gone to with his friends on their last day off or the cute girl with the bright pink hair working next to him.

That is how it started with Laia. They had been at elBulli only a few weeks when each started noticing the other across the center table. Their seats were assigned, so they didn't get to sit next to each other at family meal, but afterward, when both would run outside for a cigarette, they increasingly found themselves hanging out near each other. Finally, one night at L'Hort, it became clear that they were interested in each other. They've been together ever since. Even once she left the restaurant and returned to culinary school, they saw each other on his days off.

But romance wasn't the only reason Roger was happy at elBulli. He felt as though his efforts were being noticed; that because he worked really hard, he was beginning to stand out from the pack. He didn't have a relationship with Ferran ("He seems pretty distant and focused on his own thing," Roger said. "I've never heard him ask anyone, 'How was your weekend?'"), but Eduard and Oriol had complimented him on occasion, and even Eugeni was coming around. "At first it seemed like he would just get in your face for the sake of it," he says. "But then I realized that he has to be on top of everyone all the time and that he's in charge of family meal, too. So I respect him." The feeling was apparently mutual; in August, Eugeni named Roger as his assistant. The job entailed preparing the tasks for center table—pulling out the right knives or scissors, bringing out the product, thinking ahead to the next job so that everything would be ready by the time the stagiaires had completed the previous one. There was a reason for everything, he learned. Sergio had to have the Parmesan obulatos earlier in the day because they needed time to dry. The rabbit brains could be done whenever, but the chestnuts had to be peeled in time for them to be roasted and cooled. As he mastered the rhythms of the center table, he felt skilled and competent. Of course, he still made mistakes: one day he peeled a dozen lemons as instructed, only to discover that the skins were supposed to be sliced into long, spaghettilike threads, rather than the short, irregular strips he had cut. Eduard used him as an example: "This," he announced to the whole kitchen, "is why you always bring your work to one of us for approval. These were just lemons, so it doesn't matter, but imagine if they had been lobsters." But it happened only once; all in all, Roger felt that he was becoming known among the chefs as a stagiaire they could rely on.

And then something terrible happened to ruin all that. He got promoted.

∘ ∘ ∘

"Someone's stolen my notebook!" Andrea whispers urgently to Oriol, her face pale with distress.

"What? Are you sure?" Oriol knows exactly what notebook she's talking about.

"Yes, I'm sure. I know where I left it, and now it's gone!"

To Andrea, this is a catastrophe of unprecedented dimensions. All season long, she has been carefully noting, in her clean, looping hand, the precise proportions of and instructions for the final versions of the dishes that make it onto the menu. Hers is not the official copy—Oriol takes notes too. But his are scribbled and more haphazard; he employs a shorthand that makes sense to him alone (which is okay, since he is also the primary reader). Unfamiliar with many of the techniques that Oriol takes for granted, Andrea's notes are fuller, more exact. She uses her own version when it comes time to enter the recipes into the computer.

"Maybe someone moved it accidentally." Oriol is reluctant to assign malice, but Andrea has no such compunctions. "I'm telling you, it was stolen!" she cries.

Andrea's notebook has always been an object of longing for the other stagiaires. In it, after all, are the secrets of elBulli, the quantities and directions that are the expression of Adrià's greatness. To have a copy of that would be to have the key to the hundreds of dishes he and Oriol have tested that year, well before they are published. A young cook could make his name with the recipes included in that notebook or pass off as his own the dishes that, because Ferran had deemed them less than "magic," will never make it onto a menu or into the catalogue. He could even sell the thing. As the weeks have wound down, more and more cooks have asked if they could borrow it, just "to take some notes." Javi has even asked if he could have it for a day and get it copied. Andrea always turns them down. "It's my work," she says. "And it's taken me a lot of effort."

Halfway through service one evening, Andrea puts the notebook upstairs in Oriol and Eduard's room, on the desk where she will be entering its information into the computer. At the end of the night, she is changing to go home when she remembers she doesn't have it with her. But when she enters Oriol's room, it is gone. "It was stupid of me," she says. "I knew that there were always cooks coming and going in there—Eduard complains that their room feels like a phone booth sometimes. But I didn't think someone would actually take it."

She runs to Oriol, feeling herself becoming more and more upset with every step. He tells her to calm down, go home, get some sleep. "It's fine. It's just some recipes," he says.

Mateu is listening to the exchange, and jumps to Andrea's defense. "No, it's not fine," he says understandingly. "It's her work. It's the whole season."

Oriol pauses to consider Mateu's words. "Okay, we'll do whatever it takes. Don't worry, we'll find it."

Andrea is glad to be taken seriously, but she isn't consoled. Someone has stolen it, so why would he or she give it back? She is convinced the notebook is gone for good.

The next day she arrives early at work early to search. Oriol tells her that she doesn't have to do creativity that morning—she can just look for the notebook. At the staff meeting he is firm, urging whomever has taken it to come forward and telling the stagiaires that the restaurant considers the disappearance theft. But still, all through mise and family meal, there is no sign of it. It isn't until halfway through service that night that Pablo Pavón, the chef de partie for Small Kitchen, comes up to Andrea with what she calls "a weird look on his face." He hands her the notebook. "Diego found it in the bathroom," he says. No one asks either Pavón or Diego about the incident, which bothers Andrea a bit; she thinks whoever took it should be punished. Asked later what had happened, Pavón says he doesn't know who took it but that he wasn't surprised by the turn of events. "This happens every year—someone thinks they're going to re-create elBulli by taking the notebook and getting it Xeroxed," he confides. "They don't realize they're just notes on paper." No one communicates that to Andrea, however, and in the end she doesn't press further.

o o o

When Toni Moraga left to work at Velódromo, the chefs de cuisine didn't have to debate who they wanted to take over Starters II. By now Roger had been working as Eugeni's right-hand man for more than a month and had proven himself to be a hard worker. He had also worked service as Toni's assistant, so he knew the dishes. Not all the other stagiaires understood the choice ("He's so young," said one), but that might have been jealousy talking. Early in September, Roger found himself with his own station to run.

Suddenly his days, which had been so orderly and modulated, turned frantic. On a good day, Eduardo, one of the stagiaires from Mexico, would help him during mise. On those days, the two would crowd around their station, which was, in truth, nothing more than the cart pushed to the end of the Starters stove top. Together they roasted dozens of sweet potatoes for the gnocchi, scooping out the hot flesh and removing any fibrous strings before puréeing it in the Thermomix. They melted down the fat pared from legs of *jamón* for the canapé. They puréed the ginger to make the lemongrass sauce for the chicken canapé, a dish of which Roger was particularly fond. ("Where else in the world," he wondered, "could they get you to eat a chicken bone?") Sometimes they divided the labor for a while. And then, in the final minutes before the start of family meal, with the clock ticking down, they went down the list together to make sure that all their mise was done and all of it was in the right place.

On a bad day, Roger had to do all that by himself. Arriving in the morning, he never knew if it was going to be one of the days that was an unceasing sprint to the finish line of service or one of the days that was an unceasing sprint to the finish line with one leg tied to the other. All he knew was that he felt he was never on top of things, could never keep up. He tended to go through mise in a wrestler's half crouch, always poised to move, his mouth open in concentration. He would season food with both hands, just to get the salt in faster, and had no idea, he would freely admit, of what was happening in other parts of the kitchen. The need for perfection drove him crazy. Things were already ridiculously tight, and one mistake—a bit too much salt in the lemongrass sauce, a cockle-flavored air that wasn't stiff enough—meant throwing out the whole batch and starting over.

The most amazing thing to him was that he hadn't realized it would be like this. He had stood by Toni's side for months, always there during service and sometimes called upon, like Eduardo now, to help during mise. He had done exactly as Toni had told him, even occasionally noting the beads of sweat that would form on Toni's ample forehead but attributing them to the heat of the flattop. "I didn't know what it was like to be responsible for a station then, I was just doing what I was told," he says. "But now I'm responsible for everything. If something goes wrong, it's my fault." There might have been forty-five other people in that kitchen, but Roger has learned that being a chef—even if it's just a chef de partie—means ultimately being alone.

To help him prepare, he carries a list with him at all times, even outside the restaurant, so that he won't forget anything he has to do the next day. Most days it functions as a kind of security blanket, making him focus as he writes down items, helping him feel that he's on top of the day's chores. But then there are the days he walks into the restaurant, thinking he's got all the mise he needs prepared for that day's sea cucumber dish, only to have Eduardo tell him that the *espardenyas* looked especially good that morning, so he's added ten more.

Service, in comparison, is a breeze. "All I do during service is heat things up," he says. "Except the *espardenya*. That I have to sear." The leadership aspect—the ordering others around that was so vexing to Kim—is hardly an issue, despite the fact that it is his first time overseeing other people. "It was a little hard when Lucho was my assistant because we started at the same time. But Eduardo came later, so it's easy to tell him what to do." It's true that he misses the camaraderie of the center table a bit, that he feels a little isolated. He remembers thinking how devastating it was when Eugeni would yell at him for forgetting to smell a clam or what a pain it was to have to muck around with those tiny sticks they used to clean the pig's tails. Now those problems seem like nothing, he says. For everyone else, "things get easier and easier every day, but for me they just get harder." Sleep isn't even an escape. Almost every night, Roger has horrible dreams about the restaurant, in which he is always behind and nothing is ever done properly. "Look at me," he says one morning, his hands shaking as he tries to grasp a coffee cup. "I'm a nervous wreck."

When Roger originally learned that he was being offered a full-time position as chef de partie for 2010, he was excited. "To be able to say that you work—that they pay you to work—at the best restaurant in the world, that's really something," he says. But now he is having doubts. He would never back out of his commitment; the job is too good a launching pad for that. But he might remake his vision for the future. He had thought that he wanted, if not exactly what Ferran has, at least something that would leave open the same possibilities—a restaurant that serves haute cuisine, that is acclaimed for its food, that gets attention. But now he has come to realize that the one essential feature that makes a chef renowned—that he stands out, alone, from the rest—is precisely what is making him miserable.

"I want to do something calm and relaxing," he says. "I don't want to go to bed anymore thinking about whether I have enough ham fat for the next day." Maybe by the time he returns to elBulli in June, he will have learned how not to get so stressed out by the work. "But sometimes I wish I could go back to that first day, when we were all sitting at Si Us Plau," he says wistfully. "If I could go back to the beginning, I wouldn't have worked so hard to stand out. If I could have just done my job and stayed quietly on the center table, I would."

o o o

Few of the stagiaires will admit to longing for the kind of fame that Ferran has. "I just want to make people happy" is how Jacobo puts it, and his words are echoed, more or less exactly, by most of the apprentices. Nico is an exception. He dreams of one day owning a number of restaurants, all of them distinguished for their cuisine and all of them reinforcing the brand that his name will become. He dreams, in other words, of being a celebrity chef. "But not to be famous for fame's sake—to be famous for how good a chef I am. Like Ferran."

It's not always easy to maintain the distinction. Mario Batali may have initially risen to the forefront of the culinary scene for his delicious, updated take on authentic Italian cuisine, but he is at least as well known today for his vast restaurant empire, his television shows, his cookbooks, his friendships with the likes of the actress Gwyneth Paltrow and the musician Michael Stipe, and those damn orange shoes. Something similar has happened with David Chang; if chefs are today's rock stars, few of them more closely fit the model than the thirty-three-year-old behind the extraordinarily popular Momofuku restaurants in New York. In the six years since opening his first, Chang has been accosted by autograph seekers while working out at the gym, read reports (all untrue) of restaurants he is supposedly opening in Seoul, Tokyo, and London, listened to Martha Stewart inquire on air about his love life, and had his underwear preferences publicized in *Vanity Fair*. In a tone equally bemused and distressed, he expresses amazement with it all. "Sometimes, I just look around and think, Holy shit, how did I become this guy?"

Chang got into cooking originally, he says, because it seemed like "the last honorable profession," a job like shoemaking or glassblowing where quality and craftsmanship mattered. But these days, as he fends off investment offers from around the world and grapples with the ever-present question of whether to do his own television show, he wonders if he got it wrong. His health is suffering from the stress, and he hardly ever cooks anymore. He still cares about making delicious food, but now he sees his primary responsibility as taking care of the people who work for him, including helping them set up their own restaurants so that they, with any luck, can become famous too.

By all accounts, Ferran has managed his relationship with fame extraordinarily well. He lives modestly—"I'm not driving around in a Mercedes," he likes to point out. Although he has endorsed products, he has escaped the accusation of selling out, perhaps because he's never done a television show. He oversees a single restaurant and is there almost every night it is open. He can grow weary of the relentless barrage of requests for yet another interview and the constant demands on his time. Yet even now, with all those magazine covers and awards and invitations behind him, he still clearly enjoys the spotlight, especially when it opens new kinds of doors, such as the opportunity to teach at Harvard, participate in a prestigious art exhibition, or cook for the world leaders who gather for the semisecret Bilderberg meeting. Along with a number of other forward-minded celebrity chefs, he has been able to use his recognition to expand his role into a growing number of arenas—public policy, social welfare, environmental activism—not traditionally open to those who cook for a profession. Celebrity brings its own stresses, but for those who navigate its shoals well, Ferran suggests, it's an exciting time to be a chef.

o o o

The final days of the season witness a decline from what had been a gradual relaxation of standards to a relative free-for-all. On the penultimate day of service, Javier doesn't show up until 4:30 P.M., and no one even seems to notice. Everyone's aprons and pants are filthy; no one can be bothered to do laundry at this point. Oriol gets whacked in the head when Nico rounds a corner with a pile of trays without saying *"Quemo."* The restaurant's gossip mill starts running overtime. Quiet, unassuming Mizuho, who already confessed to kissing César early in the season, is now rumored to have hooked up with Eugeni. "I think he's cute," she says. No one in the restaurant seems to know if a relationship between a stagiaire and a chef represents some kind of breach of employee relations. Instead, Oriol, who is by now staying nightly at Eugeni's because of the cold and thus has an eyewitness view of the blossoming relationship, denies knowledge of it. "Who told you that?" he asks when queried. Begoña has apparently begun a relationship with Tato. They hardly seem to be hiding anything—at one point Tato swoops in to kiss her as he passes her in the small kitchen. The other stagiaires tease her mercilessly, sophisticated jokes along the lines of "Guess you don't need to go to the staff party since you can have your own private celebration, huh?" Begoña hushes them. "A little respect, please."

About ten days before the last service, a sheet is taped to the dressing room door. SIGN UP FOR STAFF PARTY, it reads, and describes both the location (a bar and restaurant in Empuriabrava, a few kilometers from Roses) and the contents (hors d'oeuvres; a choice of pork loin, steak, or calamari in their ink; flan, apple tart, or ice cream for dessert) of the final dinner. The party will begin at 10 P.M. on December 20, just a few hours after the end of elBulli's last service, and, because the restaurant has a club upstairs, is expected to last late into the night. Some of the stagiaires begin excitedly to list their names before they notice the fine print: they have to pay for dinner. The cost is 27 euros a person.

The news provokes outrage in the dressing room. "I find it incredible that after six months of working for him for free, Ferran Adrià can't cough up the money to buy us all dinner," says one stagiaire, as he hurries to get into his chef's jacket.

Aitor tries to defend the restaurant. "There are over seventy of us. At twenty-seven euros apiece? That's nearly two thousand euros. That's a lot of dough."

"What? You think Ferran can't afford it? Look at what he's charging the clients!"

"It doesn't matter how much it is. The fact is, we've been working for free for him. And he can't buy one fucking dinner?"

"Well, we always knew he was cheap."

"He's not cheap, he's running a business."

And so it goes. Some talk of boycotting the party altogether: "Wouldn't it be great if no one showed up?" Others fan the outrage with the rumor that Ferran usually does not attend but has decided to make an exception this year because the German documentary crew will be back filming and it's a good chance for him to make a speech for the cameras. "It's a photo op, in other words." Kim and Daniel declare that they're not going. "It's insulting that they would charge us," Daniel says. "Plus, after six months of working for free, we don't have a spare twenty-seven euros apiece." Gabriel, tears in his eyes, also says he can't afford to go.

But later in the day, the list is nearly full.

o o o

As she winds up her time at elBulli, Katie hasn't worked out the details of her romantic future. She and Felix are still engaged, and she is flying to Los Angeles to meet him for Christmas; from there they will drive cross-country to Asheville, North Carolina. They will move into the same new house as her parents and begin planning the restaurant. But no date has been set for the wedding.

In the absence of a contract from elBulli, Luke has secured one from Mugaritz, but it won't start until late in the spring of 2010—provided his visa comes through. Until then, he will go home in Korea to spend time with his mother and brother and to teach at a Seoul culinary school. He wants, he says, "to help spread avant-garde cuisine in my country."

Before, he thought that the class would focus solely on Ferran Adrià and what he had learned at elBulli. But with his idol gleaming a bit less brightly than before, he plans to include some of Andoni's techniques as well.

Andrea and her husband, Andrés, are also still waiting on their visas—Paco Pérez has yet to come through for them. Although the chef has promised them work when his restaurant reopens for its own season in March, he still hasn't turned in the paperwork, and therefore they can't legally remain in Spain past the end of the year. Andrea is distraught, both at the thought of moving to Asia—which now seems more likely—and at the thought of leaving Spain. "Andrés loves Asia, and I know that for him going there is like being in Spain is for me. But that doesn't make it any easier," she says one day after work. For the first time in a long time, she feels uncertain, and a little lost, about what the future holds. They will go back to Chicago for Christmas and see what happens from there.

When his grandfather died, Gaël calls Marc to say that he was ready to return. It is the proof Marc had been waiting for: now he knows that the grandfather story wasn't a ruse and that Gaël really is dedicated to elBulli. By then, however, there are only two services left in the season, so Marc tells him not to worry. They will see each other next year.

In the end, Hans Välimäki offers both Dan and Kim jobs at his restaurant in Helsinki. Dan is excited, but Kim keeps putting off the decision. And not just putting it off: she won't even talk about it. "I'm kind of getting the message she doesn't want to go there," Dan admits. "But what am I going to do? Leave her to go work there on my own?" The two will end the season with no clear plans for their future, beyond spending the holidays with their families.

And Roger? He is so stressed out by the last few months that he has decided to retreat for at least part of the time before he returns to elBulli. "I'm going to go back to my family's farm," he says. "Maybe I'll take a job with the village butcher. Someplace quiet and tranquil."

o o o

The last service of the year is a lunchtime meal. That morning, Kim stops at the bakery to pick up bread. Knowing that the last few days were likely to be crazy, she and Dan had "done a week's worth of mise," as she puts it, for the meals they would eat when they got home from work. Today's menu, on the last day of service, is sausage and peppers, which is why she needs the bread. Does that mean they're really not going to the party that night? She says they still haven't decided.

Service the night before had been rough. Two different servers dropped plates, and Ferran became furious. Rafael Ansón, the Royal Spanish Gastronomic Academy president, was back—that was his other tradition, to come at the end of the season as well as the start—and that increased the pressure as well. One table showed up about an hour late, which meant that no one left until 2 A.M. But here it is, 9 A.M. on a cloudy, chilly December 20, and the dressing room is raucous. Stripping off their jeans and sweaters as quickly as they can against the cold, the cooks prepare for their last day of work by making promises about how much they're going to drink that night. Some of them convey this information in a weird, singsong voice. Yesterday Juli came into Small Kitchen and half sang something, and ever since, the cooks—first those in Small Kitchen and later everyone else—have been imitating it, transmitting even the most matter-of-fact information in an irritatingly cloying tune.

For the final meeting, the stagiaires take their regular places around the edge of the kitchen. Marc is waiting for them, ready to explain what the days after the restaurant's close will be like. Yes, there's a party tonight, but remember, he says, tomorrow is a workday, and we expect you here at 10 A.M. Both Monday and Tuesday, in fact, will be full days dedicated to cleaning the kitchen completely, breaking it down, and packing things up until next year. Eduard offers his own warning: "Let's have fun tonight, but I don't want anyone losing his head."

Mise en place comes off without incident, though just to keep things interesting, an eight-person film crew is on site, shooting a feature film in the dining room, complete with 1940s period dress. Later, the director plans to turn the cameras on in the kitchen during service. Family meal that day is a hodgepodge of leftovers: potato salad, guacamole, roast chicken from two days ago. The air is humming. As they line up to receive their meal for the last time, someone says, "It smells like a party," and a little cheer runs through the line. Today the stagiaires have only fifteen minutes to eat, but they interrupt the meal to take pictures of one another and horse around.

With food out of the way, Ferran calls everyone back into the kitchen. An immense cake has appeared on the bar, designed and delivered by the famous Barcelona *pastelería* Escribà. It has the name of every stagiaire—including Luke's real one—piped on an individual piece of white chocolate. Ferran lights the candles, which shoot off flames like firecrackers, and everyone claps. He makes a little speech. "I want to thank you for all the effort and all the passion you have brought to your work. It's people like you, the ones who have passed through this kitchen, that make elBulli what it is. I know working here is hard, but now you can say you worked in the place that changed the face of gastronomy." With that, he passes the knife off to Eugeni, who cuts the cake into slices. The stagiaires file by to pick up a slice, looking for their white chocolate name tags. And then, as they are still wiping the crumbs from their faces, Eduard steps to the front of the kitchen. "Okay, *señores*, let's begin."

Uncharacteristically, no clients are waiting at the gate when the restaurant opens. For a long ten minutes, Ferran Adrià stands alone at the pass like a premonition, waiting. Finally the first table walks in. For this last service, all the stagiaires are more or less back in their regular places. Jacobo has called in sick, so Aitor has returned to the head of Cold Station. Kim, in turn, takes back the reins at Starters I, and because Ivan had left a few days earlier, Nico acts as her assistant. Roger is in his regular half crouch, ready to sprint through the marathon of service. In Pastry, Katie is again on the pass, the same place she was when she started the season. One of Luke's wishes has come true, and he is working in *cuarto frío*. Emma never did get the chance to learn spherification, but she has taken over Luke's place making yubas and Parmesan ravioli skins during mise and finds the work to be some consolation. "I don't know what it is, maybe having responsibility for something, but I feel like I'm in a whole different restaurant."

Each dish that goes over the pass that day marks the end of something. First to go are the *cañas*, the sugarcane cocktails that were elBulli's signature opener from the first night of the 2009 season. As Diego inserts mint leaves into their ends and places the marinated sticks in their heap of ice, Pablo runs to his side and issues a sort of papal blessing. There are still a few sticks left in the bag, however, so Diego hands out *cañas* to everyone in the small kitchen, then rushes over to Sergio's station to begin bartering with the rest. "I'll give them to you if you give me some *ortiguillas*," he says, then thinks again. "Or the mimetic peanuts." By now Txema is finishing up the yubas on the soy plate. "Txema," says Lorenzo, passing by, "those are the last three yubas of your life." Roger rushes by, saying "*Quemo*. For the love of God, *quemo*," but you get the sense that even he, at this point, is kidding. Sergio, who has a free moment, pokes his head into the small kitchen to sing, in that same annoying tune, "This is all over." Txema responds in kind, "We already know that."

The season's signature dishes keep coming: now it's the rose, which Begoña paints with tiny squares of silver; then it's the lentils. "This is the fastest service ever," says Kim as she rushes by on her way to the *plonge*. Before they know it, the first dishes in the game series are going out, and here, miraculously, is the meringue raft that Oriol couldn't get right at the beginning of the season; it has been reincarnated as a bed for the woodcock. The kitchen fills with the scent of shaved truffles—a sign that the savory dishes are almost done. And sure enough, at 4:45, Small Kitchen starts breaking down. Andrea rushes by, dressed not in her chef's whites but in the black servers' jacket. Weeks earlier, she asked to work the front of the house in the hope of understanding what a dinner at elBulli was like for the diners. Now she is ecstatic. "It's so amazing watching their faces as they try these new things," she gushes. "I feel like I have a whole new understanding of what happens here. I feel like I finally get why it matters." Listening to her enthusiasm, Kim can't refrain from a wisecrack: "Just remember, Andrea. When you're walking through the dining room with a tray in your hands?" She pauses for emphasis. "Don't *quemo* the clients."

By 5:45, the main kitchen is breaking down. There's a carelessness to the staff now—Roger breaks a plate as he cleans his station, and Oriol somehow manages to cut himself, dripping blood all over his apron. Fifteen minutes later, Mateu sends out the first chocolate *pañuelos,* those crisp but undulating sheets that so vexed Katie. Now he tells her to keep focused—she's been cleaning instead of finishing up the plating. A waiter rolls up the gold cloth on the main pass. Jacobo takes the leftover ice *estanques* out of the freezer, and Lorenzo and Mike take turns cracking them with a spoon. After several minutes in the walk-in, Kim staggers out. "I just ate half an ounce of caviar," she says. But it is Eduard who signals the end with what may be the most shocking breach of self-imposed protocol yet: he begins to snack on some leftover pistachios. A server comes up and shakes his hand.

Andrea Correa, Emma Leftick, Kim Floresca, Daniel Ryan, Sunny Jin, and two servers at the final party (Debbie Sanchéz)

The party goes off just as expected. From the moment it starts, the atmosphere is determinedly riotous, and almost everyone, including—or especially—Eduard and Oriol is quickly drunk. The German film crew is indeed there, but as guests—the only cameras are the ones the stagiaires themselves have brought. The women from the front of the house show up looking more voluptuous than anyone has ever seen them, decked out in high heels, skintight dresses, and lots of makeup. The Catalans break into song every few minutes, and the Americans try to retaliate with a hastily composed ditty built around an infelicitous mix of the word *quemo* and the Village People's classic "YMCA." No one notices the food. Ferran is there, dressed in a sports coat and slacks, a little awkward as he stands alone for much of the party—this might be his family, but they aren't his friends. Nonsensical prizes are awarded, and a lot of drunken confessions of fraternal love are made. At 4 A.M., the party is still going strong.

The next day, no one arrives at the restaurant on time, not even Oriol, who staggers in fifteen minutes late wearing a sweater and jeans. Mateu goes straight for the coffee machine and starts turning out *cortados*. Even Katie, normally so punctual, oversleeps and has to frantically call around Roses in the hopes of getting a ride (she still manages to get there before anyone else). The rest shuffle in over the next hour. Marc is there handing out certificates ("I get a lot of people calling to check references of people who say they worked here but haven't," he notes dryly). It is a bitterly cold, drizzly day, and as the stagiaires go to work scraping a season's worth of grime from the smoke ducts, scrubbing down the refrigerators, and wrapping plates, the kitchen seems unrecognizably melancholy.

The night before, at the party, Ferran made another a speech. Once again, he thanked everyone for their efforts and then went through each of his permanent staff and thanked them personally. The front of house, he said, was the best in the world—something his clients were always telling him. He congratulated Eugeni on having proven himself through hard work and welcomed him to the ranks in which he considered the chefs de cuisine—as one of "ours," as a permanent responsibility. Of Eduard he said, "This is the person whose labor is least rewarding, who has to be the bad guy so that I don't. He fights every day so that we are all better." Mateu came in for similar accolades as Ferran praised him for his masterful running of pastry that year and for his own, burgeoning creativity. Of Oriol he said, "I've had the great luck to work with two geniuses in my time: my brother Albert and Oriol Castro. People who have had the fortune to work with him will never be the same."

It was a surprisingly intimate speech, tinged, no doubt, by Ferran's knowledge of elBulli's future. As he spoke, the stagiaires glanced around at one another. Clustered along the edges of the room, they were in much the same positions they took during the morning meetings, and it wasn't hard to imagine their thoughts. They knew now who the strongest among them were, and each had his or her own opinion on who from their group would be the next Redzepi or Achatz. They had differing ideas of what the past six months had meant; most were grateful for the experience, though some, it is true, wished they had never come. But they knew that they too, now, were part of history. And if they felt as though they had come through a trial by fire, at least in that moment of wine-fueled bonhomie and congratulations, they felt they had triumphed.

And so, despite all the disappointments and exhaustion, they watched Ferran with the same rapt attention they had brought to that first meeting six months earlier. Turning away from his chefs, Adrià addressed the group at large, noting that they would all be hearing news about the restaurant at the end of January. He wanted to assure them now that any future changes detracted not one bit from the sacrifices they had made and the meaning of the work they had done. The changes, he promised, would all be made with the welfare of those who had fought for elBulli in mind. Then he said something that, in their discussions the next day about the party and in the weeks and months to come, the stagiaires would all remember, though few of them at the time understood what he meant. "Be brave," he said looking around the table at their young faces. "Because the world is not for cowards."

The author with elBulli's 2009 brigade

(Francese Guillamét)

It is barely fifty degrees outside, but in the kitchen Emma Leftick is sweating. As she wraps shallow bowls of béarnaise custard in plastic, she glances repeatedly at the clock overhead. A cook asks for her help, and she stops what she is doing to flip quickly through a binder and locate a recipe for him. Soon she is poking nervously at the custards again. Once service begins, however, she is calm and controlled. As orders start to come in, she acknowledges each one, then turns to begin deftly putting together the delicate plates. She picks up a pair of surgical tweezers to place a few fragile leaves around a thin swath of raw salmon, then turns to reach up and brown thick slices of brioche under the salamander. It's a familiar gesture for her, the upward reach followed by a quick rise on her toes to see if the product is warming properly; she did it nightly for months on end, heating strawberries stuffed with wasabi, taking the chill off the artichoke roses. But this time when an order comes, she no longer answers, *"Oído."* Instead, when her chef, Corey Lee, calls, "Two salmon, two monk," she answers in kind. "Two salmon, two monk."

While she was at elBulli, Emma was one of the least contented stagiaires. Before arriving, she had worked at the French Laundry, a restaurant that she loved and that had left her with the same dedication to exactitude for which Thomas Keller is known for. "If you can't find the time to do it right, when will you find the time to do it again?" she once wrote on her Facebook page, and the sentiment summed up her general attitude toward cooking. Asked what most impressed them about elBulli, the other stagiaires would invariably say, "The organization." But Emma disagreed. "Nothing is ever where it's supposed to be," she said one day back in July. "It's called mise en place for a reason." The comparative laxness wasn't the only thing that bothered her. Emma also disliked Ferran's relationship with his chefs and the fact that the stagiaires weren't necessarily exposed to everything going on in the kitchen; unlike at the Laundry, which draws up a curriculum for its apprentices, station assignments at elBulli were random, and a stagiaire might spend six months at the restaurant without ever learning, say, to spherify. Emma herself had never rotated through *cuarto frio* (that would have been awkward in any case, since she was dating its chef de partie), which meant that she never had the chance to work with some of the restaurant's most daring techniques. As late as October she complained, "I came here without any experience in molecular gastronomy, and I still feel like I don't have any." She was bored half the time and annoyed at not being given more responsibility. Sometimes she wondered why she had come.

To keep her mind occupied while she peeled pistachios or dipped rose petals at elBulli, Emma used to daydream about San Francisco: she would picture herself walking down the street, on her way to work in the new restaurant that Lee (her former chef de cuisine at the French Laundry) would be opening. Now that she is doing just that and Lee's Benu is the hottest debut of the 2010 season, she is mostly happy—both with her work (she runs *garde-manger*) and her new boss, with whom she has a close, if still deferential, relationship. But in the process of leaving Spain, getting a visa to work in the United States, breaking up with her boyfriend, Aitor, and helping to open the new restaurant, something has changed: Emma no longer looks at her time at elBulli with the same sense of frustration as before. "Just being in such a different environment and a legendary restaurant will always stay with me," she says. "The food really is mind-blowing, and there really is no other place like elBulli. I came back with so much more than what I arrived with."

Although Emma would confess that she felt a lot of stress during Benu's opening night (she was responsible for twelve dishes, and the béchamel custards weren't coming out right), she moved efficiently through the gleaming new kitchen, making none of the superfluous motions that betray a novice. Watching her, it was hard not to think that she was more assured, more skilled even, than just a year ago. Like almost everyone who spends time there, Emma had been changed by elBulli.

o o o

Once an ambitious young cook would go to France for his *stages* and then return home to begin laboring as a line cook in someone else's restaurant. But now that France is no longer the sole locus of serious cuisine, the whole world has opened up, and a chef in training may well choose to keep moving. These days, the young cooks of the world are a truly international class, traveling from country to country, restaurant to restaurant, in search of the newest technique, the most exciting kitchen, the best education, or, more practically, the highest-paying job. They meet, form friendships over work, then separate, only to run into each other again later in another kitchen in another place.

A year after they first came together in the glaring sunlight of Roses' boardwalk, elBulli's 2009 stagiaires have scattered back around the globe. Jorge Puerta, still bearing the scars of his hot oil burn, spent the first few months after the season ended helping his fellow stagiaire Txema Llamosas convert his parents' traditional restaurant in the Basque Country into something more modern (complete with airs and liquid nitrogen on the menu). He then left to work at a resort in St. Barts before returning home to Caracas, where he planned to open a gastropub. Txema, meanwhile, had bought a new space where he hoped to branch out on his own within a couple of years. Mizuho Nakamura, who had surprised everyone when she came in third at the ICEX competition, was back in Japan working at the highly acclaimed Ryugin in Tokyo but was also busy drawing up plans to open a Japanese tearoom—"I want it to be REAL Japanese," she wrote, "though with plated desserts"—in

Barcelona or New York. After he left elBulli, Frederico Ribeiro went to work for William Hickox, whom he had met earlier when the two *staged* together at Martín Berasategui in San Sebastián. Hickox had recently opened a Scottish gastropub called Highlands in New York's West Village, and Frederico soon worked his way up to executive sous chef. Less than a year later, he would help oversee the opening of Hickox's second restaurant, Mary Queen of Scots. Diego Corrado—the one Ferran referred to as "Messi"—was in Mexico City, advising a restaurant group. Sunny Jin was offered a position in New York but couldn't convince his wife to move there on a sous chef's salary; instead they went to Newberg, Oregon, where he became executive chef at Jory, a restaurant in the Allison Inn. César Bermúdez, the pastry cook, spent several months working at a hotel in Lugano, Switzerland, before signing on to work for one of Madrid's most important bakeries. Luca Balboni had returned to his family and girlfriend in Modena, Italy, and was running a catering company. When he wasn't consulting for restaurants in his native Galicia, Spain, Mike Álvarez was traveling around South America, learning about new products. And Perfecto, who had dropped out of his *stage* so early in the season to help Julian Serrano open his restaurant in Las Vegas? Perfecto quickly learned that he hated Vegas and moved to San Francisco instead, where he found work as chef de cuisine at the well-established restaurant Campton Place. But he didn't stay long; within a few months, he was working at Eric Ripert's four-star restaurant Le Bernardin, in New York. There too, he soon grew tired of the conditions—in that case, he says, it was the cold that bothered him—and, at the suggestion of a friend, put in a call to the Beverly Wilshire hotel in Los Angeles. "I called them up and said, 'If you want a good chef, someone who can make the restaurant run well, you should hire me,'" Perfecto recalls. He is now executive chef. A few months ago, he served breakfast to the visiting Barack Obama.

Three of the 2009 stagiaires stayed at elBulli, returning for the 2010 season as chefs de partie. Antonio Romero, who used to daydream at the center table about his nights out on the town, took over the meat station; Jacobo Astray, after spending the off-season working at Albert Adria's tapas bar Inopia, returned to oversee *cuarto frio*. And Roger Alcaraz, who struggled so hard in 2009 to master the demands and stress of being chef de partie when he was promoted to it as a stagiaire, was now running Starters II with the confidence of a veteran. The three of them were supposed to have been joined by two other repeaters. But Javi Izquierdo, who had made such a point of saying he didn't like elBulli's food, had apparently decided he didn't like preparing it either. And Gaël Vuilloud, who earlier in the year had been so excited to be returning to the restaurant where he had had to cut his *stage* short, had also changed his mind. In his case, his enthusiasm for working at elBulli was tempered when he learned that those hired for the 2010 season would also be expected to stay on for 2011, now that the two seasons would be running back-to-back. "It's one thing to be away from my job and my girlfriend for six months," he said. "But twelve? And for twelve hundred euros a month? I don't see how anyone who isn't from the area can do it."

A similar concern with finances led Kim and Dan to briefly consider taking jobs in Las Vegas. Prior to their *stage,* they had spent six months on the ICEX program, earning nothing while they slowly ate through their savings. "We need to make some money," Kim said as the season came to an end. "And that's a good place for it." But however much they could justify the move as an opportunity to work in some creative places (they were especially interested in the casual place that Pierre Gagnaire was opening), they still felt sheepish about considering Vegas, as if they were selling out the training they had just completed. In the end, they got lucky and avoided the possibility: each got a job in Napa Valley, Kim as sous chef at Meadowood and Dan as pastry sous chef at the French Laundry. For Kim, the new position was both daunting—she quickly had to learn to break down a pig, for example—and exciting, not least because Meadowood would earn its third Michelin star in October 2010. She especially liked the fact that the restaurant grew most of its own produce. "To go out first thing in the morning, when there's still mist on the fields and pick the vegetables you're going to be cooking with that day—there's nothing better than that," she said. They were both working five days a week, but most of the time their days off didn't coincide, so they saw each other only briefly in the morning before Kim left to start her shift or late at night when they both arrived home. Sometimes they had to rely on Facebook to communicate with each other.

As much as she had resisted leaving Europe, Andrea found herself surprisingly happy in Singapore. She became a line cook at the Michelin-starred Iggy's, the same place where her husband, Andrés, was working as pastry chef. She liked her bosses there and had enough responsibility and independence to feel that she was growing in the job. She had also begun to understand Andrés's love of Asia, and together they were considering staying there for an extended period of time. But in August 2010, their relationship took an abrupt turn for the worse, and soon Andrea was on a plane home to Colombia, where she would try to figure out her next step. "You think I felt lost when elBulli was about to end?" she wrote. "That was a joke compared to this. But one thing is for certain. I WILL BE COOKING." Sure enough, she was. By October, she had secured a position as line cook at noma.

For his part, Luke was still in Korea, waiting for the visa to come through that would allow him to return to Spain and take up the job that Andoni Luis Aduriz had promised him at Mugaritz. As for Katie, she received an abrupt education in the vagaries of starting a restaurant from scratch. When she began her *stage* at elBulli in June 2009, she had confidently predicted that the new place she would run with her parents, Ted and Liz, and her boyfriend, Felix, would be up and running by the spring of 2010. In fact, although her parents lived in New York and Felix in Los Angeles, they had all chosen to move to Asheville, North Carolina, in part because they believed the city's relative smallness and laid-back charm would diminish the hassles involved in buying property and starting a new business. But deals on the first two potential locations fell through, and it was only in June 2010 that they were able to close on a property: a former shop, perfectly located on Asheville's main street. They would have to put in a kitchen, and between problems with designers and the difficulties involved in meeting building standards, they still hadn't begun construction in August. Without money to support themselves, Katie and Felix were living with her parents, and although the house was beautiful and fairly ample, the close proximity, Felix admitted, "had caused some tensions." Samples of dishware lay stacked in the basement, and with no kitchen in the restaurant yet, Katie had to do all the recipe development at home. But they had found a talented Spanish sous chef who was looking for a way to move to the United States and were hopeful that they could find their place in the Asheville market. Katie had abandoned her earlier idea of cooking avant-garde cuisine and instead decided to specialize in straightforward Spanish food. They had also settled on a name for their new locale: Cúrate, which they thought worked nicely in both English (curate) and Spanish (heal yourself). Katie hoped they would be open by the end of the year.

Most of the stagiaires, then, had already received the most immediate benefit of a stint at elBulli—they had gone on to good jobs, and their reputations would continue to reap the benefit of their association with the restaurant for as long as they remained in the field. Katie put it best: "I feel like, having been through elBulli, I'm on the fast track now."

But what else? Did they get what they had come for? Even before a year had passed since the end of their *stages*, many of the former apprentices were able to reflect on the less tangible impacts those months at elBulli had had. For the few who had arrived with little experience, the *stage* had been their first trial by fire. Asked what the experience meant to him, Sergi Palacín, the young cook with the nipple ring, proudly recalls what Oriol said to him on his last day: You came here as a boy, but you left as a chef. "And that," says Sergi, "pretty much defines my time in Roses."

Others learned what they did not want to do. Cesare Marazzi, one of the three stagiaires who had left elBulli just weeks into his *stage*, had taken a position as chef de cuisine in a small inn in the Italian Alps, where foragers brought him wild mushrooms they had collected that morning in the woods and shepherds brought their homemade cheeses. "When I tell people about dishes like the Easter Egg that I made at elBulli and how I had to use a syringe to fill a balloon with coconut milk and blow it up, then spin it in liquid nitrogen," he recalls, "they look at me like I was crazy. But I learned that a kitchen as frenetic as that is not for me and that I want to work in a more relaxed way." Nico, who had gone on to *stage* first at the Alicia Foundation and then at Paco Roncero's Terraza del Casino in Madrid, was still ruffled by the way he had been treated. But he was trying to make peace with it. "That the experience only lasts six months, and after that you can't continue to be bitter," he says. "In the future, I want the option to keep working in a place."

Some of the stagiaires garnered positive lessons they expected to use in the future. Those were less about individual dishes—for all of elBulli's fame as a place of spectacular techniques, few of the stagiaires felt changed by the methods they had acquired—than about overarching structures and approaches to food. "Organization," responded at least a dozen of the apprentices when asked what they would take with them. Despite the difficulties many of them had had in forging themselves into a machine, most had come to see a certain beauty in elBulli's form of production. Daniel, who, among all the stagiaires, had secured one of the more prestigious jobs as pastry sous chef at the French Laundry, was especially thoughtful. "The organization of European restaurants is different than restaurants in America," he said. "Here we breed the individual, there they breed the team. Believe it or not, I actually miss elBulli."

Others were left with a new sense of their own abilities. Andrea, once so cautious in the kitchen, was astonished to find herself inventing new dishes—dishes good enough to make it onto Iggy's menu. "Three or four of them," she says with wonder in her voice. "They're on the menu now. If before elBulli you had told me I would be creative in that way, I never would have believed you." Meanwhile Luke, though still enamored of great chefs, had come to think of his discipleship as a discrete period of time—one it might be time to leave behind. "I think I'm ready for a real job, not a *stage*," he says. "A real job with pay."

Katie still didn't have full confidence in her abilities. Asked where she'd like to be in fifteen years, she answers, "I'd like to be comfortable calling myself a chef." But she has come a long way. "I learned about endurance, I learned to work with other people, and I learned what makes a great dish," she says. "I'll never forget Mateu telling me not to get too complicated—include only one element in a dish that's surprising, and leave the rest alone." She pauses and gestures toward the empty storefront that will, one day soon, house her first restaurant. "I know I wouldn't be here without my experience at elBulli. It made me feel like I can do anything."

Font of approval and disciplined object of a quest; source of nurture and a staging ground for artistry; a place to prove oneself and make oneself stand out—food became all this, to differing degrees, for the stagiaires of the 2009 season. And there was one other thing that nearly all took with them: gratitude for elBulli's family meals. "Those were the best staff meals of anyplace I've staged," says Nico, who has staged in quite a few. Emma agrees. "Those noodles? The food was so good!" she gushes. "If I learned one thing, it's the difference a good family meal can make."

o o o

The stagiaires weren't the only ones changed by the 2009 season. Ferran may have known even before the season opened that he would be reinventing elBulli, but it wasn't until he was halfway through the season that the reinvention began to take concrete shape. Indeed, when he finally announced at Madrid Fusion that he would be closing the restaurant and reopening it two years later as a foundation, it quickly became clear that many of the crucial details had yet to be hammered out. He initially referred to the future enterprise as an "academy," which had many media outlets running stories about how he was going to open a cooking school. But what Ferran had in mind was closer to a think tank. "This is about creativity more than cooking," he said. "We're not going to be teaching anyone how to break down a cod."

The main question on everyone's mind remained unresolved: would there be anything to eat? Ferran was adamant that elBulli would no longer be a restaurant, but he was just as clear that it would still feed people. What he and Juli hadn't figured out yet was how. They briefly entertained the idea of only opening for charity events, before Ferran remembered that he really wanted some form of feedback for the research that was under way. He thought of opening for a couple months each year and offering limited dinners that would allow invitees to sample the fruits of the fellows' research, but that, he thought, might seem too much like the present elBulli. He thought about inviting just a single table each night but worried that that would be too elitist. He thought of inviting the press to impromptu tastings and of opening for breakfast. For a while, he was certain that the foundation would serve roughly sixty meals a year in the formal style of, well, a restaurant, but that too seems to have come up for revision. These days, Ferran will say only that they won't decide for sure until 2013.

Many other pieces of the plan have fallen into place, however. The foundation will award fellowships annually to twenty or so young cooks so that they can spend a year working with elBulli's permanent staff (all of whom have been invited to stay on), investigating new techniques and developing new flavors. Discussions led by prominent visiting chefs and leaders in the worlds of art and design will complement their research. Each year, the foundation will release a book and video that catalogue that year's discoveries, and every night, it will post the results of that day's experiments online. To accommodate these new endeavors, elBulli will expand its physical structure. Although the sleek kitchen and homely dining room will remain untouched, Ferran and Juli have already met with architects to draw up plans for an audiovisual room, a library, and a new outdoor space. All this with a very specific goal in mind: "Our dream," says Ferran, "is that each year, we'll turn out one or two chefs who will be extremely important for the future of cuisine."

Now that he and Juli have decided on a closing date for the restaurant—they will run the two remaining seasons back-to-back, so that the final service will fall on July 30, 2011—Ferran is absolutely percolating with ideas. The foundation will have its own garden and a museum. It will press its own oil. The experimental kitchen will be open to any chef who wants to use it; if Grant Achatz and Andoni Aduriz want to come, they are invited to take any ideas they discover there and apply them at home. They will start a social network too and launch a kind of world creativity team that will travel the globe, spreading ideas. "I don't have money to give away," says Ferran. "But I can give away what I do have, which is my creativity."

That creativity is not confined to the foundation. Ferran and his brother, Albert, have begun work on a new tapas bar in Barcelona that will combine the conviviality of Inopia with the creativity and theatricality of elBulli. If it succeeds (and how could it not?), they might try to expand to other cities around the world. There is talk of turning the Harvard course into a permanent collaboration. Governments and corporations alike are approaching Ferran with offers of sponsorships and requests for projects he would like to launch. There are also simpler goals: to spend more time with his family, to be able to travel for pleasure with his wife, Isabel. "You know what else I'm going to do with the time off?" he says one day. "I'm going to learn English."

There is one other change as well. For all the care it takes in documenting its creations, elBulli has never kept very close track of the individuals who have come through its kitchen. Certainly the staff knows and maintains regular contact with the Spanish cooks who worked for years as employees, just as they certainly know which cooks have gone on to make big names for themselves. But the rest? The hundreds, if not thousands, of former apprentices who might today be running their own restaurants or toiling in someone else's in Boston or Bangkok or Brussels? Asked for a list of stagiaires from even five years ago, Marc was at a loss—he simply didn't compile that kind of information. But now there are signs that Ferran is beginning to think differently. In the summer of 2010, elBulli posted a notice on its website, asking former stagiaires to send the restaurant details of their careers to date for a database it plans to compile.

As the restaurant nears its final service, Ferran is adjusting his understanding of his contribution to culinary history. Until now he always thought that it lay in the techniques he has invented and even more in the philosophy that has guided him. But maybe, he sees now, his true legacy lies with the people he has trained who have, in turn, helped make elBulli what it is. Perhaps it lies with is stagiaires.

o o o

On opening night of the 2010 season, I went back to elBulli. By then the closing date had already been set, and the new group of stagiaires had been invited to work the two back-to-back seasons. Some had declined the offer, but most had not, and so the young men and women working tensely at the center table that night comprised elBulli's last real batch of stagiaires. As I stood there watching, I was struck by an overwhelming sense of déjà vu: clearly, I had been here before. There was Eugeni, snapping at one stagiaire for overloading a tray he was carrying to the *plonge*, and there was Eduard, instructing another in the finer points of sweeping. At the center table, the ingredients and faces had changed, but the actions remained the same, right down to the collective flinch that went down the line when, at exactly 7:30 P.M., Ferran said, "*Señores*, let's begin."

But there was one noticeable difference. The stagiaires were as nervous as ever, fumbling into one another as they awkwardly tried, on this first night, to figure out where they should be. But the permanent crew, from Ferran on down, were noticeably calmer. Ferran shouted at the kitchen to quiet down a few times, but otherwise he was in a jovial mood. Oriol and Eduard were also relaxed, even managing to smile at each other even when a stagiaire did a particularly stupid thing. As I watched the customers come into the kitchen, table by table, and watched Ferran greet them warmly (the first table of the night was American; once again, the last was Ansón and his family), I was reminded of a night a few months earlier when I was in London, attending the awards ceremony of the S.Pellegrino World's 50 Best Restaurants. As the announcer reached the final two places on the list, a gasp went through the room: for the first time in four years, elBulli had fallen to second place, beat out of the top slot by noma. As René Redzepi and his crew joyfully took the stage to receive the award, a food journalist seated next to me asked me how I thought Ferran had taken the news. "I think there's some nostalgia there," I answered. "But mostly, I think he's delighted." It was true. I had seen Ferran earlier in the day, soon after he'd learned the results, and instead of disappointed, he'd seemed absolutely ebullient. I commented on his surprising response to his wife, Isabel. "Don't you see?" she asked. "He's been set free."

Ezra Pound, he of the "Make it new!" dictum, also wrote, "The artist is always beginning." In the twenty-five years that he has been at elBulli, Ferran has had innumerable beginnings. There are the actual ones: the ones that the arrival of each year's new batch of apprentice cooks mark. There are historical ones: the time they stopped serving two meals a day, the time they invented foam. And then there is the beginning that Ferran himself represents, the one that guarantees his place in the history of cuisine and that, not incidentally, explains why so many young cooks want to learn from him, and why so many who have had that opportunity go on to share his passion. The beginning that says: food can be whatever you imagine it to be.

A friend once said to me that a truly great restaurant is always about something more than what it serves. ElBulli is about change.

KITCHEN
Ferran Adrià, executive chef and co-owner

CHEFS DE CUISINE
Oriol Castro
Eduard Xatruch (pronounced sha-TROOK)
Mateu Casañas

JEFE DE PRODUCCIÓN
Eugeni de Diego

CHEFS DE PARTIE
Luis Arrufat
Toni Moraga
Aitor Zabala
Pablo Pavón
Anthony Masas
Sergio Barroso
Andrés Conde

KITCHEN STAGIAIRES
Roger Alcaraz
Mike Álvarez
Jacobo Astray
Luca Balboni
Nicolas Bejarano
César Bermúdez

FRONT OF HOUSE
Juli Soler, co-owner

FRONT OF HOUSE DIRECTORS
Lluís García
Lluís Biosca

SOMMELIERS
Ferran Centelles
David Seijas

MAÎTRE D'HÔTES
David López
Pol Perelló
Xus Gónzalez

STAFF COORDINATORS
Marga Fuentes
Débora Sánchez

DINING ROOM STAGIAIRES
Julio Barluenga
Natzarí Canals
Erik Alejandro De Anda
Marta Farré
Arantxa Fernández
Victor García

Katie Button
Eduardo Carmona
Diego Corrado
Andrea Correa
Kimberly Floresca
Luis "Lucho" Frey
Alfonso Gómez
Laia Guinó
Javier Izquierdo
Myungsan "Luke" Jang
Sungho "Sunny" Jin
Emmanuelle Leftick
Txema Llamosas
Pablo Martín
Begoña Martínez
Cesare Marazzi
Lorenzo Melchiorre
Juan Pablo Mellado
Mizuho Nakamura
Sergi Palacín
José Luis Parra
Miguel Alexander Pérez
Jorge Puerta
Daniel Ryan
Frederico Ribeiro
Perfecto Rocher
Antonio Romero
Iosu Sainz
Ralph Schelling
Gabriel Vidolin
Gaël Vuilloud

Daniel González
Hugo González
Diana Ilincic
David Rius
Mauricio Rodríguez
Carles Ros
Rita Soler
Adam Torrent
Manel Vehí

The label "genius" is applied so regularly to Ferran Adrià that it is worth recalling the word's origins. Long before it referred to a person with extraordinary intellectual or creative ability, "genius" signaled a kind of guardian spirit—sometimes benevolent, sometimes mischevious—who wielded an often disproportionate influence over his charge. The addition of this second, earlier definition seems to me to resolve any doubt over whether the word can in fact be applied to a cook; for, if we consider cuisine to be the charge in question, and then Ferran clearly qualifies as its instigator and protector. Add it to his unique creativity, and both meanings are united.

But this book is not about Adrià's genius, or at least not primarily. As I explained to him when I first brought up the possibility of this book, I wanted to write about the human side of elBulli. He not only bravely agreed to the prospect but was and continues to be consistently enthusiastic about it, granting me full access to him, his staff, and his kitchen. That access—in the end I spent about seventy days in the kitchen—meant that I witnessed not only the fascinating techniques, precise organization, and spectacular dishes for which he is deservedly renowned but the foibles and occasional failures as well. The portrait of him that emerges is based in part on the perspective of those who work for him, and is therefore necessarily more complicated than often seen. But I hope it is no less admiring; in addition to convincing me of his genius, the time I spent at elBulli revealed to me the great depth of Ferran's intelligence and courage. I am truly grateful to him.

Everyone on the permanent staff at elBulli is so good at what he or she does that each of them qualifies for the label of genius in his or her own right. The multitalented Marc Cuspinera has been unfailingly helpful to me throughout the process of writing this book—from the beginning, when he sent me that first, tentative list of 2009 stagiaires, until just last week, when we filled in a few more blanks in the long history of elBulli's personnel. So exceptional is the work of Oriol Castro, Eduard Xatruch, and Mateu Casañas that none could ever receive the recognition he deserves, but I'd like to try to start here. On more than one occasion, each of them has made me wonder how it is that a single kitchen could compile such remarkable talent. Juli Soler, elBulli's co-owner and all-around good guy, and the two Lluíses (Biosca and the astonishingly gracious García) persuaded me that the front of the house is touched by its own genius. And everyone, front or back, including Marga Fuentes, Débora Sánchez, and Eugeni de Diego not only generously tolerated my presence and answered my questions patiently but made me feel part of the elBulli family. Perhaps no one more than the sommeliers and maître d's with whom I, with great good luck, was assigned a seat at family meal: Pol Perelló, Ferran Centelles, David Seijas, and David López.

I'm not sure what the thirty-two stagiaires who showed up at Si Us Plau on June 10 thought of me at that initial encounter—I suspect that, with so many other new things to learn, they barely noticed me at all. But over the course of the season, they kindly accepted my interest in everything from their knife skills to their sex lives, and opened themselves up to what were, I'm sure, at times annoying questions. Some of them risked getting in trouble to show me a particular technique, and many of them forwent an extra hour of sleep to meet me for early morning coffee and interviews at Sant Pau. Without exception, each of them has impressed me with his or her dedication and passion, and I know that I will be following what are sure to be their exciting careers for a long time to come.

In the course of this research, a number of chefs were kind enough to talk to me about their own experiences as either stagiaires or the bosses of stagiaires: Andoni Luis Aduriz, Juan Mari Arzak, Mario Batali, Claude Bosi, Daniel Boulud, David Chang, Roberto González, Thomas Keller, Denis Martin, Josean Martínez Alija, Nuno Mendes, Paco Morales, Daniel Patterson, René Redzepi, Paco Roncero, and Pedro Subijana. Dan Barber went further than any of them, not only sharing his own memories and vast knowledge of the culinary world but providing a source of inspiration for which I still don't thank him enough.

I owe much to my editor Leslie Meredith for her enthusiasm in this project before it had been drafted and her insight and advice after. Like her assistant, Donna Loffredo, she has helped make the end product markedly better. To David Black, my agent, I am tremendously grateful for both his convivial encouragement and his clear-sighted direction. Andrew Friedman has been both colleague and good friend, generously sharing with me not only some crucial contacts and ideas but, as the accomplished author he is, providing me with some much needed perspective on the daunting process of getting an idea into print.

I'd also like to thank my colleagues, past and present, at *Time* magazine. Although I've set foot only once in that office on Sixth Avenue, they have made this freelancer feel a valued part of a great institution. I've had such exceptionally good luck in editors that I've begun to suspect that, like elBulli itself, the magazine has a genius for attracting talent. In particular, I'd like to thank James Graff, Simon Robinson, Jumana Farouky, and fellow elBulli *aficionado*, Howard Chua-Eoan for their encouragement and support.

Over the many years I've known Geoff Pingree, he has consistently believed in me; this book owes much to that faith. I'm also grateful to my siblings, Emily Piassick and Andy Abend, and my parents, to whom this book is dedicated, for the opportunities they created for me and the loving support they continue to give.

Lastly, I'd like to thank Victoria Burnett, who not only came up with this book's title but acted as enthusiastic cheerleader in the early days of its germination. Mary Alice Hurvitt has provided decades of friendship and one much needed respite with her lovely family. Amy Serafin was my other great discovery of 2009—a new and lasting friend who, at the last, critical moment, also revealed herself to be an expert editor. And Carolyn Fraser has been many things: soother of nerves, font of ideas, tireless listener, adventurous travel companion, source of much laughter. A woman couldn't ask for better friends.

NOTE: Italic page numbers refer to picture captions.

Abellán, Carles, 229

Achatz, Grant, 6, 107, 132, 161, 260, 272

Aco, Rick, 203

Ad Hoc (Napa Valley restaurant), 211

Adriá, Albert, 50, 73, 81, 169, 224, 231, 238, 260, 266–67, 273

Adriá, Ferran: advice to stagiaires by, 260; Almodóvar compared with, 176–77; anger/shouting of, 121–22, 123–24, 157; appearance of, 18–19, 182; as artist, 189–90, 191; backlash against, 180–83; biography of, 77; chair of, 119–20, 156; closing of elBulli by, 1–2, 271–73, 274; contribution to culinary history of, 273–75; creation of new dishes and, 141–49; creativity of, 3–4, 43; culinary evolution/transformation of, 175, 190; culinary tours of, 106, 143; defense of elBulli by, 186–92; endorsements by, 234–35, 251; expansion of public role of, 251; fame/reputation of, 1–2, 3, 5, 78, 105–6, 141, 190, 229, 234–35, 250–51; as genius, 191; goals of, 163, 271–73; greeting of diners by, 93–94, 93, 274; hierarchy and, 21, 22, 23, 118, 119–20; home of, 205; initial attraction of cooking for, 77; introduction to new stagiaires by, 17, 18–20; legacy of, 273; memory of, 75, 125; new vocabulary and language

for cooking and, 3; opening day of 2009 season and, 49–50; pencil of, 46; personal life of, 273; personal and professional background of, 74–75, 82–83, 175; personality of, 20–21, 44, 77; pictures of, 5, 113; pressures to innovate on, 141; quality emphasis of, 186–87; reputation of Spanish food and, 12; as revolutionary, 176–77; role models for, 233; Santamaria's criticisms of, 43–44; science and, 190; self-image of, 190; staff photo and, 132; *stage* with Figueras of, 153–54; as stagiaire at elBulli, 69, 75; stagiaires views about, 157. *See also specific person or topic*

Aduriz, Andoni Luis, 6, 112, 132, 191, 209, 254, 268, 272

agar-agar, 128, 135, 147, 235

Alcaraz, Roger (kitchen stagiaire): ambitions of, 249–50; appearance of, 236; daydreaming of, 244; Eduard and, 235–36, 244, 245; Eugeni and, 244–45, 249; Ferran's relationship with, 244; first staff meeting for, 18; first week of training for, 38; Laia's relationship with, 58, 133, 244; last service of 2009 season and, 256, 257, 258; leadership abilities of, 249; media interview of, 229–30; mistakes of, 245; opening of 2009 season and,

54; Oriol's compliments about, 244; personal life of, 58, 133, 243, 244; personal and professional background of, 18, 235–37, 241–42; picture of, 230; post-stagiaire plans of, 200, 231, 249–50, 254, 267; promotion for, 245, 247–50, 267; reflections about elBulli of, 244; responsibilities of, 245, 247–50; Starters I assignment for, 37; Starters II assignment of, 229–30, 247–50, 267; stress of, 230, 231, 247–50, 254; work ethic of, 244

Alicia Foundation, 190, 270

Alinea (Chicago restaurant), 14, 42, 107, 161, 208

Almodóvar, Pedro, 176–77

Álvarez, Mike (kitchen stagiaire), 30, 38, 83, 258, 266

American Café (Atlanta restaurant), 149

Andrés, José, 18, 20–21, 69, 70–71, 74, 125, 132, 199, 219

Andrews, Colman, 77

Ansón, Rafael, 45, 51, 63, 255, 274

Arola, Sergi, 181, 241

Arora, Saurabh (kitchen stagiaire), 170

Arrufat, Luis (chef de partie): at Café Atlántico, 70; first 2009 staff meeting and, 18; first day of training for 2009 stagiaires and, 26; as floating chef de partie, 218, 243; guests visits to kitchen and, 93, 94; Kim's relationship with, 217–18; leave of absence of, 216–17; as Mateu's assistant, 231, 243; Nico as assistant to, 216; opening day of 2009 season and, 49, 54; quemo use by, 10; station assignments for stagiaires and, 37

artichoke rose, 5, 65–66, 65, 111, 131, 143, 152, 169, 184, 243, 257

Arzak, Juan Mari, 4, 66, 238, 239–40

Arzak (San Sebastián restaurant), 18, 28

asparagus canapé, 29, 144

Astray, Jacobo (kitchen stagiaire), 53, 152, 200, 231, 243, 250, 256, 258, 266–67

Atherton, Jason, 132

Auberge de Vouvry (Switzerland restaurant), 173–74, 175

Balboni, Luca (kitchen stagiaire): development of new dishes and, 162; discontent of, 134; doubts about returning to elBulli of, 242; first staff meeting of 2009 for, 18; Kim—Dan relationship comment of, 224; personal life of, 218–19; personal and professional background of, 18, 79; personality of, 170; post-stagiaire activities of, 266; return of, 170; tasting complaint of, 85; Thanksgiving celebration and, 225, 227; tiramisù of, 193; views about stage at elBulli of, 12

Barber, Dan, 12, 72, 108–9, 125

Barceló, Miquel, 155

Barroso, Sergio (chef de partie), 18, 37, 52, 221, 245, 257

Batali, Mario, 72–73, 250

The Bazaar (Los Angeles restaurant), 18, 74

Bejarano, Nicolas "Nico" (kitchen stagiaire): ambitions of, 232, 250; creativity class comments of, 162; Eduard—stagiaires relationship comment of, 215; final days of 2009 season and, 252; first day of training for, 28–29; food/cooking views of, 191; Kim and, 216, 217, 218, 232, 256; last service of 2009 season and, 256; as Luis's assistant, 216; motivations for coming to elBulli of, 30; personal and professional background of, 28–29; personality of, 216; post-stagiaire plans of, 200, 232; reflections about elBulli of, 232, 269–70, 271; sauce preparation by, 195; Starters I assignment of, 37, 216, 217, 218, 232, 236; tasting complaint of, 85

bell jar recipe, Katie's, 86–88

Benno, Jonathan, 117–18

Benu (San Francisco restaurant), 264, 265

Berasategui, Martín, 28, 153, 204, 266

Bermúdez, César (kitchen stagiaire), 79, 81–82, 123, 161, 171, 227, 228, 243, 252, 266

Beverly Wilshire Hotel (Los Angeles), 266

Biko (Mexico City restaurant), 18

Blanc, Georges, 82

Blue Hill (New York City restaurant), 12

Blumenthal, Heston, 106, 168

Bocuse, Paul, 233

Bocuse d'Or contest, 174, 223, 241

Boqueria market (Barcelona), 3, 46, 101, 187, 225, 236

Bosch, Eduard "Lalo," 101, 154

Bosi, Claude, 125

Bottura, Massimo, 6, 18, 160, 181

Boulanger, M., 77

Boulud, Daniel, 107–8

Bourdain, Anthony, 75–76, 77, 78, 163

Braendle, Martial, 174, 177

Bras, Michel, 106

Broadmoor Hotel (Denver), 203, 208, 220

Buckhead Dinner (Atlanta restaurant), 149–50

Buford, Bill, 148

Bukhara (New Delhi restaurant), 105

Button, Katie (kitchen stagiaire): ambitions of, 61, 86; barbecue sauce of, 193; bell jar recipe of, 86–88; creativity of, 86–88, 99; crisis of faith of, 61–62; culture at elBulli and, 79; Felix's relationship with, 70, 74, 79, 88, 134, 219, 253, 268; final days of 2009 season of, 237, 256, 258, 259; first staff meeting of 2009 for, 18; group photo and, 134; hierarchy and, 86, 117; Iuzzini stage of, 73–74; last service of 2009 season and, 256, 258; Mateu as teacher of, 55–56, 80, 81, 82, 85, 86, 87, 221; Mateu's advice to, 270–71; motivations of, 62; notebook of, 85; opening day of 2009 season and, 48; pastry focus of, 73; personal and professional background of, 18, 55, 60–62, 67–68, 69–70, 79, 85; personality of, 85–86, 88, 135, 259; picture of, 57; plan of, 71–72, 73; post-elBulli plans/activities of, 88, 134, 171, 253, 268–69; quemo use by, 10; reflections about elBulli of, 269, 270–71; relationships among stagiaires and, 85, 102, 216; self-doubts of, 88, 270; serving stage at elBulli of, 70–72; sexism and, 221; stress of, 219; Thanksgiving

celebration and, 225, 227, 228; wedding plans of, 134–35, 171, 219, 253

Button, Liz, 61, 67, 68, 87, 88, 134, 171, 219, 268

Button, Ted, 60, 61, 62, 88, 268

Café Atlántico (Washington, D.C. restaurant), 62, 69–70

Campton Place (San Francisco restaurant), 266

Can Fabes (Barcelona restaurant), 180

Can Jubany (Barcelona restaurant), 238

Capelli, Mauro, 173

Carême, Marie-Antoine, 77, 189

Carmona, Eduardo (kitchen stagiaire), 133, 137, 247–48, 249

Casañas, Mateu (chef de cuisine): Andrea's missing notebook and, 246; César's relationship with, 243; as chef de cuisine of pastry, 7, 18, 21, 80, 81, 99; creativity class and, 161; creativity of stagiaires and, 86; documentary about elBulli and, 41; family life of, 204; Ferran and, 119, 122–23, 124, 206, 259–60; first staff meeting of 2009 and, 18; hierarchy and, 21, 23, 119, 120; Japanese visitors and, 198; Katie and, 55–56, 80, 81, 82, 85, 86, 87, 221, 270; last service of 2009 and, 258; Luis as assistant to, 231; morale of, 171; motivations for becoming chef of, 7; new dishes and, 199; opening day of 2009 and, 47, 48, 49, 50, 52; pañuelo of, 87–88; personal life of, 81; personal and professional background of, 80–81, 154; picture of, 80; reputation of, 206; responsibilities of, 21; at staff party, 259–60; stagiaires' relationship with, 117–18; tasting by, 84; as teacher, 81–82; Thanksgiving celebration and, 225, 227

Castells, Pere, 190

Castro, Oriol (chef de cuisine): ambitions of, 185; Andrea as assistant to, 38, 130–31, 135–36, 148, 157–58, 164, 165, 243, 245–47; Andrea's missing notebook and, 245–47; appearance of, 153; authority of, 10–11; as chef de cuisine, 21, 154; creativity class and, 161, 162; creativity of stagiaires and, 86; cuisine as passion of, 156; culture at elBulli and, 119; dinner guests visits to kitchen and, 93; documentary about elBulli and, 41; Eduard's relationship with, 40, 154, 155; elBulli living conditions for, 205; Eugeni–Gaël contest and, 184; Eugeni–Miso relationship and, 252; family life of, 204–5; Ferran and, 119–20, 124, 153, 154, 155–56, 164–65, 204, 206, 260; final days of 2009 season and, 252; first staff meeting of 2009 and, 18, 20; first week of training for stagiaires and, 23–24, 25, 26, 32, 38–39, 40, 41; Gaël and, 185, 194, 242; health care at elBulli and, 171; hierarchy and, 21, 23, 119, 120; illness of, 158, 219; Jorge's burning accident and, 137; July training of stagiaires by, 58; Katie's bell jar and, 87; Kim and, 118, 197, 215, 217, 221, 222; last day of 2009 season and, 259; last service of 2009 and, 258; as Luke's role model, 127; missing spoons and, 46; new dishes and, 65, 136, 142, 143, 144, 146, 148, 152–53, 154–56, 158, 164, 193, 199–200, 217, 257; notebooks of, 152, 200; opening of 2009 season and, 45, 46, 47, 48, 50, 52–53, 54; opening of 2010 season and, 274; personal life of, 155, 156, 204–5, 219; personal and professional background of, 153–54; personality of, 136, 154, 155; Petroleum dish and, 130; pictures of, 17, 156; plating demonstrations by, 38; pressures on, 159; reputation of, 206; responsibilities of, 1, 21, 40, 185, 199–200; Roger and, 235–36, 244; as role model for stagiaires, 154; sacrifices of, 204–6; salary for, 206; Sergi's reflections on advice from, 269; staff meetings and, 90; at staff party, 258; as stagiaire at elBulli, 154; stagiaires relationship with, 117–18, 154, 198, 214; tasting by, 84; Thanksgiving celebration

and, 226–27; visitors to kitchen and, 198, 238, 240
catalogue, elBulli, 153, 199–200, 238
center table, elBulli: artichoke rose preparation at, 66; assignment of stagiaires and, 37; characteristics of good stagiaires and, 59; Eduard's responsibilities and, 215; Eugeni's responsibilities for, 133; Ferran's defense of technology and, 183; former stagiaires return to, 204; Gaël at, 183; Luke's assignment at, 112, 126; opening of 2010 season and, 274; picture of, 36; responsibilities of stagiaires at, 38, 47, 245; Roger and, 245, 249, 250; rules for, 170; stagiaire relationships at, 115, 197, 243–44, 249; visiting chefs at, 198
Chang, David, 66, 117, 123, 188, 250–51
Charlie Trotter's (Chicago restaurant), 151
chefs de cuisine, 21, 22, 43, 117–18, 132. *See also specific person*
chefs de partie: aprons for, 22; Gaël applies for position as elBulli, 184–85, 194; hierarchy and, 22; opening day at elBulli and, 46; post-elBulli plans of, 231; staff photo and, 132; stagiaires applications for, 200; stagiaires assignments and, 37; stagiaires relationships with, 118; tasting by, 84; two 2009 stagiaires returning in 2010 as, 266–67. *See also specific person*
Child, Julia, 67, 68
chocolates, elBulli, 13, 53, 82, 92, 94, 99, 199, 237, 258
cocktails, 45, 47, 50, 63–64, 199, 223, 257
Cold station (*cuarto frío*): Aitor at, 10, 256; as desirable assignment for stagiaires, 36–37, 58; first serving day of 2009 season and, 50, 53, 54; Jacobo as chef de partie for, 243, 266–67; July training of stagiaires and, 66; new dishes at, 162; opening day of 2009 season and, 50, 53, 54; stagiaires assignments and, 37, 58, 264; stagiaires relationships at, 157
Colicchio, Tom, 204

Comerç 24 (Barcelona restaurant), 29
Conde, Andrés (chef de partie), 18, 243
cooking: aesthetics of, 151–52; as art
    form, 189–90, 192; discipleship
    in, 107–8; as "feminine" craft, 220;
    as form of self-expression, 192;
    payment/salary for, 7; philosophical
    approach to elBulli, 83; science and,
    3; status of, 7, 72–73; vocabulary
    and language for, 3. See also cuisine;
    food; specific dish
cooking contests, 96–97, 128, 174–75,
    222–24, 265. See also Junior
    Culinary Olympics
cooks. See chefs/cooks; specific person
Corrado, Diego (kitchen stagiaire):
    Andrea's missing notebook and,
    247; appearance of, 197; chefs
    de cuisine–stagiaire relationship
    comment of, 118; creativity class
    comments of, 162; early departure of
    stagiaires and, 133; family meals and,
    210; Ferran's relationship with, 124;
    first week of training for, 23, 27, 28,
    38, 41; last day of 2009 service for,
    257; opening day at elBulli and, 54;
    post-stagiaire activities of, 200, 266;
    rules of elBulli and, 197; station
    assignments and, 103; visitors to
    kitchen and, 240
Correa, Andrea (kitchen stagiaire):
    accepted as elBulli stagiaire, 152;
    Albert's birthday celebration and,
    169; ambitions of, 149, 150; Andrés
    relationship with, 135, 151, 219, 268;
    appearance of, 135; creativity class
    comments of, 161–62; creativity
    of, 135, 158–59, 270; crying in the
    kitchen by, 221; feelings about
    elBulli of, 131, 135, 157, 160, 163–64;
    Ferran's work with, 158–59; final
    days at elBulli of, 237; first staff
    meeting of 2009 and, 17, 18; first
    week of training for, 26, 28, 37–38;
    front-house work of, 243, 257;
    notebook of, 130, 159, 245–47;
    opening day of 2009 season and,
    52; as Oriol's assistant, 38, 130–31,
    135–36, 148, 157–58, 164, 165,
    243; personal and professional
    background of, 18, 136–37, 139–40,

149–52; personality of, 136; pictures
    of, 132, 156, 258; post-elBulli plans/
    activities of, 200–201, 243, 254, 268,
    270; reaction to elBulli documentary
    by, 42; Redzepi and, 123, 151;
    reflections on elBulli of, 270;
    responsibilities of, 157–58, 159, 243;
    self-doubts of, 131; self-image of, 135;
    sexism and, 221; at staff party, 258;
    stagiaires relationships and, 102,
    133, 159, 164; station assignment
    for, 37–38; views about Ferran of,
    163–64
creativity: codification of, 141;
    comparison of Ferran and
    Almodóvar and, 176–77;
    development of new dishes and,
    141–49; and elBulli change from
    restaurant to foundation, 271–73;
    Ferran's advice to Luke about, 106;
    Ferran's businesslike approach to,
    141–42; Ferran's class for stagiaires
    about, 160–63; Ferran's views about,
    131, 141, 152, 186–92; sources of new
    ingredients and, 142; technology
    and, 141–42; trial and error process
    in, 146–47
cuisine: avant-garde, 152, 163, 178, 179,
    180, 181, 182, 186, 191, 208, 241,
    253, 269; classic French, 75, 82–83,
    180, 182; history of, 7, 176, 273, 275;
    nouvelle, 69, 83, 175, 182; of product
    versus elaboration, 188; Spanish,
    181, 191, 269
Culinary Institute of America, 6, 84,
    150, 220
Cuspinera, Marc (permanent staff
    member): advice to Katie of,
    270–71; as chef de cuisine at elBulli,
    13; database of past and present
    associates and, 273; early departures
    of stagiaires and, 58, 59; as elBulli
    stagiaire, 14, 28; elBulli's reputation
    and, 43; first day for stagiaires and,
    15–16, 17, 19; first week of training
    for stagiaires and, 35, 37; Gaël and,
    242, 254; institutional memory of,
    43; Iosu's departure and, 242; Jorge's
    burning accident and, 138; last day
    of 2009 season and, 259; Luke and,
    112, 127–28, 231, 232; opening day

of 2009 season and, 50, 53; personal
and professional background of, 154;
personality of, 14; responsibilities
of, 13–14, 238; rocks at elBulli and,
28; as role model, 127; selection
of stagiaires and, 14–15, 112; staff
meeting and, 255; staff photo and,
132; as *stage* program head, 13–14, 116,
122; stagiaires assignments and, 37;
stagiaires relationship with, 14, 116

Dacosta, Quique, 132, 199
database, elBulli, 63, 273
Dawes, Gerry, 12
A Day at elBulli (documentary), 41–42, 235
Die Schwarzwaldstube (German
restaurant), 105
Diego, Eugeni de (jefe de producción):
demonstrations by, 31–32, 33, 34–35,
40; Emma and, 116, 170; family
meals and, 212–13, 255; Ferran's
comments about, 116, 259; first staff
meeting of 2009 and, 18; first week
of training for stagiaires and, 24–25,
26, 32, 33, 34–35, 39, 40; Gaël and,
166, 183–84, 193; hierarchy and, 21–
22, 116; Jorge's burning accident and,
137, 138; July training of stagiaires by,
58, 64, 66; Kim and, 214; last family
meal of 2009 season and, 256; Lucho
as assistant to, 170, 197; Luke's
relationship with other stagiaires
and, 126; Mizuho's relationship
with, 252; opening of 2009 season
and, 46, 50, 51, 52, 53–54; opening
of 2010 season and, 274; Oriol's
relationship with, 205; personal
life of, 252; personality of, 115–16;
preparation of new dishes and, 66;
relationships among stagiaires and,
103, 157, 244; responsibilities of, 21–
22, 115, 116, 212–13, 245; Roger and,
244–45, 247, 249; as sous chef, 21;
stagiaires relationship with, 115–16,
197, 198; stagiaires tasting and, 84;
Thanksgiving celebration and, 225,
227; two-tiered stagiaire system and,
133
dishes: aesthetics of, 131; change of
season opening at elBulli and, 170;
creativity class and, 162; development

of new, 1, 136, 140–49, 152–53,
154–56, 158–59, 199; documenting
new, 152, 153, 156; as emblem of
restaurant, 24; most beloved 2009,
188; naming of, 148–49, 152; new
ingredients for, 154–55; photographs
of, 212, 240; preparation of, 31,
63–65; returned elBulli, 131; that
don't work out, 213; unintended
discoveries for, 147–48. *See also*
specific dish
Drolma (Barcelona restaurant), 181
Ducasse, Alain, 11, 42, 204, 208, 226

Easter Egg, 193
El Bulli. *See* elBulli
El Celler de Can Roca (Gerona, Spain),
198
El Poblet (Valencia restaurant), 209
elBulli: as Best Restaurant in the
World, 2, 4, 43, 274; birthday
celebrations at, 169; change as
characteristic of, 63, 275; changing
of season at, 44, 168, 169–70; as
classroom, 59–60; closing of, 1–2,
83, 271–73, 274; control system
at, 100–102; critics scrutiny of,
168, 185–92; culture/character of,
4–5, 19–20, 25–26, 91, 100–102,
118–19, 125, 237; database of,
63, 273; documentaries/filming
about, 15, 41–42, 235, 253, 255;
early days of, 68–69; evolution of,
78; fame/reputation of, 8, 29–30,
91, 229, 233; funding for, 272; as
gastronomical foundation, 1–2,
271–73; group photos of staff at,
131–32, 134, 261; hiring at, 231–33;
institutional memory at, 43; interior
design of, 91; language at, 118–19;
last service of 2009 season at,
255–58; legacy of, 8; location of,
12, 16–17, 68–69, 168; as locus
of culinary revolution, 3; as losing
money, 234; as matchmaker, 219;
menus at, 4, 31, 63, 69, 71, 140, 158,
169–70, 199, 239; Michelin stars
for, 1, 69, 78, 80, 163–64; mistakes
at, 121–24, 133; myths about, 182;
nouvelle cuisine at, 83; opening of
2009 season at, 39–42, 44–54;

elBulli (*cont.*): opening of 2010 season at, 274; philosophical approach to cooking at, 83; physical structure of, 272; reservations at, 4, 12, 164, 168; road to, 16–17, 168; rocks surrounding, 28–29, 113; as second Best Restaurant in the World, 274–75; shopping for, 101, 186–87; signature techniques of, 114, 257; stations at, 22; ten-day sequence at, 62; as think tank for gastronomic creativity, 1–2; use of first names at, 117–18. *See also specific person or topic*

Eleven Madison Park (New York City restaurant), 208

Escoffier, Auguste, 3, 21, 24, 77, 83

Escribà (Barcelona sweet shop), 134, 256

Essex House Hotel (New York City), 208

Euro-Toques International, 180–81

Faces dishware, 235

family meal: elBulli, bonding of staff and, 210; cake at final 2009, 256; cigarette break after, *239*; cost of, 213; dishes that don't work out at, 213; documenting of, 212–13; Eduard's instructions about, 24; Eugeni's responsibilities for, 245; Ferran at, *113*, 118, 127; Ferran's views about, 213–14; final 2009, 255–56; on first 2009 training day, 26–27; food at, 210, 213; kitchen breakdown for, 26–27; picture of, *113, 210*; planning for, 211; recipe notebook for, 211; reflections of stagiaires about, 271; setup and breakdown times for, 40, 58; small kitchen as responsible for, 36; systematization of, 211

Fast Good (Spanish fast-food chain), 235

Fat Duck (Bray, England, restaurant), 14, 106

50 Best Restaurants in the World, 220, 274

Figueras, Jean Luc, 153

flavor, 187–89, 191

Floresca, Kimberly "Kim" (kitchen stagiaire): abalone sauce by, 195–97; ambitions of, 230; Benno relationship with, 117–18; chefs respect for, 214; creativity class comments of, 162; Dan and, 203, 208, 223–24, 225, 228; first staff meeting of 2009 and, 18; first week of training for, 27; hierarchy and, 214; ICEX cooking competition and, 222–24; ICEX scholarship for, 208–9, 222, 267; in Junior Culinary Olympics, 202–3; last service of 2009 for, 255, 256, 257, 258; leadership abilities of, 218, 249; Luis's relationship with, 217–18; as Luis's replacement, 216–18; Nico's relationship with, 216, 217, 218, 232, 256; opening day at elBulli and, 42, 45; Oriol and, 118, 197, 215, 217, 221, 222; personal and professional background of, 18, 201–3, 208–9, 220, 227; personality of, 201, 202, 203, 214, 215–16, 218, 221, 224; pictures of, *196, 226, 258*; post-elBulli plans/activities of, 225, 254, 267–68; responsibilities of, 195–97, 216–17; rules and, 216; self-doubts of, 218; self-image of, 215; sexism and, 220, 221; Spanish eating tour of, 209; staff party and, 253, 258; stagiaire relationships and, 243–44; at Starters I, 216–18, 256; Sunny's competition with, 243; Thanksgiving celebration and, 225–27, 228; work ethic of, 214, 218

foams, 54, 140, 141, 162, 182, 187, 275

fondue, 167, 192–93

food: as art, 179, 189–90; as evolving canvas, 185; flavor of, 187–89, 191; functions of, 2–3; meanings of, 2–3; modern obsession with, 2, 6–7; movies compared with, 176–77; as political issue, 2; quality of, 186–87; reputation of Spanish, 12; revolution in Spanish, 238; as source of entertainment, 2. *See also* cooking; cuisine; *specific dish or type of cuisine*

Food Network, 201, 234

French Laundry (Napa Valley restaurant), 11, 18, 19, 107, 171, 208, 263, 264, 267, 270

Frey, Luis "Lucho" (kitchen stagiaire), 29, 53, 110, 169, 170, 197, 249

front-of-house staff, elBulli, 70, 118, 213, 243, 257, 259. *See also specific person*

Gagnaire, Pierre, 106, 267
Gambero Rosso (Italian restaurant), 105
García, Dani, 209
García, Lluís (front of house director), 63, 89, 122, 154
García, Rubén, 199
García, Victor (dining room stagiaire), 133, 170
Gasol, Pau, 4
gazpacho, 140, 175, 209, 211
gender: of chefs/cooks, 76, 116–17, 219–20; of elBulli stagiaires, 15, 214, 219–21
Giacomello, Terry, 199
Gilmour, David, 69
gnocchi, 38, 158, 164, 170, 188, 248
Goldfarb, Will, 132, 148
Gómez, Alfonso (stagiaire), 133, 172
González, Roberto, 146–47, 203
González, Xus (maître d'hôtes), 52
Gourmet magazine, 67
Guérard, Michel, 107, 233
guests, elBulli, 63, 89–95, 110, 130–31, 141, 168–69
Guillamet, Francesc (house photographer), 132
Guinó, Laia (kitchen stagiaire), 34, 38, 53, 58, 102, 133, 138, 219, 244
Guy Savoy (Las Vegas restaurant), 180

Hacienda Benazuza (Seville hotel/restaurant), 199
Hamilton, Richard, 155
Harvard University: Ferran's teaching at, 190, 251, 273
Harvey's (San Francisco restaurant), 76
Hickox, William, 266
hierarchy, 10–11, 21–22, 86, 116–20, 121–24, 125
Highlands (New York City restaurant), 266
Hibiscus (London restaurant), 125
history: culinary, 7, 176, 273, 275; role of chefs in, 7; of *stage*, 12–13
Hotel Playafels (Spain), 77
Hôtel Restaurant Le Saint-Christophe (Switzerland), 173
Howard Johnson chain, 72
Hughes, Robert, 189
Humm, Daniel, 208
hydrocolloids, 187–88

ICEX program, 208–9, 222, 224, 265, 267
Iggy's (New York City restaurant), 268, 270
Imitate the Chef (TV show), 179
Inopia (Barcelona bar), 81, 231, 267, 273
internship. *See stage*
Iron Chef (TV show), 4
Iuzzini, Johnny, 73–74, 168
Izquierdo, Javier "Javi" (kitchen stagiaire), 200, 231, 246, 252, 267

James Beard awards, 208
Jang, Myungsun "Luke" (kitchen stagiaire): ambitions of, 127–29; camping near elBulli of, 112; at Cold Station, 256; cooking contests and, 96–97, 128; criticisms of, 113; discipleship of, 107, 126, 231, 270; discontent of, 127–29; elBulli's hiring practices and, 232–33; Ferran's influence on, 106, 107, 112, 127, 231, 254; financial affairs of, 30; first staff meeting of 2009 and, 18; first week of training for, 33, 38, 39; food/cooking views of, 191; kimchi cooking by, 193; last service of 2009 season and, 256; mentor search of, 105–6, 111, 112; as model for elBulli chefs, 114; as Mugaritz stagiaire, 112; nickname for, 106; opening day of 2009 season and, 42, 46; personal and professional background of, 18, 95–96, 97–98, 104–5, 111; personality of, 113–14; pictures of, *98, 113*; post-stagiaire plans/activities of, 127–28, 200, 231–32, 253–54, 268, 270; reflections on elBulli of, 270; rejection for position at elBulli of, 231–32; relationships among stagiaires and, 103, 126, 127, 209; responsibilities of, 126–28, 129; return to elBulli of, 112; role models for, 127; spherification by, 114–15, 126–27; visit to elBulli by, 106; work ethic of, 111, 112, 113–14, 115, 126, 127, 128–29; working conditions at elBulli and, 99
Japan: influence on Adrià/elBulli of, 4, 33, 52, 142, 147

Japanese chefs: as visitors at elBulli, 198–99

Jean-Georges (New York City restaurant), 73–74, 85

Jin, Sungho "Sunny" (kitchen stagiaire): anticipation of 2009 opening by, 42; first staff meeting of 2009 and, 18, 19; first week of training for, 36, 37; food/cooking views of, 191; hierarchy at elBulli and, 23; illness of, 242–43; Jorge's burning accident and, 137, 138; July training of, 64; Kim's competition with, 243; personal and professional background of, 18, 19; personality of, 19; picture of, 258; post-elBulli plans of, 237; reflections about elBulli of, 171, 198; relationships among stagiaires and, 243–44; as short-term stagiaire, 133; at staff party, 258; station assignments for, 37; sugarcane cutting by, 64; Thanksgiving celebration and, 225, 227, 228

Jory (Oregon restaurant), 266

Jubany, Nandu, 238

Junior Culinary Olympics, 174–75, 177, 202–3

Keller, Thomas, 19, 26, 37, 106–7, 203, 211, 227, 263. See also French Laundry; Per Se

Kennedy, Diane, 168

Kennedy, John F., 72

Kitchen Confidential (Bourdain), 75–76, 77

kitchen, elBulli: accidents in, 137–38; change from restaurant to foundation and, 272; crying in, 221; culture of, 74, 78–79, 157, 237; as family, 207; Ferran's absence from, 204; hedonism of, 78; hierarchy in, 10–11, 21–22, 86, 116–20, 121–24, 125; illness among staff in, 171; Jorge's burning in, 137–38; media crews in, 229–30; metaphors for, 40; picture of, 93; rules of, 74, 134, 170, 197–98, 216; setting up of, 23–24; shared purpose in, 207; shouting/screaming in, 121–24; staff of, 5–6; visitors to, 49, 77–78, 92–95,

198–99, 238–40; working conditions in, 237

kitchens: dangers in, 137–38; formation of second family in, 207; macho culture of, 75–78; open, 77–78

La Broche (Madrid restaurant), 18, 241–42

Lacombe, Jean-Paul, 125

Lagrava, Teresa, 236

Lam, Francis, 77–78

language: at elBulli, 118–19; Gaël's skills with, 15, 183–84; hierarchy and, 118–19

Lara, Andrés, 135, 151, 152, 200–201, 219, 254, 268

La Vanguardia, 181, 229, 233

Le Bernardin (New York City restaurant), 266

Lee, Corey, 171, 263, 264

Leftick, Emmanuelle "Emma" (kitchen stagiaire): artichoke rose preparation and, 66; Eugeni and, 116, 170; as "expert in roses," 111; Ferran's relationship with chefs and, 264; first staff meeting of 2009 and, 18; first week of training for, 34, 37, 40–41; food/cooking views of, 191–92; July training of, 66; last service of 2009 season for, 256; opening day of 2009 season and, 51, 53; personal life of, 103, 219, 264; personal and professional background of, 18, 227, 263–64; pictures of, 34, 258; post-elBulli plans/activities of, 171, 263–65; reflections about elBulli of, 264–65, 271; relationships among stagiaires and, 103, 197, 215, 243–44; responsibilities of, 170; sexism and, 221; at staff party, 258; station assignments for, 37, 184; Thanksgiving celebration and, 225, 227, 228

L'Hort restaurant (Sabadell-Spain), 58, 78, 85, 244

liquid nitrogen, 53, 94, 182, 187, 188, 193, 265

Llamosas, Txema (kitchen stagiaire), 18, 37, 40, 171–72, 257, 265

locavore, 185–87, 191

López, David (maître d'hôtes), 93, 94, 235

Madrid Fusion: Ferran announces closing of elBulli at, 271

Maison Pic (Valence restaurant), 82

maître d's, elBulli, 43, 90, 93. *See also specific person*

manipulation, 144, 188–89

Marazzi, Cesare (kitchen stagiaire), 36–37, 58–59, 269

Martin, Denis, 18, 177–80, 185, 188, 193, 231

Martín, Pablo (kitchen stagiaire), 34, 50, 58, 257

Martínez, Begoña (kitchen stagiaire), 18, 25, 191, 209, 219, 221, 252, 257

Martínez, Josean, 132

Mary Queen of Scots (New York City restaurant), 266

Masas, Anthony (chef de partie), 37, 50

MasterChef (TV show), 4, 6

Maximin, Jacques, 106

Meadowood (Napa Valley restaurant), 267

Meana, Felix, 70, 74, 79, 88, 102, 134, 219, 253, 268–69

media: chefs as celebrities and, 125, 204; closing of elBulli and, 2, 271; elBulli change from restaurant to foundation and, 272; Ferran/elBulli reputation and, 78, 190, 230, 233, 234–35, 271; Roger's interview by, 229–30. *See also specific organization or person*

Melchiorre, Lorenzo (stagiaire), 103, 127, 171, 257, 258

Mellado, Juan Pablo (kitchen stagiaire), 124, 125

Mendel, Janet, 12

Mendes, Nuno, 132, 191

mentors, 105–6, 107–8, 111, 112. *See also* discipleship

Mesón de Cándido (Segovia restaurant), 209

Miramar (Spanish restaurant), 200

"molecular gastronomy," 3, 179, 182, 185, 188, 191–92, 264

Momofuku (New York City restaurants), 117, 123, 250

Montjoi lentils, 109–11

Moraga, Toni (chef de partie), 18, 27, 39, 50, 229, 247, 248

Morales, Paco, 191

Moy, Miquel, 75

Mugaritz (San Sebastián restaurant), 18, 112, 209, 219, 231, 232, 253, 268

Nadal, Rafael, 4

Nakamura, Mizuho "Miso" (kitchen stagiaire): Eugeni's relationship with, 252; final days of 2009 season and, 252; ICEX cooking competition and, 222, 223; Mateu as teacher of, 81; morale of, 171; opening day of 2009 season and, 47; personal life of, 252; personal and professional background of, 79, 81; post-elBulli activities of, 265–66; relationships among stagiaires and, 102–3, 209; sexism and, 221; Thanksgiving celebration and, 227–28

Nandron, Gerard, 108

Negresco (Nice restaurant), 106

Neichel, Jean-Louis, 69

Nestlé, 172

The New York Times, 74, 182

The New York Times Magazine, 4, 181

NH (hotel chain), 235

Noack, Ruth, 189

noma (Copenhagen restaurant), 11, 18, 123, 151, 268, 274

Obama, Barack, 266

obulato, 39, 52–53, 86–87, 144, 158, 245

oído, usage of term, 11, 224

omelette surprise dessert, 34, 39, 53, 54

ONCE (Spanish organization), 233

Ortega, Simone, 176

Osteria Francescana (Modena restaurant), 18, 181

Palacín, Sergi (kitchen stagiaire), 31–32, 41, 51, 52, 58, 126, 133, 221, 245, 257, 269

Palacios, Angel, 241–42

Pàmies (product supplier), 143

pañuelo (snack), 87–88, 99, 144

Parmesan, 46, 58, 71, 128–29, 135, 147, 158, 161, 176, 256

Parra, José Luis (kitchen stagiaire): 18, 20, 38, 39, 45, 102, 133, 162

Pastry station, elBulli: in August, 99; July training of stagiaires and, 66;

Pastry station, elBulli (cont.): Katie's assignment to, 79, 86–87; Luis as Mateu's assistant in, 231; Mateu as chef for, 7; as one of elBulli stations, 22; opening of 2009 season and, 48, 54; professional background of stagiaires in, 73; stagiaires relationships in, 157

Patterson, Daniel, 72

Pavón, Pablo (chef de partie), 18, 38, 40, 50, 58, 247

Pellegrino, S., 274

Pépin, Jacques, 72, 76

Perez, Isabel (Ferran Arià's wife), 112, 205, 275

Per Se (New York City restaurant), 14, 18, 107, 117, 208, 223

Perelló, Pol (maître d'hôtes), 52, 64, 93, 94, 235

Pérez, Miguel Alexander (kitchen stagiaire), 35, 41, 44, 47, 57–58, 115, 133, 219

Pérez, Paco, 200, 201, 254

perfection, 25–26, 123, 152, 244, 248

permanent staff, elBulli, 18, 43, 118–19, 259–60, 261, 272, 274. See also specific person

Petroleum (dish), 130–31, 153

plating, 36–39, 36, 38, 51, 58

Pound, Ezra, 275

prep work, 31–35

Pricci (Atlanta restaurant), 150

protein dishes, 144–45

Puck, Wolfgang, 49, 233

Puerta, Jorge (kitchen stagiaire), 30, 32, 38, 137–38, 162, 184, 237, 265

Puig, Fermi, 75, 77, 181

quemo: as all-purpose warning, 9–10; Andrea's front-of-the-house service and, 257; hierarchy and use of, 10–11; as joke, 138; variations in use of, 10–11

Rafa's (Roses restaurant), 89, 134

Ramsay, Gordon, 121

ravioli, 53, 63, 135, 147, 158, 162, 179, 256. See also Shabu Shabu

Rayner, Jay, 234

recipes: Andrea's missing notebook and, 245–47; development of

elBulli, 140–49; Katie's views about, 73; Sardines on the Plancha with Refried Garlic, 212; unintended discoveries for, 147–48. See also creativity

Redzepi, René, 6, 100–101, 123, 125, 132, 135, 151, 191, 260, 274

Restaurant Magazine, 4, 220

Restaurante Calima (Spain), 209

restaurant(s): as business propositions, 163; dishes as emblem of, 24; distinction between good and bad service at, 101–2; failure of, 163; first, 77; great, 275; impact of French tradition on, 22–23; modern system for, 21–22; organization of, 270; set menus at, 239; sexism and, 220–21; working conditions in, 220–21

rhubarb, 33, 40, 46, 147

Ribeiro, Frederico (kitchen stagiaire), 122, 198, 266

Ripert, Eric, 266

risotto, 145, 146, 169

Ritz Carlton Hotel (Amelia Island, Florida), 202

Robuchon, Joël, 181

Roca, Joan, 132

Rocher, Perfecto (kitchen stagiaire), 29, 59, 266

Romero, Antonio (kitchen stagiaire), 38, 40, 115, 133, 171, 266

Roncero, Paco, 238, 270

rose petals. See artichoke rose

Roses, Spain, 13, 89, 119

Rostang, Michel, 108, 125

Royal Spanish Gastronomic Academy, 45, 51, 255

rules, elBulli, 74, 134, 154, 170, 197–98, 216

Ruscalleda, Carme, 123, 204

Ryan, Daniel "Dan" (kitchen stagiaire): ambitions of, 208; anticipation of 2009 opening by, 42; appearance of, 224; creativity class question of, 161; ICEX cooking competition and, 222–24; ICEX scholarship for, 208–9, 222, 267; Kim's relationship with, 203, 208, 223–24, 225, 228; last service of 2009 season for, 255; Mateu as teacher of, 81; morale of, 171; personal and professional

background of, 42, 79, 102, 161,
203, 207–9; personality of, 207,
224; pictures of, *226, 258*; post-
elBulli plans/activities of, 224–25,
254, 267–68; reflections on elBulli
of, 102, 270; Spanish eating tour
of, 209; staff party and, 253, *258*;
Thanksgiving celebration and, 225,
228
Ryugin (Tokyo restaurant), 265

Sadler (Milan restaurant), 150
Sagristà, Xavier, 154
Sánchez, Débora (staff coordinator), 213
Sainz, Iosu (kitchen stagiaire), 27, 35,
44, 47, 57–58, 134, 171, 197, 242
Sant Pau (Roses restaurant), 58, 123,
198, 204
Santamaria, Santi, 43–44, 180–81, 186,
187, 191
Sardines on the Plancha with Refried
Garlic (recipe), 212
Schelling, Ralph (kitchen stagiaire), 17,
25, 42, 51, 53, 133, 222
Schilling, Hans, 68–69
Schilling, Marketta, 68–69, 205
science, 3, 190
Sergi Arola Gastro (Madrid restaurant),
181
Serrano, Julian, 59, 266
sexism, 220, 221
Shabu Shabu (dish), 63, 144, 146,
148–49
Shah, Paras, 123, 223
Si Us Plau (Roses, Spain), 88, 250
Small Kitchen (elBulli station), 22, 36,
37, 50, 54, 59, 240, 255, 257
Soler, Juli (co-owner/front of the
house), 21, 69, 77, 80, 118, 132, 255,
271, 272
soy milk, 160–61, 198
Spago (Los Angeles restaurant), 233
spherification, 3, 22, 38, 114–15, 126–27,
158, 162, 187, 232, 256
spoons, tasting, 45–46, 84
staff meetings, elBulli, 17–20, 44–45,
57, 62–63, 90, 119, 247, 255
staff party, elBulli, 252–53, 255, 258–60,
258
staff photographs, 131–32, 134, *261*
stage program, 6, 12–14

stagiaires, elBulli: aprons for, 22;
benefits of training for, 6, 12;
characteristics of, 6, 33, 59–60;
database of, 273; as legacy of Ferran/
elBulli, 8, 273; length of training for,
12, 13; Marc as head of program for,
13–14; opening of 2010 season and,
274
stagiaires, elBulli 2009:
accommodations for, 16; age of, 14;
anticipation of season opening by,
41–42; applications for positions
as, 6, 12, 13, 14; chefs relationships
with, 117–18, 120, 125, 197–98, 252;
competition among, 102–3, 157,
243; complaints of, 84–85; creativity
class for, 160–63; culture of elBulli
and, 100–101; difficulties facing,
31–32; dish preparation and, 31–32;
early departures of, 58–59, 133, 170;
expertise as goal of, 111; feelings
about elBulli of, 260; Ferran's
advice to, 260; Ferran's creativity
and, 190–91; Ferran's relationship
with, 124–26; financial affairs of,
12, 30–31; first day for, 15–21; first
day of training for, 23–29; first
week of training for, 23–42; gender
and, 15, 214, 219–21; hierarchy
and, 11, 22, 120; illness of, 242–43;
influence of elBulli cooking on,
191–92; instruction/criticism of, 11,
114, 116; lack of knowledge about
classical French cooking of, 82; last
service day for, 255–58; military
background of, 133; mistakes of,
100–101, 121–24, 133; morale of,
171; most important learning of,
111; motivations of, 8, 29–31, 101–2;
oído use by, 11; Oriol's relationship
with, 117–18, 154; personal life
of, 78–79, 218–19; personal and
professional background of, 15, 57,
133; personalities/egos of, 59–60;
picture of, *261*; piecemeal quality
to education of, 83; post-elBulli
plans of, 171–72, 200–201, 231–33;
prep work by, 31–33; reaction to
criticisms of superiors by, 123–24;
reflections about elBulli of, 264,
269–71; relationships among,

stagiaires, elBulli 2009 (*cont.*): 58, 79,
85, 102–3, 126, 127, 133, 157, 159,
164, 197, 209, 215–16, 221, 243–44;
responsibilities of, 6, 12; return
of earlier, 199, 231; as returning
as 2010 chefs de partie, 266–67;
romantic relationships among, 252;
rules for, 16, 19–20, 39, 60, 134,
154, 197–98; sacrifices of, 30–31;
selection of, 14–15, 112; short-term,
133, 198, 238; station assignments
for, 36–37, 103, 264; tasting by,
84–85; transportation for, 16–17;
two-tiered system among, 133;
working conditions for, 30–31, 94,
99, 110–11, 134, 157, 203–4, 237;
worst experience for, 111; yelling in
kitchen and, 123–24. *See also specific
person*
Starck, Philippe, 155
Starters I (elBulli station), 22, 216–18,
232, 243, 256
Starters II (elBulli station), 22, 184,
229–30, 247–50, 267
Streisand, Barbra, 168
Subijana, Pedro, 238–39, 240
sugarcane cocktails, 45, 47, 50, 63–64,
257
sweet potatoes, 158, 164, 170, 188, 248

technology, 141–42, 183, 187–88
Terraza del Casino (Madrid restaurant),
238, 270
Tetsuya's (Sydney, Australia restaurant),
11, 18, 19, 104–5, 107
Texturas, 181, 235
Thanksgiving celebration, 225–28, *226*
Time magazine, 4
Top Chef (TV show), 4, 13, 227
Tramonto, Rick, 208
Tru (Chicago restaurant), 208

Välimäki, Hans, 225, 254
Velódromo (Barcelona restaurant), 229,
247
Vidolin, Gabriel (kitchen stagiaire),
124–25, 200, 227, 232, 237, 253
Vinay, Jean-Paul, 69
visitors, elBulli, 49, 198–99, 238–40
Vongerichten, Jean-Georges, 73–74, 84.
See also Jean-Georges

Vuilloud, Gaël (kitchen stagiaire):
ambitions of, 172, 177–78, 185;
anticipation of opening day at
elBulli by, 42; anxiety of, 192–93,
242; appearance of, 172; chefs as
artists views of, 185; in cooking
contest, 174; cooking/food views
of, 192–94; Eduard and, 166–67,
184, 192, 193; Eugeni and, 166,
183–84, 194; Ferran's comments
about, 184; first staff meeting of
2009 and, 18; first week of training
for, 40; fondue cooking by, 192–93;
influence of elBulli on, 192; Jorge's
burning and, 184; July training of,
58; language skills of, 15, 183–84;
leave for family reasons of, 242, 254;
Luke's criticism of, 127; opening day
of 2009 season and, 52; personal life
of, 231; personal and professional
background of, 18, 172–75, 177–80,
183; personality of, 184; picture of,
167; post-stagiaire position as chef
de partie position for, 184–85, 194,
200, 231, 242, 267; responsibilities
of, 183–84; self-confidence of, 185;
tasting complaint of, 85; on TV, 179,
193; working conditions at elBulli
and, 99

Wakuda, Tetsuya, 104–5
War of the Stove Tops, 180–81
White, Marco Pierre, 76, 234
workshop, Ferran's Barcelona, 3, 73,
143, 160

Xantana, 147, 159, 182, 183, 187, 188,
222, 235
Xatruch, Eduard (chef de cuisine):
anticipation of 2009 opening day
by, 39–41; authority of, 10–11; at
center table, 215; as chef de cuisine,
18, 21; creativity class and, 161;
cuisine as passion of, 156; culture
at elBulli and, 119; demonstrations
by, 46; documentary about elBulli
and, 41; elBulli living conditions
of, 205, 246; Ferran and, 119, 120,
121–22, 124, 204, 206, 259; first
staff meeting of 2009 and, 18; first
week for 2009 stagiaires and, 18,

20, 23–24, 25, 26, 27, 39, 41; former stagiaires return and, 204; Gaël and, 166–67, 184, 192, 194; health care at elBulli and, 171; hierarchy and, 21, 119, 120; illness of, 171; Iosu's relationship with, 197; Jorge's burning accident and, 138; July training of stagiaires by, 58, 64; Kim and, 196, 214–15, 221; last service of 2009 season and, 255, 256, 259; Luke and, 114, 127; menu design by, 63; new dishes and, 65, 142, 144, 148, 199; opening of 2009 season and, 44–45, 46, 47, 48, 50, 52, 54; opening of 2010 season and, 274; Oriol's relationship with, 40, 154, 155; personal life of, 156, 204–5, 219; personal and professional background of, 214; personality of, 118, 121–22; pictures of, 17, 228; reputation of, 206; responsibilities of, 21, 39–40, 49, 65, 214; Ribeiro car accident and, 122; Roger and, 235–36, 244, 245; role at elBulli of, 214; rules of the kitchen and, 134; sacrifices of, 204–6; salary for, 206; at staff party, 258; stagiaires relationship with, 117–18, 214–15;

station assignments for stagiaires and, 103; tasting by, 84; ten-day sequence meeting and, 62; Thanksgiving celebration and, 225, 227; views about how kitchen should work of, 40, 41; visitors to elBulli kitchen and, 49, 199, 238, 240; work ethic of, 214–15

yubas, 33–35, 34, 44, 54, 57, 160, 256, 257

Zabala, Aitor (chef de partie): assignments for stagiaires and, 37; at Café Atlántico, 70; at Cold Station, 10, 256; criticism of stagiaire by, 114; Emma and, 103, 264; first staff meeting of 2009 and, 18; first week of training for stagiaires and, 40; illness of, 243; last service day for 2009 and, 256; opening day of 2009 season and, 50, 51, 52, 53; relationships among stagiaires and, 103; spherification and, 114; staff party and, 253; at Starters I, 243; Thanksgiving celebration and, 227
Zafra, Rafael, 199

about the author]

LISA ABEND is a journalist based in Madrid. Since 2005, she has been *Time* magazine's correspondent in Spain. She also contributes to a number of newspapers and magazines, including *The Atlantic*, *The New York Times*, *Food & Wine*, *The Nation*, *Saveur*, *Wired*, and *Slate*. In a previous life (that is, about six years ago) she was a professor of Spanish history at Oberlin College.